Sum… University of Kent, and Honorary Consultant Psychiatrst at Chase Farm Hospital, Enfield. **David Ndegwa** is Clinical Director for Forensic Psychiatry at Lambeth Health Care NHS Trust. **Melba Wilson** is Race and Mental Health Adviser to MIND.

Forensic psychiatry, race and culture

Suman Fernando, David Ndegwa and Melba Wilson

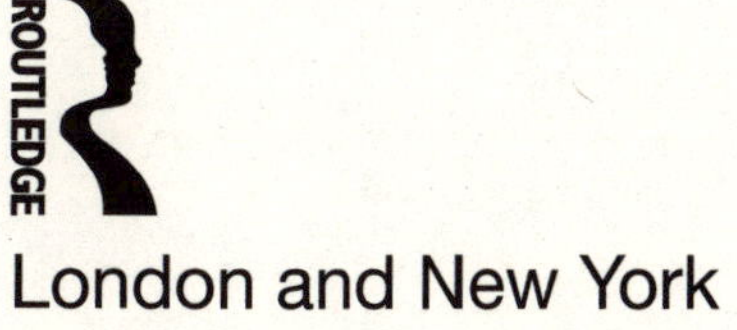

London and New York

First published 1998 by Routledge
11 New Fetter Lane, London EC4P 4EE

Simultaneously published in the USA and Canada
by Routledge
29 West 35th Street, New York, NY 10001

Typeset in Times by Routledge
Printed and bound in Great Britain by TJ International, Padstow, Cornwall

British Library Cataloguing in Publication Data
A catalogue record for this book is available from the British Library

Library of Congress Cataloging in Publication Data
Fernando, Suman.
Forensic psychiatry, race and culture/Suman Fernando, David Ndegwa, and Melba Wilson.
Includes bibliographical references and index.
1. Forensic psychiatry – Cross-cultural studies. 2. Psychiatrist – Attitudes. I. Ndegwa, David. II. Wilson, Melba. III. Title. [DNLM: 1. Forensic Psychiatry. 2. Cross-Cultural Comparison. 3. Race Relations. 4. Mental Disorders – ethnology. W 740 F364f 1998]
RA1151.F53 1998
614'. 1–dc21
DNLM/DLC
for Library of Congress 97-42754 CIP

ISBN 0–415–15321–2 (hbk)
ISBN 0–415–15322–0 (pbk)

To all those who have experienced the psychiatric services:

I am loud – that's unacceptable; I dress differently – that's considered strange. I eat different foods – that's frowned upon. My English is not good – they don't try and get an interpreter. I am discriminated against – they say I have a chip on my shoulder.

(Woman, aged 42, given a diagnosis of schizophrenia,
Wilson and Francis,1997)

I was a foreigner. Now I am a mad foreigner.

(Man, aged 34, given a diagnosis of manic depression,
Wilson and Francis,1997)

Contents

Illustrations

BOXES

FIGURE

Contributors

Suman Fernando has been writing on race and culture in psychiatry/mental health for some years and was a member (for nine years) of the Mental Health Act Commission, for which he chaired the National Standing Committee of Race and Culture and was a member of the Commission's Central Policy Committee. He was a consultant psychiatrist in Enfield until July 1993 and is now a part-time senior lecturer at the Tizard Centre, University of Kent at Canterbury, and honorary consultant psychiatrist at Chase Farm Hospital, Enfield. He is Fellow of the Royal College of Psychiatrists.

David Ndegwa has been involved in both research and clinical work in Birmingham and Hackney (London) where there are relatively large populations of African-Caribbean people. Formerly, clinical director of forensic psychiatric services in the City and Hackney Community NHS Trust, he has recently been appointed as clinical director for forensic psychiatry and consultant forensic psychiatrist at Lambeth Health Care NHS Trust/honorary senior lecturer at the United Medical and Dental Schools (UMDS), London. He is a member of the Royal College of Psychiatrists and a member of the executive committee of its faculty of forensic psychiatry.

Melba Wilson is actively involved in community projects in mental health for black people. As a health journalist, she was the editor of papers for the NHS Mental Health Task Force Regional Race Programme and she then worked in the policy department of MIND (National Association for Mental Health), developing its policy on the criminal justice system and people with mental health problems. She is now race and mental health adviser at MIND and has been conducting research into issues concerning the mental health of black people.

Preface
The basic facts

Suman Fernando

Forensic psychiatry works closely with the criminal justice system (CJS). A good description of the current legal and administrative framework within which it functions in the UK has been provided by Herschel Prins in the second edition of his book *Offenders, Deviants or Patients?* (1995). As a preface to the main book, this section will present some basic facts about both the CJS and forensic psychiatry appertaining to issues of race and culture. It is a noticeable fact that there is a paucity of hard ethnic data about forensic psychiatry compared to that available about the criminal justice system.

CRIMINAL JUSTICE

In the 1960s and 1970s confrontations and disturbances occurred in prisons all over Western Europe and North America, many involving black prisoners. The relative over-representation of black people in American prisons had been noted for many years and, following prison riots in USA, Angela Davis (1971) wrote (in Sim, 1990): 'Prisoners – especially Blacks, Chicanos and Puerto Ricans – are increasingly advancing the proposition that they are *political* prisoners. They contend that they are political prisoners in the sense that they are largely the victims of an oppressive politico-economic order, swiftly becoming conscious of the causes underlying their victimisation' (1971: 37).

The over-representation of black people in British prisons has been noted for many years. A recent review, *Race and Criminal Justice* (Penal Affairs Consortium, 1996), brought together the following information about race differences among prisoners:

1 The prison population contains a disproportionately high number of black prisoners – 18 per cent of all prisoners, 17 per cent of male prisoners and 24 per cent of female prisoners are from minority ethnic groups. The high number of women is partially explained by the many foreign women serving prison sentences for drug smuggling.
2 Twelve per cent of total prison population, 11 per cent of males and 20 per cent of females are classified as 'black' of African-Caribbean origin (while only 1.5 per cent of general population are A–C). Three per cent of all prisoners are south Asians (compared with 2.7 per cent of the general population). Three per cent of all prisoners are 'Chinese and other' (compared to 1 per cent in population).

These observations should be considered against a background of the following findings:

1 A recent Home Office Research study *Young People and Crime* (Graham and Bowling, 1995) analysed self-reported crimes admitted by a random sample of young people aged 14 to 25 in confidential interviews with researchers. They found that African-Caribbean and white young people had similar rates of offending while Asians had lower rates than either African-Caribbeans or whites. Also, white youngsters were more likely to use illegal drugs than African-Caribbean youngsters.
2 Black people entering prison have on average fewer convictions than white prisoners (Penal Affairs Consortium, 1996) indicating that black people who commit offences are more likely to end up in prison than comparable white offenders.
3 Evidence from studies in the early 1990s suggested strongly that for the same type of offence, black people (compared to white) were more likely to be stopped by police, cautioned, prosecuted and remanded in custody (National Association for the Care and Resettlement of Offenders, 1991).

An extensive analysis of the effects of race in the criminal justice system is contained in a study of the outcome of a large number of people who had been convicted and sentenced at Crown Courts in the West Midlands of England (Hood, 1992). This study found that indirect (racial) discrimination operated through various processes. In comparing equivalent samples of black and white people:

1 Black people were less likely to forgo their right to challenge

prosecution and so more likely to plead not guilty. And, in the case of people who make such a plea (compared to those who plead guilty), social reports are not done on them, and, even more importantly, they receive higher sentences. Forty-two per cent of blacks and 43 per cent of Asians (compared to 28 per cent of white offenders) were sentenced without a social inquiry report (SIR) being available.

2. Black people were more likely to be remanded in custody (even allowing for charge and background). Those in custody were less likely to be able to show mitigating circumstances (e.g. by getting a job and keeping clean).
3. Black people were disproportionately charged for drug related offences, especially cannabis possession, and most of these charges arose from police activity rather than complaints from the public.

In calculations based on his research, Dr Hood found that:

1. Black people had a 5–8 per cent greater overall chance of going to prison.
2. Black adults were given sentences higher up on the tariff than were whites (more so in some courts than in others) and that, in cases of medium gravity (where judges had greater discretion than in most serious cases), the difference was 13 per cent.
3. Eighty per cent of the over-representation of black men in the prison population was due to the disproportionate number of them appearing before Crown Courts (reflecting, of course, decisions made at all previous stages of the criminal justice process) and the seriousness of their cases.

Conclusions

As far as it is possible to discern, the ethnic breakdown of prisoners is very similar to that of people detained in forensic psychiatry institutes (special hospitals and regional secure units). This strengthens the contention, based on general impressions, that forensic psychiatry and the criminal justice system are jointly involved in law and order, especially when issues of 'race' are involved. It could be argued that the 'medical component' of forensic psychiatry is debatable when the total picture is considered, although clearly questions of 'illness' apply to all people detained in forensic institutes and to only a minority of prisoners.

FORENSIC PSYCHIATRY

Although there is some overlap in the fields covered by general psychiatry and forensic psychiatry, the latter is generally seen as being totally responsible for the special hospitals in England and Wales, namely Broadmoor, Rampton and Ashworth and the regional secure units (RSU) spread around the UK. Also, it is increasingly the case that forensic psychiatry services hold outpatient clinics, sometimes located in general psychiatric settings, to follow up people discharged from forensic psychiatry institutes and carry out assessments of people both in the community and ordinary psychiatric units. Most patients in the special hospitals have been found guilty of serious offences but about one-third of others (Prins, 1995) are there because they have been deemed disruptive or 'dangerous' in ordinary psychiatric hospitals. In all instances, a person detained in a special hospital or RSU would have been assessed at some stage by a forensic psychiatrist and deemed to require treatment in conditions of special security.

Another setting, apart from the special hospitals and RSUs, generally regarded as 'forensic', although often not designated as such, is the growing number of private institutions that claim to provide 'secure' or 'medium secure' hospital settings and are often used by National Health Service (NHS) patients on the basis of 'extra-contractual' referrals, i.e. referrals arranged outside the usual contracting process within the NHS. At present in England and Wales, there are five such institutes owned by Partnerships in Care (Kneesworth House Hospital, Llanarth Court, Redford Lodge, Stockton Hall and St John's) and a sixth, St Andrews Hospital in Northampton.

In addition to working in institutes specifically 'forensic' in type, forensic psychiatrists also provide a service within the NHS of advising on issues of dangerousness in people who are detained in, or considered for admission to, ordinary psychiatric hospitals. So, when someone is referred to a general psychiatric service, a decision may be made that a forensic opinion is required because of possible 'dangerousness'. Thus, in the UK, the responsibility for determining the 'dangerousness' of a person who may be seen to be suffering from mental health problems, is generally taken on by forensic psychiatrists; they are the 'specialists' in dangerousness, the arbiters of those who should be kept in hospital under secure conditions.

The ethnic breakdown of people detained under the forensic

system has not been published. An official discussion document issued by the Department of Health and Home Office in the UK (1994a) entitled *Review of Health and Social Services for Mentally Disordered Offenders and Others Requiring Similar Services*, vol. 6, *Race, Gender and Equal Opportunities*, states that 'black mentally disordered offenders are more likely than white mentally disordered offenders to be: remanded in custody for psychiatric reports; subject to restriction orders; detained in higher degrees of security for longer; be referred from prison to medium secure units or special hospitals' (1994a: 18).

Studies in the West Midlands found an over-representation of African-Caribbean people (compared to whites) among people admitted to a medium secure unit (Cope, 1989) and among the latter, African-Caribbean patients were more likely to be referred from prison while on remand while white patients were more often admitted from NHS and special hospitals (Cope and Ndegwa, 1990). A recent survey of first admission to RSU beds in the North Thames Forensic Psychiatry Service over a period of twelve years from 1 November 1983 (Mohan *et al.*, 1997) found that African-Caribbean people formed 37 per cent, compared to 2.3 per cent in the general population of the area (Office of Population Censuses and Surveys (OPCS), 1993) and Asian people formed 6 per cent (compared to 10.4 per cent in the population). There is considerable anecdotal evidence known to the authors of this book of the serious over-representation of black people, especially African-Caribbeans, in both RSUs and special hospitals. Informal inquiry revealed that in 1997, 22 per cent of all patients in Broadmoor Hospital are from ethnic minorities, with 66 per cent of this group being African-Caribbean, and that 17 per cent of patients at Ashworth Hospital in Liverpool are from ethnic minorities. The general impression is that discrimination in the forensic system may be very similar to that in the criminal justice system (CJS) in that it may occur at various levels and hinges to a great extent on the issue of a person's dangerousness as perceived by police, magistrates, judges, mental health service providers, and the general public.

Acknowledgements

All three authors acknowledge the insights they have gained from discussions with numerous colleagues and users of forensic psychiatric services. Special thanks are due to Professor Herschel Prins, who made useful comments on some of the chapters in Part 1; Professor Graham Thornicroft for encouraging remarks on Part 2; Ann Meskell for secretarial assistance with Part 2, and Liz Sayce, MIND's policy director, for her help with early drafts of Part 3.

Introduction

Suman Fernando

Issues of badness *vs.* madness have been the subject of comments and concern for centuries. As psychiatry widened its horizons and penetrated legal systems of criminal justice, forensic psychiatry developed as the speciality within psychiatry that attempted to address the practical problems involved in dealing with people who committed offences. And hand-in-hand with this was the development of forensic institutes i.e. special hospitals and (more recently in the UK) regional secure units (RSU), sometimes called 'medium secure units', and locked wards in private hospitals that take in-patients contracted out by the National Health Service (NHS) – wards which are often little different to special hospitals in terms of the types of people who are admitted there as patients.

As mental health care in general changes from being institution based to being based in the community ('de-institutionalisation'), issues of dangerousness in relation to disturbances of mental functioning have become matters of concern to the public. As a result, the concept of 'community care' is sometimes criticised as not adequately addressing dangers posed by people deemed to be 'mentally ill' in psychiatric terms. The reaction of forces in power in the UK has been to devise systems of supervision allied to 'risk assessment' aiming at a balance between maintaining 'human rights' and instituting what is seen as 'treatment' based on 'diagnosis' (in psychiatric terms).

The *Oxford Textbook of Psychiatry* (Gelder *et al.*, 1989) states:

> The term forensic psychiatry is used in two different senses, one narrow and one broad. In its narrow sense the term is applied only to the branch of psychiatry that deals with the assessment and treatment of mentally abnormal offenders. In its broad sense

> the term is applied to all legal aspects of psychiatry, including the civil law and laws regulating psychiatric practice, as well as the subspeciality concerned with mentally abnormal offenders.
>
> (1989: 858)

The situation in the UK (and in most other Western European countries) is that clinical psychiatrists deal with two sets of people – those seen in 'ordinary clinical practice' and 'mentally disordered offenders'. In the USA the situation is somewhat different: unlike in Europe, people who call themselves forensic psychiatrists are predominantly concerned with their role as experts to courts and tribunals and are 'less than enamoured at the prospect of being plunged into taking responsibility for the armies of the mentally ill in the penal institutes of the USA, and the mass of the assaultative and fear-inducing individuals in the public psychiatric hospitals' (Mullen, 1995: 366).

With the shift from institutional psychiatry to community psychiatry that has taken place since the 1950s (Scull, 1984), the involvement of (medically trained) psychiatrists in the care of and organisation of services for, people with mental health problems has undergone considerable change. Today, psychiatrists are usually (important) members of multidisciplinary teams that include social workers, clinical psychologists, occupational therapists, etc., with much reduced powers (in comparison to what they were fifty years ago) in terms of decision-making over treatment and even diagnosis. However, the exception to this rule occurs in the field of forensic psychiatry, where if anything, the power of the psychiatrist – usually the 'forensic' psychiatrist – is as evident today as it has ever been in the history of psychiatry. And, not only (medically trained) psychiatrists but other professionals, such as clinical psychologists and nurses ('forensic psychologists' and 'forensic nurses'), working in forensic settings exert the sort of control over (what are called) 'mentally disordered offenders' that is more in keeping with the prison system than with a medically based 'caring' system.

The involvement of (medical) psychiatrists in the care of people with learning difficulties has changed rapidly during the past twenty years with the shift to community care and a multidisciplinary approach being even more marked than in the case of people deemed to have 'mental disorder'. Thus, services for people with learning difficulties are largely managed by professionals without a basic medical training – care managers, psychologists, etc. However, if a person with learning difficulties is categorised as being a 'mentally disordered offender', the power of the (medically trained) psychiatrist 'in charge' of the person becomes paramount over that of everyone else in the multidisciplinary team. In such situations, psychiatrists, sometimes together with clinical psychologists, become the main determiners of controls and restrictions placed upon people with learning difficulties.

Thus, both in the field of learning difficulties and in mental health generally, forensic psychiatry as a medical influence exerts to a large extent the power that was evident in psychiatry as a whole until the middle of the twentieth century. The empire ruled over by forensic psychiatry in the UK, once limited to the special hospitals (such as Broadmoor), now covers numerous 'regional secure units' and sometimes even units in general psychiatric settings that have reached *de facto* secure status. This is especially true of units in private hospitals run for profit although used mainly by the National Health Service. In terms of beds for patients (the traditional measure of the power of a psychiatrist), the scope of the forensic empire is one that is steadily expanding even as general psychiatry contracts as a result of becoming de-institutionalised.

Clearly, forensic psychiatry – or indeed *any* psychiatry or psychology – is about real people living in real societies, and many societies in Western Europe and North America are 'multi-ethnic' in nature. However. what this actually means for the practice of forensic psychiatry is often ignored – and it is the overall function of this book to address this issue. The term 'ethnic' primarily involves concepts of both 'race' and 'culture' (Fernando, 1991) and so people who constitute a 'multi-ethnic' society carry, to a greater or lesser extent, racial and cultural identities. Even more importantly, there are definite differences in the way people in such societies are viewed, depending on their perceived ethnicity – their 'race' and/or their 'culture'. However, race and culture are often confounded both in terms of theoretical considerations and in the way people are perceived and treated.

In a very general sense, 'culture' denotes a way of life (i.e. family life, patterns of behaviour and belief, language, etc.), related to tradition and background but also derived from current living conditions. Further, there is often constant change and interchange, especially in communities where people from several cultural backgrounds are living together in the same community, socialising and sharing common facilities such as schools, hospitals and social centres, although the amount of interchange may well depend on the extent of mixing and inter-marriage, the degree to which there is ethnic separation (segregation), etc.

Reference to race does not necessarily imply support for the thesis that people are *inherently* 'different' psychologically because of certain inherited characteristics that are related to skin colour, but it does imply that people are perceived as 'different' because of skin colour and often advantaged or disadvantaged as a result. In other words reference to race implies that racism exists. In popular language 'race' is synonymous with colour and 'we speak casually of Africans (or African-Caribbeans) as one race, Asians as another, Europeans or whites as a third' (Malik, 1996). These everyday perceptions, rather than providing any scientific or biological evidence, form the basis for the term 'black people' as used in this book. Another way of describing the use of this term (in this book) is by reference to its 'political sense' – i.e. as indicating people who trace their ancestry to populations that were and/or are subjugated and exploited etc. by people who are known as 'white people'. Thus, in the UK, Africans, African-Caribbeans, Arabs, Bangladeshis, Greek and Turkish Cypriots, Indians, Iranians, Palestinians and Sri Lankans, may be seen as black people. In this book, the authors generally use the term 'black people' in this 'political sense' but accept that this is not always the case in other places. Furthermore, the use of the term 'black' may be different in some instances (even in this book), referring specifically to people who are seen as, and usually identify, as being of African and African-Caribbean descent, but not people who are seen as (or identify as) 'Asian' or 'Chinese' or 'Turkish'. The exact meaning given to the term 'black' will be clear from the context.

A recent development is the emphasis given in the UK to the (ethnic) 'diversity' of its population, rather than to racial differences between British people that are reflected in the use of the term 'black' or to their geographical origin, or that of their ancestors, implied in terms such as 'Asian' and 'African'. In such a context, the term 'visible minority communities' has gained some currency among some individuals and organisations in order to emphasise the discrimination and disadvantages faced by people because of (what is seen as their) 'race', reflected in differences in problems and experiences encountered by the 'diverse' communities in the UK.

In keeping with the expansion of forensic psychiatry in the UK, the past ten years has seen the publication of many books directed at professionals working in this field. However, none have sought to address in any detail or depth one of the most important issues evident to anyone, whether a patient or professional, participating in this area: the issue of 'race', linked inevitably to questions of cultural difference. A discussion document issued by the Department of Health and Home Office (1994a) for the committee under Dr John Reed that reviewed health and social services for (so-called) mentally disordered offenders, highlighted many racial and cultural issues that needed to be considered by that committee. The question of whether they were adequately considered by the committee itself is another matter. Reports of several inquiries that have attracted public interest, for example that into the care and treatment of Christopher Clunis (Northeast Thames and Southeast Thames Regional Health Authorities, 1994), have either overtly or implicitly addressed issues of race and culture, often in an inadequate and insensitive manner. However, one particular inquiry – that into the deaths of black patients at Broadmoor Hospital (Special Hospitals Service Authority, 1993) – did delve into this otherwise 'no-go' area for inquiry reports. Although the fact that race and culture are involved fairly intimately in the anomalies and difficulties evident in the field of forensic psychiatry is openly voiced and commented upon, little or no attempt has been made so far to analyse, or explore, the issues in a British or European context. The primary aim of this book is to redress this omission.

The history of the emergence of forensic psychiatry as psychiatric interest in issues of criminality in nineteenth-century European society shows that, from the very beginning, not only did forensic psychiatry overlap with the dispensation of criminal justice, but that the boundary between the two systems was blurred. Also, from the beginning the role of forensic psychiatry centred on decision-making about dangerousness and individual responsibility for crime. Since a psychiatric approach focuses on the individual, his/her emotional state (seen in terms of 'illness' and health) and his/her psychology, judgements on people thought to be dangerous or criminal become personalised once forensic psychiatry, or any other psychiatry, gets involved, i.e. judgements focus on *the person* rather than on his/her behaviour *per se*, or the context in which the behaviour occurs. Thus, the person's beliefs, attitudes and ways of thinking – his/her culture – become scrutinised and judged against a norm derived from within the psychiatric system. In a multi-ethnic society this is not a simple matter of applying well established norms, but rather of allowing for differences and, more importantly, ensuring that racist perceptions do not influence the judgements made. This is why a deep understanding of issues of race and culture are essential for the practice of forensic psychiatry. This book attempts to provide the basis for such an understanding. It does not provide easy answers, blueprints for change, or panaceas. It does, however, bring into the public domain many issues that are often left unsaid – sometimes because people are afraid of being criticised for being merely 'politically correct', sometimes because what is said may be misused, and sometimes because of the fear of being thought of to be 'racist'.

This book has been written by three authors, each bringing a unique perspective to the task at hand and tackling one particular aspect of the whole. Inevitably, the individual parts differ in style and to some extent in approach. In Part 1 Suman Fernando, a general psychiatrist, examines the *Background* to current issues; in Part 2 David Ndegwa, a forensic psychiatrist, considers *Clinical practice*; and in Part 3 Melba Wilson, a health journalist, analyses *Public policy*. Finally, in Part 4, all three authors consider *Future prospects*, examining what aspects of forensic psychiatry need to be changed and providing practical suggestions for such change. Each part is able to stand alone; the last part is a consensus statement of all three authors. The book as a whole has been edited by Suman Fernando.

Forensic psychiatry has evolved over many years in Europe and North America in a context generally described as 'Western'. Chapters 1 to 4 explore its development, analysing the concepts, theories and ideologies that are important to the issues involved in considering issues of race and culture in forensic psychiatry today. Chapter 1 discusses concepts of race and culture, together with their corollaries, leading on to examine ways in which both forensic psychiatry and the criminal justice system developed historically. Chapter 2 traces the roots of forensic psychiatry as it emerged as an offshoot of general psychiatry linked closely with attitudes towards the punishment of offenders. In Chapter 3 the permeation of racism into the popular construct schizophrenia is outlined and in Chapter 4 the ways in which 'race' has become involved in issues about dangerousness, both in the USA and the UK, are considered from various angles that seem relevant to the issues central to the book.

Forensic psychiatry is generally considered a clinical discipline within a medical framework. Chapters 5 to 9 examine issues of race and culture from such a clinical perspective, setting it against what is known about the operation of the criminal justice system. Chapter 5 sets the field in which the clinical process functions, examining the interplay between, on the one hand, the services themselves, and on the other, black people who live in the UK. Chapter 6 reviews issues about crime and violence that affect the clinical practice of forensic psychiatry. But since clinical practice is ostensibly based on research, Chapter 7 addresses issues of bias in the way information is collected and the research carried out in the fields of race and culture. The medical model that clinicians use always includes diagnosis, although the importance given to it may well vary from place to place and clinician to clinician. Chapter 8 poses the likelihood that racist ideology and misperceptions may result in the schizophrenia diagnosis being over-used for people seen as 'black', and discusses ways round this for the sensitive clinician. Finally, Chapter 9 addresses issues around race in connection with specific clinical processes – admission to institutions, medication, seclusion, etc.

Psychiatric systems, and forensic psychiatry more than any other, are a part of society and, to a large extent, reflect society. The problems faced by people in the forensic system mirror the problems they face in society at large. Also, the assessments made by professionals in the forensic system – judgements about people, their behaviour, motivations etc. – are influenced by attitudes in society. Chapters 10 to 13 examine public policy around forensic psychiatry in terms of (public) perceptions, attitudes and activities (such as the media), in so far as they affect matters around race and culture in forensic psychiatry. Chapter 10 explores the reasons behind the stereotypical images of black people that affect decision-making in forensic psychiatry. In Chapter 11 the effects of these images on public policy at an institutional level are discussed. In Chapter 12 issues arising from public pressures that influence the pathways that black people follow – or are made to follow – into the forensic system are discussed in examining lessons to be learned from the (many) inquiries into events that have hit the media and affected government policy. Chapter 13 reviews the attempts being made by black communities to reclaim for themselves the field of mental health, and by black professionals to help this process.

The field covered in this book is a complex and controversial one. It requires a balanced approach based on knowledge that is deep and far reaching, rather than being merely medical, social or political in a narrow sense. Therefore, the last part of this book seeks to address at least some of the problems alluded to in the earlier parts. Chapter 14 gives an overall picture of the issues that should be addressed and Chapter 15 pin-points the areas where change *can* and *should* occur sooner, rather than later – not just in the interest of black people alone but in the interest of society as a whole and in the interests of the discipline of forensic psychiatry.

Part I

Background

Suman Fernando

Chapter 1

Race and cultural difference

Historically, ideas about 'race' based on skin colour occurred in a context where the words 'black' and 'white' had been associated in the English language with heavily charged notions of good and bad and went hand in glove with prejudice from the very beginning. Then came slavery and colonialism feeding into racial prejudice and vice versa. Today, racism is fashioned by racial prejudice and underpinned by economic and social factors; when implemented and practised through the institutions of society, often without people involved even being aware that they are being racist, it is called 'institutional racism' (Wellman, 1977). Concepts of cultural difference are often distorted by racist perceptions and 'culture' is often confounded with 'race' both historically and in modern Western thinking (see Fernando, 1988). This chapter will attempt to pick out some of the issues around race and culture that form a background to discussions about the emergence of forensic psychiatry that will follow in Chapter 2. Of all historical situations that have fashioned modern European thinking about race and cultural difference, the most significant events centre around the transatlantic slave trade and the colonial era, so this chapter will start with a brief overview of these two shameful and tragic episodes in European history. Then, the concepts of 'race', 'culture' and 'ethnicity', and racism will be discussed. Finally, the chapter will consider other issues, such as multiculturalism where racism is implicated in issues around cultural difference, that may help in understanding the theses presented in the succeeding chapters of this part of the book.

SLAVERY AND COLONIALISM

Slavery had existed in Europe and Africa for a long time before the transatlantic slave trade started (Pieterse, 1995); it was well established in ancient Greece and slaves had been an important European export to the world of Islam and to Byzantium. 'What changed in the course of the sixteenth and seventeenth centuries was that slavery acquired a colour' (1995: 52). Slavery of black people by white people happened outside Europe to a large extent but it contributed significantly to the accumulation of capital in Europe that brought about the Industrial Revolution and it affected European thinking about race.

Initially, slavery thrived on greed and in turn fuelled racism and soon England became the foremost slave trading nation in the world. According to Fryer (1984) 'it was their drive for profit that led British merchant capitalists to traffic in Africans. There was money in it. The theory came later' (1984: 134). And the theory of racism based on skin colour was articulated most strongly by European philosophers of the eighteenth century. As a corollary of the slave trade, black people became a visible minority in British cities by the final decade of the sixteenth century. As England's black community grew in numbers, there were calls for expulsion of blacks by the then monarch. Fryer (1984) quotes an open letter in 1596 from Queen Elizabeth I to the Lord Mayors of major cities stating that 'there are of late divers blackamores brought into the realm, of which kind of people there are already here to manie', and recommending 'that those kind of people be sent forth from the land' (1984: 10). Apparently the Queen's call met with no response in spite of it being repeated in 1601 (Bygott, 1992).

With the abolition of the slave trade in 1807, racism became a crucial ingredient of colonialism. In his classic book *Asia and Western Dominance*, Panikkar (1959) traces the progress of European imperialism in Asia. . By the middle of the seventeenth century, the economic prosperity in Europe, as a result of slave labour and the plunder of the USA, led to the demand for superior goods from the advanced economies of the East – mainly in China and India. Trade gave way to conquest and colonisation, with Britain leading the way. As India was colonised, its industry was suppressed and destroyed and by the mid-nineteenth century, India had been changed from an exporter of manufactured goods to a producer of raw materials and later a source of indentured labour for other parts of European empires. Meanwhile, starting with the 'opium wars' between 1839 and 1842, successive raids into China by British, French and Portuguese forces, often accompanied by acts of vandalism (such as the burning of the Summer Palace in Peking by Lord Elgin in 1860), led to China becoming a semi-colonial state by 1900.

Christian missionaries from Europe started going to India about 1813 supporting a view of the superiority of Europe over Asia. According to Geoffrey Moorhouse (1983), William Wilberforce, a leader of the fight against the slave trade, considered that the conversion of India to Christianity was a cause greater than the abolition of slavery. In the debate which preceded the new India Act, he told the House of Commons in 1813 that he saw the subcontinent as a place which would 'exchange its dark and bloody superstition for the genial influence of Christian light and truth', the gods of the Hindus being 'absolute monsters of lust, injustice, wickedness and cruelty. In short, their religion is one grand abomination' (1983: 69).

In the mid-nineteenth century the final onslaught on Africa began. Historian Basil Davidson (1984) describes how explorers were followed by the missionary drive and European coastal traders. An invasion of the mainland of Africa followed, Europeans were often impressed by the widespread violence and insecurity they found in some parts of Africa and they used this as moral justification for their invasions. But from the very first encounter, they established as a principle their alleged racial superiority over black Africans – an attitude among invaders that was new to Africans (Davidson, 1984):

> However various the methods of colonial enclosure, the results were in one great aspect the same. They brought a new subjection by peoples who, unlike all previous and internal conquerors, regarded themselves as naturally superior to Africans, and who were also able to apply methods of oppression and exploitation of a range and intensity never known before.
>
> (1984: 286)

An agreement to divide up the continent (the 'scramble for Africa') was concluded by European powers at the Berlin conference in 1884/5, but full subjugation of Africa was not completed until about 1920. At that time, African society was organised in social groups – tribes – claiming descent from a common ancestor

(Rodney, 1988). All the large states of nineteenth-century Africa were multi-ethnic and 'their expansion was continually making anything like "tribal" loyalty a thing of the past' (1988: 228). As European powers moved into Africa in force, the nation states were destroyed and tribalism – loyalty to small social groups – encouraged in the interests of cheap colonial rule (Davidson, 1984). In spite of vast profits being made by European firms and European farmers, education and responsibility were withheld from blacks except for elites most of whom 'were content to accept the values of their masters' (1984: 305). The overall result of colonialism was the disintegration of African economies, virtual eradication of African political power and the loss of 'vital aspects of culture' (Rodney, 1988: 232).

Slavery was legally ended within the British Empire on 1 August 1834, but the emancipated black slaves in British colonies in the Caribbean were subjected to a period of 'apprenticeship' that tied them to work on the sugar plantations for a further four years (Fryer, 1988). Then, ex-slaves left the plantations and soon set up communal villages 'through a remarkable process of self-help and solidarity' (1988: 29). Meanwhile European planters imported indentured labourers from British India to develop a 'coolie' system 'built on the foundations laid by the slave system' (1988: 27). However, following an outcry from Indian public opinion, this system was abandoned. The British colonies in the West Indies were left with a multi-ethnic population of people with cultural roots in Africa, Asia and Europe – the vast majority being racially defined as 'black people'.

Resistance

In *Black People in the British Empire* (1988), Peter Fryer states that: 'nowhere within the British Empire were black people passive victims. On the contrary, they were everywhere active resisters. Far from being docile, they resisted slavery and colonialism in every way open to them. Their resistance took many different forms, both individual and collective. It ranged from a watchful and waiting pretence of acceptance – a subtle if elementary form of individual resistance to slavery – right up to large-scale mass uprisings and national liberation movements' (1988: 85). These movements in the Asian, African and West Indian colonies came to a head in the 1930s and 1940s. Then, with the weakening of two major European colonial powers, namely the UK and France, during the so-called 'Second World War' 1939–45 (defeat of Japan), Asian colonies started to become independent and the winds of change soon reached Africa and the West Indies. The final chapter was written in 1993 with the liberation (from white settler rule) of South Africa. But the aftermath of colonialism and slavery had clearly led to massive problems, especially in Africa, allowing the economic plunder – neo-colonialism – to continue throughout the second half of the twentieth century.

RACE

The classification of people into racial types on the basis of physical appearance has a long history in Western culture. And from the very beginning, skin colour was the most popular physical characteristic used for this purpose. In the eighteenth century, Linnaeus (1758) divided homo sapiens into the following varieties: *americanus*, *europaeus*, *asiaticus*, and later identified them in terms of being red, white, yellow and black, and *ferus* and *monstrosus* were identified by general characteristics. In the book, *On the Natural Varieties of Mankind* (1776 [1969]), Blumenbach, a German physician and anthropologist, coined the term 'Caucasian' to refer to what he thought was the ideal race best exemplified by people (Georgians) who then lived on the southern slopes of the Caucasian mountains. He advocated the theory that other races, which he named as Mongolian, Ethiopian, American and Malayan (using skin colour as the main criterion for so doing but adding hair, form, facial characteristics and the shape of skull), had 'degenerated' from this ideal 'Caucasian' type. (This concept of degeneration was taken up in the next century informing the construction of schizophrenia – see Chapter 2). Later, 'Caucasian' became a term applied to people from Europe, North Africa and the Middle East, but is now used loosely to mean 'white-skinned'.

In 1853–5, de Gobineau's pioneering *Essay on the Inequality of the Human Races* (Essai sur l'inegalité des races humaine) which was well received in Europe (Proctor, 1988), claimed scientific status for casting 'race' 'as the primary force in world history' (1988: 12). And, 'scientific racism' thrived in the eighteenth and nineteenth centuries. Darwin's theory of evolution in the mid-nineteenth century gave rise to a new concept of 'race' as a subdivision within the same species: 'domestic races of the same species differ from each other in the same manner as, only in most cases in a lesser degree than do, closely-allied species of the same genus in a state of nature' (Darwin, 1859: 16). By analogy with his description of numerous 'races' within each species, the idea developed that, while human beings as a whole were a 'species' with fertile mating within it, individual (human) 'races' were 'varieties' or 'subspecies' with partial reproductive isolation from each other (Banton, 1987). Each race was seen as being subject to continual modification and development rather than to a static set of inherited characteristics. Although the idea of race as a subspecies promoted the concept of geographical race, it did not exclude the view that races may become separate types: it was held that a subspecies may evolve to a point where it is no longer able to interbreed with other forms and hence become a species.

This new view of race was a flexible and egalitarian one compared to that espoused by de Gobineau, although in *The Descent of Man and Selection in Relation to Sex* (1871) Darwin wrote about the likely extinction of 'savage races' because of their inability to change habits when brought into contact with 'civilised races'. However, Darwin's ideas in *On the Origin of the Species by Means of Natural Selection: or the Preservation of Favoured Races in the Struggle for Life* (1859) were used to develop 'Social Darwinism' that argued for racial hierarchies. In Germany, social Darwinists, like Ploetz, 'an anthropologist of repute' (Bonger, 1943: 24), voiced fears that 'racial degeneration' may come about as a result of 'medical care for the weak' and the rapid multiplication of the poor and misfits of society (Proctor, 1988: 15). The idea that crime and psychosis had a racial basis became such a fundamental belief in Germany by the turn of the nineteenth century that Näcke, described by Bonger (1943) as a well known criminologist, 'very much taken in by the milieu-as-cause theory of crime' (1943: 23), was quoted by him as stating in 1906:

> If one believes in the dissimilarity of the races in physical and psychical respect, then, consequently, one must conclude that the physical and psychical abnormalities and deficiencies in conscience will show certain quantitative and qualitative variations. And this, indeed, seems to be the case, especially where crime and psychosis are concerned.
>
> (1943: 23)

And Social Darwinism fed into the racial hygiene movement which then developed hand-in-hand with eugenics and the construction of schizophrenia as an illness.

As a result of the genocide of Jews and Gypsies in Germany during the 1940s, theories about racial differentiation and overt racism itself became unpopular after the military defeat of Germany in 1945. Post-war science rallied round anti-racism. But new forms of Darwinism, popularised recently by human ethologists (e.g. Robert Ardrey, 1967) and sociobiologists (e.g. Richard Dawkins, 1970), have revived racist ideas (see Barker, 1990). Both ethology and sociobiology suggest that 'it is biologically fixed that humans form exclusive groups, and that these groups succeed internally in so far as they close up against outsiders' (1990: 18). Robert Ardrey (1967), arguing that 'aggression' (identified by ethologists as represented in a variety of animal behaviours) is '*innate*', postulates that its exhibition towards outsiders is a natural condition because 'the biological nation is the supreme natural mechanism for the security of a social group' (1967: 253). Richard Dawkins (1976) writes that 'racial prejudice could be interpreted as an irrational generalisation of a kin-selected tendency to identify with individuals physically resembling oneself and to be nasty to individuals different in appearance' and that this tendency 'could have positive survival value' (1976: 8). Having invented the concept of 'kin altruism' as an extension of 'the selfish gene' sociobiologists appear to argue that it is natural to maintain ethnic boundaries with aggression towards competitive outsiders. Race thinking is implied and racism – and indeed aggression towards outsiders – is justified in both modes of thought.

Recent scientific advances have enabled geneticists to identify human genes that code for specific enzymes and other proteins. It is now possible to use information on the distribution of polymorphic proteins (i.e. proteins that have alternative forms that exist in varying frequencies in the human species) in order to calculate differences between individuals and between defined populations. J. S. Jones (1981) notes that eighty-four per cent of all genetic variation results from genetic difference between individuals belonging to the same tribe or nationality, six per cent from differences between tribes or nationalities, and ten per cent from genetic divergence between 'racial' groups. 'In other words the genetic differences between the classically described races of man are on the average only slightly greater than those which exist between nations within a racial group, and the genetic differences between individual human beings within a population are far larger than either of these' (1981: 189). Thus the genetic differences between (say) indigenous populations of France and Spain, or between different tribes of Africa, are similar to those between so-called races. A way of thinking that includes together in one 'race' everyone who has a particular skin colour or hair type or some other aspect of physical appearance, assigning borderline cases according to traditional ideas (e.g. that 'white' skin colour is pure and 'non-white' is caused by an admixture that corrupts that purity), is no longer biologically acceptable or useful in scientific practice.

The myth of race has been exploded but race as a social reality persists. Thus, in popular lore, and even in medical and scientific circles, racial differences are still seen as indicating biological differences – or at least physical ones that are inherited genetically – and skin colour remains the most popular basis for distinguishing one race from another. Continuing to use the concept of 'race' (defined in social terms by certain aspects of physical appearance) inevitably leads to problems of communication. For example, since the idea that pure races exist is a myth, there cannot be such a thing as hybrid or mixed races (unless the whole human race is thought of as 'hybrid' or 'mixed' racially) and a person cannot be described as being 'of mixed race' – although the *parents* of a person can be described as 'mixed' in that they are perceived as being from different races.

While the assumption that racial groups are biologically distinct from each other is incorrect in scientific terms, race as a marker may be useful in a very limited way. For example, certain genetically transmitted conditions, such as Tay-Sachs disease (infantile amaurotic idiocy), sickle cell trait or sickle cell disease, and cystic fibrosis may be suspected when there is evidence of East European Jewish, West African and north European ancestry respectively (Molnar, 1983), and race may be used as an initial indicator to detect people who may be vulnerable to these conditions. But this use of 'race' in no way challenges the overall conclusion that scientifically, 'as a way of categorising people, race is based upon a delusion' (Banton and Harwood, 1975: 8).

CULTURE

Culture was originally seen as 'something out there', a social concept, but it is now often seen as something 'inside' a person – a psychological state (D'Andrade, 1984). Culture may be described in terms of accumulation of knowledge among people constituting a social group, of 'conceptual structures' that determine the total reality of life within which people live and die, or of social institutions such as the family, the village and so on. In a broad sense, the term culture is applied to all features of an individual's environment, but generally refers to its non-material aspects that the person holds in common with other individuals forming a social group. For example, it refers to child rearing habits, family systems, beliefs and ethical values or attitudes common to a group – a mixture of behaviour and cognition (in a wide sense) arising from what Leighton and Hughes (1961) call 'shared patterns of belief, feeling and adaptation which people carry in their minds' (1961: 447).

All these definitions are within European thinking – Eurocentric notions of human existence, meaning of life, worldviews, etc. Such an understanding usually fails to address what is referred to by people versed in other ('non-European') cultural traditions as 'spirituality'. In other words (modern) Western thinking, maximising its emphasis on rationality and 'scientific' thinking, tends to exclude 'spirit' from the trilogy mind–body–spirit in definitions of 'culture' as much as in many other aspects of (what goes for) knowledge. Yet, in multi-ethnic societies, such as those in Western Europe and North America, spirituality is a part of what many people would consider their 'culture' and cannot be ignored.

Edward Conze (1957), a Western scholar of Eastern traditions argues that 'the word "spiritual" seems vague nowadays . . . it is easier to state by what means one gets to the spiritual realm than to say what it is in itself' (1957: 12). In Western reductionist thinking (e.g. even within anthropology) spirituality is seen as (and often dismissed as) a belief system – religious ideas concerned with the soul or spirits, rather than a state of mind, an emotional or cognitive state. But in other (non-Western) ways of thinking (what is conceptualised as) spirituality is central to human experience and cannot be allocated to some 'part' of it – as a 'belief' or a 'cognition', or even as an emotional state. Conze refers to Buddhism as an 'Eastern form of spirituality. . . . Its doctrine, in its basic assumptions, is identical with many other teachings all over the world, teachings which may be called "mystical"' (1957: 11). Yet, Buddhism, as a system for understanding the human condition, is akin to (Western) psychology rather than (Western) ideas of religion. Safaya (1976) thinks that Indian psychology, embedded in Indian philosophy, has a number of 'divergent philosophical systems or thought-currents . . . but there is a common current of idealism and spiritualism running through all of these' (1976: 2). Nobles (1986) believes that the integration of mind, body and spirit is characteristic of the worldviews derived from African thinking, and indeed what Du Bois (1904 [1970]) calls 'Spiritual Strivings' in his classic *The Souls of Black Folk*, characterises much of the cultural life of black (African) Americans today. And the same would go for many black people whose cultural roots are from Asia and Africa.

The concept of 'culture' is often confused with ideas about race. People seen as racially different are assumed to have different cultures and the value judgement attached to the race is transferred to the culture. Thus, all too often, cultures are seen in racist terms and racist ideas camouflaged as views about cultural difference. In fact, racism has so distorted European views of culture that cultures seen as 'non-European' are often thought of as inferior and skin colour, designating race, is an important dimension in all cross-cultural group interactions in many European settings. The perception of a society as 'multicultural' is not the same as its designation as 'multiracial'. A multicultural society is one composed of people with different backgrounds, traditions and worldviews – not necessarily the same as a multiracial society, although a particular racial group may also sometimes be a cultural group (as discussed later in the section on ethnicity).

The term culture is sometimes applied to describe the ethos or ways of functioning of professional groups or institutions. So, reference may be made to the culture of social work, psychiatry or psychology. The culture of Western psychiatry has been described elsewhere (Fernando, 1995a) as being characterised (basically) by a mind–body dichotomy, a mechanistic view of life, a materialistic concept of mind, a segmental approach to the individual, illness meaning a bio-medical change, and a natural cause of illness (1995a: 13). It is from the 'ethos' contained in these roots that psychiatry functions. In order to understand the roots it is necessary to trace its origins (see Chapter 3).

But a culture is never static – whether of family, community or institution. In the case of the culture of a family or community, changes may (and nearly always do) occur over time, in successive generations, or as new ideas affect the group of people involved. In the case of institutions, new ways of functioning can be introduced through training or education. Further, external pressures, especially those derived from racism, play a significant part in determining certain aspects of culture – even the very formation of 'culture' of a group (as noted above); the culture of a community, family or group may be determined as much by social circumstances (e.g. poverty, racial harassment, segregation) as custom, and the culture of an institution may change as a result of social and political pressures.

ETHNICITY

Ethnicity is a term that lacks precision but alludes to the definition of both cultural and racial groups. The bonds that bind together people of an ethnic group are often subtle and unclear; they are not definable in terms of physical appearance (race) or social similarity (culture) alone, although both may be involved. The overriding feature of an ethnic group is the sense of belonging together that the individuals within it *feel*; it is basically a psychological matter. This feeling may be promoted, or even initiated, by the way society at large perceives people. If certain persons are seen as belonging together – for whatever reason – and are treated as such, a sense of being part of a group may develop. If the bonds that seem to bind them together are seen as 'cultural' or 'racial', or both, an ethnic group is identified. Thus, cultural similarity, real or imagined, may engender or even determine a sense of belonging that determines ethnicity. But this sense of belonging may well arise for different reasons: for example, a sense of belonging that emerges in a racist society is likely to be based on race as perceived by society at large, rather than culture as experienced by the group members. But, if racially identified people become isolated or alienated – and especially if they tend to live in segregated communities – a characteristic 'culture' would emerge.

In the UK, the term 'ethnic' is taken to mean a mixture of cultural background and racial designation, the significance of each being variable. (It was, and still is, used differently on mainland Europe.) It is essentially about self-perception – how people see themselves. A government paper (in this case about collecting health statistics) states: 'Ethnic group describes how you see yourself, and is a mixture of culture, religion, skin colour, language, the origins of yourself or your family. It is not the same as nationality' (NHS Management Executive, 1993).

So, if racism is felt as a powerful force in society, people from various backgrounds and cultures may see themselves largely in racial terms (e.g. as 'black people'), but also (or alternatively) in 'cultural' terms of religion or parental origin (e.g. as 'Muslims' or 'Asian'). The UK has seen a significant change in the ethnic composition of its population over the past forty years, mainly as a result of migration from countries that were formerly British colonies in Asia and the Caribbean. So, most societies within the UK are made up of various ethnic groups – i.e. they are multi-ethnic. In the 1991 census of the UK, an ethnic question was included for the first time, each person being asked to identify himself or herself in terms of ethnicity. The main broad ethnic groups referred to in population statistics, health surveys and research are African-Caribbeans, Africans, Asians and whites, the two largest minority ethnic groups being Asians (predominantly referring to South Asia) and African-Caribbeans. In the UK, the term 'black people' is applied quite often to mean either all ethnic minorities or more often to Africans and African-Caribbeans, but in other places (e.g. the USA and Canada) the term 'people of colour' is preferred and in many European countries the pejorative term 'migrant' is still used. However, in the 1990s, the categories of ethnicity applicable to British populations is changing – a matter discussed below.

RACISM

Although racism pre-dates slavery and colonialism (Fryer, 1984), these two historical events clearly played an important role in consolidating the dogma of European racism. The crude notions of white racial superiority that developed during slavery were refined and confirmed into a lasting ideology integrated into European culture. And it was while colonial exploitation and plunder was in full swing in the mid-eighteenth century that 'scientific' justification for racism emerged. Myths, stereotypes and superstitions about black people and about cultures seen as 'non-European', 'Oriental', or 'African' became integrated into European culture and thinking. As Europe entered the period of its 'Enlightenment', 'numerous writings on race by Hume, Kant and Hegel played a strong role in articulating Europe's sense not only of its cultural but also of its racial superiority. In their writings, '"reason" and "civilization" became almost synonymous with "white" people and northern Europe, while unreason and savagery were conveniently located among the non-whites, the "black," the "red," the "yellow," outside Europe' (Eze, 1997: 5). For example, the Scottish philosopher David Hume in 1753 added in a footnote to an essay written in 1748 and quoted by Fryer: 'I am apt to suspect the negroes, and in general all the other species of men (for there are four or five different kinds) to be naturally inferior to the whites. There never was a civilized nation of any complexion than white, nor even any individual eminent either in action or speculation. No ingenious manufacture among them, no arts, no sciences' (1984: 152).

In the nineteenth century, the histories and achievements of African, native American and Asian cultures were largely discredited in the West, although (for example) West Africa in the sixteenth century was a highly developed region economically, politically and artistically with at least one state, the Wolof Empire, which could muster 10,000 cavalry and 100,000 infantry (Davidson, 1984), and (as noted above) India and China were much more advanced industrially (compared to Europe) before the colonial conquest. In the first volume of his seminal book *Black Athena* (1987), Martin Bernal has shown how racism affected the writing of history in the nineteenth century – the heyday of colonialism. And it is this distorted history that continues to be taught to black and white people in multi-ethnic societies. As Europe entered the nineteenth century, 'Virtually every scientist and intellectual in nineteenth century Britain took it for granted that only people with white skin were capable of thinking and governing' (Fryer, 1984: 169). In the twentieth century, racism is deeply embedded in all aspects of European culture and permeates the psyche of every European person, black or white. Fanon (1952), a black psychiatrist who was educated in France, writes:

> *In Europe, the black man is the symbol of Evil. . . .* The torturer is the black man, Satan is black, one talks of shadows, when one is dirty one is black – whether one is thinking of physical dirtiness or of moral dirtiness. . . . The Negro is the symbol of sin. . . . In the remotest depths of the European unconscious an inordinately black hollow has been made in which the most immoral impulses, the most shameful desires lie dormant. And as every

> man climbs up towards whiteness and light, the European has tried to repudiate this uncivilized self, which has attempted to defend itself. When European civilization came into contact with the black world, with those savage peoples, everyone agreed: Those Negroes were the principle of evil.
>
> (original emphasis, 1952: 188–90)

Modern racism

The concept of 'race', meaning some biologically determined entity recognisable by external appearance (or rarely by nominal religious affiliation or language), has been dismissed in scientific circles as a basis for dividing up the human race (J. S. Jones, 1981). As *Not in Our Genes* (Rose *et al.*, 1984: 127) states: 'Human "racial" differentiation is indeed only skin deep. Any use of racial categories must take its justification from some other source than biology'. However, the tendency to think of people in terms of their 'race', or 'race thinking' (Barzun, 1965) persists and affects individual and group behaviour. When racism is implemented and practised through the institutions of society, often without people involved even being aware that they are being racist, it is called 'institutional racism'. Many sociocultural systems fashioned in the West, such as psychiatry, social work, clinical psychology and counselling, show aspects of institutional racism.

In the late twentieth century, in post-slavery, post-colonial Europe, racism shows little signs of losing its hold. Clearly, economic and political factors feed into racism, and psychological needs of the people who stand to gain from racial classification play a part too. It persists because dominant groups, whether as nations or ethnic groups, need it in order to divide, rule, oppress and control (often) more numerous but economically weaker groups. The fact is that racial categorisation on the basis of mainly skin colour is a powerful social reality. But, when a group of people are perceived as belonging to a racial group, the assumption is of common ancestry. When a society is referred to as 'multiracial', the implication is that it contains people whose ancestries vary; but more importantly, it implies that these ancestries are related to different skin colours represented in people's appearance or in their heritage – their 'blood'.

Racism in psychology and psychiatry is as old as the disciplines themselves (see Fernando, 1991). Publications (for example) by

Jensen (1969) and Eysenck (1971), revived the racist IQ movement in the 1970s and psychologists have shown a remarkable persistence in pursuing racism; the latest books, *The Bell Curve: Intelligence and Class Structure in American Life* by Murray and Herrnstein (1994) and *The g Factor* by Brand (1996), published and then withdrawn in the UK both argue for a hierarchy of races, although now the 'Orientals' from Japan come out on top! Today racism continues to emerge in scientific guise, sometimes expressed in cultural language, sometimes in terms of arguments about intelligence or personality. In his book *The Race Gallery: the Return of Racial Science* (1995), M. Kohn documents the continuing message of racism in scientific circles: 'Race remains embedded in science at many levels, as do the hardline race scientists themselves' (1995: 57).

As biological thinking lost its scientific backing from the 1970s onwards, the way racism is manifested in contemporary Western society appears to have revived a racist 'culturalism' that was always there in European thinking. Malik (1996: 143) notes that the casting of racist discourse in cultural terms can be traced to French thinkers of the late nineteenth century. The current situation has been documented in the writings of sociologists (Gilroy, 1987, 1993; Bhabha, 1994). According to Gilroy (1993) British racism now 'frequently operates without any overt reference to "race" itself or the biological notions of difference which still give the term its common-sense meaning'. 'Culture', seen as an immutable, fixed property of social groups (which it is not), has become confounded with 'race', and racism is articulated in cultural terms. Malik quotes Todorov (1993) on this issue:

> Modern racialism . . . replaces physical race with linguistic, historical and psychological race. It shares certain features with its ancestor, but not all; this has allowed it to abandon the compromised term 'race'. . . . Nevertheless it can continue to play the role formerly assumed by racialism. In our day racist behaviours have clearly not disappeared, or even changed; but the discourse that legitimises them is no longer the same; rather than appealing to racialism, it appeals to nationalist or culturalist doctrine, or to the 'right to difference'.
>
> (1996: 143, in Todorov, 1993: 156–7)

The contention that British racism is now marked by the importance given to 'culture rather than biology' (Gilroy, 1993) means that the concept of 'multiculturalism', in going along implicitly with a definition of race as culture, emphasising 'cultures' of essentially 'racial' groups, may well collude with (or even implement) British racism.

NEW ETHNICITIES

Race, culture and ethnicity are interrelated in complex ways depending on historical, political and social factors. For example, the experience, post-slavery, of black people in the USA has shaped a black consciousness – a sense of belonging to a group – as well as a recognisable black culture (Richardson and Lambert, 1985). In the post-empire UK, black people find themselves trapped under a system of 'internal colonialism' within cities (Pryce, 1979). And these 'internal colonies', sometimes identified geographically as 'ghettos', have provided the material base for a cultural revival of a 'West Indian consciousness' extending into a more generalised 'black consciousness' (Hall *et al.*, 1978).

In the light of the discussions about modern racism and ethnicity, it is necessary to examine the category 'black' when applied to people with diverse subjective positions, social experiences and cultural identities – represented by categories used for identifying ethnicity. As Stuart Hall (1992) points out, it is no longer adequate politically to contend 'that all black people are *the same* (1992: 254, original emphasis). The challenge today is to 'be able to build those forms of solidarity and identification which make common struggle and resistance possible but without suppressing the real heterogeneity of interests and identities, and which can effectively draw the political boundary lines without which political contestation is impossible, without fixing those boundaries for eternity' (1992: 254–5). The issue now is one of representation of each person in a particular context that takes account of background, experience, gender, 'race' and everything else that is worthwhile to the individual and/or the family. It is about the meaning of being British or US or European; it is about the lack of representation as the title of Gilroy's first book states so bluntly, *There Ain't No Black in the Union Jack* (1987).

MULTICULTURALISM

Although the racist nature of British society is not often talked about very openly, there are few qualms in referring to the UK as multicultural. The liberal-minded aim underlying multiculturalism is to foster cultural plurality accepting that all cultures are equally valid. Positively, multiculturalism is a corrective to a predominantly Eurocentric vision of society. The promotion of 'multicultural education' has been actively pursued in schools in both the UK and parts of North America (e.g. Canada) for many years and many health authorities in the UK too have provided 'cultural education' to acquaint professionals with cultural differences. As the 'melting pot' ideology of assimilation of cultures within an all-encompassing 'US culture' has given way in the USA to the promotion of cultural diversity, there too multiculturalism has been promoted. In writing about the current US scene, bell hooks (1995) points out that in a context of racism, multiculturalism can promote 'coalition building between people of color' to resist white supremacist pressures (1995: 203) or 'become a breeding ground for narrow fundamentalism, identity politics, and cultural, racial, and ethnic separatism' (1995: 201). She appears to see the need to recognise cultural plurality of US society and the limitations of adhering to 'static notions of black identity' (1995: 243), advocating a version (of multiculturalism) that 'embraces both a broadbased identity politics which acknowledges specific cultural and ethnic legacies, histories etc. as it simultaneously promotes a recognition of overlapping cultural traditions and values as well as an inclusive understanding of what is gained when people of color unite to resist white supremacy' (1995: 203).

In the UK, anti-racist movements that developed in the late 1960s generally accepted multiculturalism as a positive step towards recognition of the cultural diversity and individuality of people lumped together as 'black people'. In the late 1970s there were some warning signs that all was not well with the cultural discourse. For example, Margaret Thatcher, then leader of the Opposition in the House of Commons made the following statement on 30 January, 1978:

> people are really rather afraid that this country might be swamped by people with a different culture. And, you know, the British have done so much for democracy, for law, and done so much throughout the world, that if there is fear that it might be swamped, people are going to react and be rather hostile to those coming in.
>
> (Fitzpatrick, 1990: 249)

It is evident that, although multicultural policies may have created better understanding in some instances, they have often exacerbated and reinforced racism. One reason is that, although the concept of 'race' (referring to biological difference) and that of 'culture' (arising from historically derived differences between groups of people) may appear to be clearly differentiated in European thinking, this has never been the case – at least not for a long time. And so, in going along implicitly with a definition of race as culture, emphasising 'cultures' of essentially 'racial' groups, in a context of modern racism (discussed earlier), 'multiculturalism' implemented in a racist context may well collude with (or even implement) racism. For example, in the UK, the emphasis on multi-culturalism by emphasising 'difference' without confronting racism, has helped define national identity in 'racial' terms, articulating it in cultural language – sometimes with very little attempt to disguise the racist message. In fact, racism is a major part of the ideology underlying the current discourse about nationality and belonging – about being 'British' or 'European'.

Today, multiculturalism as a policy for a multi-ethnic society where racism is a powerful force, has serious problems. K. Malik (1996) writes:

> How can we understand the difference between racial difference and cultural relativity, given that the latter seems to embody both racist and antiracist perspectives? To arrive at the answer we need to pull together a number of different threads. First, at the heart of the discourse of cultural relativity . . . there lies a hostility to . . . universalism as implacable as that in the discourse of race. Second, the discourse of race and that of culture express two very different forms of hostility to universalism. Third, the key to understanding the difference between the concept of race and that of culture lies in the different ideas of social progress embodied in each.
>
> (1996: 145)

In more direct political language, emphasis on multiculturalism can divide communities (for example, by inducing competition for funds and favours from statutory bodies), although they should be using each other's strengths for the pursuit of liberty and justice for all. After all, the promotion of just such divisions was used by Western imperialism in divide-and-rule policies in the colonies.

CONCLUSIONS

'Race', 'culture' and 'ethnicity' are difficult to disentangle in practical situations; confusion between them is rife in many areas of thought – from politics to scientific research. In short, race is perceived as primarily physical although it is a social construct: culture is entirely sociological and ethnicity is largely psychological. 'Race' is a social entity which has powerful effects on almost all aspects of society, including the practice of forensic psychiatry. Culture and ethnicity are dynamic entities that are constantly changing in relation to social and political forces, personal likes and dislikes, etc. Racism does not refer to racial prejudice alone, but, more importantly, to 'institutionalised racism' that informs many of the social systems in Europe and North America, including psychology and psychiatry The pervasiveness of racism in the processes that have shaped the development of psychiatry with its models of illness, and then in the conditions that formed the background in which forensic psychiatry emerged, is complicated and not always overt. However, this is exactly what the next three chapters in this part of the book will attempt to examine.

Chapter 2

Mental illness and criminality

The aim of this chapter is to explore the background to the current concepts of mental illness and criminality in order to trace the origins of assumptions about the association between them, especially the current popular tendency to see connections between (what is understood as) schizophrenia and perceptions of some people as 'dangerous'. The chapter will outline the history of Western psychiatry which, in the nineteenth century, developed the concept of schizophrenia and also incorporated the idea of the 'dangerous man' – both emerging in the context of various forces in European thinking. It will then discuss the extent to which images of race – and indeed racist images – influenced ideas about schizophrenia and the concept of 'dangerousness' itself.

ORIGINS OF PSYCHIATRY

In the sixteenth century Descartes established a strict division between mind and body setting the style of (Western) psychology (Murphy, 1938). Since then, Western thinking has increasingly split thought from affect (emotion) (Fromm *et al.*, 1960): 'thought alone is considered rational – affect, by its very nature, irrational; the person, I, has been split off into intellect, which constitutes myself, and which is to control *me* as it is to control nature' (1960: 79). Western psychology, aping the physical sciences, has dissected human nature, reducing complex systems of emotional and intellectual life in order to 'find' laws, basic 'facts', natural tendencies, etc. – the reductionist approach to gathering knowledge. Later, psychology took on the mechanistic approach of Newtonian physics, analysing human feelings in terms of cause-and-effect, 'forces', etc. In adopting this mode of thinking characteristic of nineteenth-century science, anything to do with supernatural influences and spirituality was excluded.

Prior to the seventeenth century, medical ideas about insanity were associated in European thinking with the terms phrenitis, mania and melancholia – indeed 'mania' was used as a general term for madness (Jeste *et al.*, 1985). In England, medical interest in matters to do with the mind was represented by books such as *A Treatise of Melancholy* (1586) by T. Bright and R. Burton's *The Anatomy of Melancholy* (1621). And then came what Foucault (1967) has called the 'great confinement' which resulted in moves across Europe and North America to institutionalise various groups of people considered deviant in one way or other. His analysis of how this came about purports that around the middle of the seventeenth century, 'the formulas of [social] exclusion' that had been applied to people with leprosy for the previous two or three centuries was repeated in the case of 'poor vagabonds, criminals and "deranged minds"' (1967: 7). According to Foucault, it was a response to 'an economic crisis that affected the entire Western world: reduction of wages, unemployment, scarcity of coin' (1967: 49).

In France, the great confinement was largely instituted by the state in a centrally managed policy. However, this may not have applied to the same extent in England and even less so in Scandinavia, Spain, Portugal, Ireland and eastern Europe (Porter, 1990). According to Scull (1993), what happened in England was that, 'after a brief flurry of activity in the late sixteenth and early seventeenth centuries, the poor, including the insane poor, continued to be dealt with on a local parish level' (1993: 15) until the early eighteenth century. Even then, many of the lunatic asylums that were built in London, Manchester and York were charitable trusts rather than state institutions and the large-scale building of asylums by the state occurred much later – in the early nineteenth century (Porter, 1990).

What did happen, however, all over Europe and North America was that places where 'the mad' were confined came under medical jurisdiction to an increasing extent; the landmark in France was the 1656 decree founding the Hôpital General in Paris (Foucault, 1967) and in England the appointment in 1632 of a medical governor at the Priory of St Mary of Bethlem – an institution that had been taking in lunatics since 1403 (see Porter, 1990). However, it was not until the eighteenth century that the medicalisation of madness really took place; medical practitioners began to specialise in 'mad-doctoring' (Scull, 1993: 180), analysing the causes of insanity in medical terms and later prescribing treatment. So, although psychiatry as a discipline had its origins in Europe of the mid-seventeenth century, it did not take on a medical role until the early eighteenth century. It should be noted (Castel, 1988) that 'making madness a medical matter' was not essentially one of establishing a relationship between the doctor and the sick person, but represented 'the development of a hospital technology, the exercise of a new kind of power within the institution, the acquiring of a new social mandate from practices based at first upon the bastion of the asylum' (1988: 46).

The great confinement occurred as European thinking entered the 'age of reason . . . [when] . . . all beliefs and practices which appeared ignorant, primitive, childish or useless came to be readily dismissed as idiotic or insane, evidently the products of stupid thought processes, or delusion and daydream' (Porter, 1987: 14–15). People exhibiting such attitudes and behaviour – 'outsiders' – were identified as disturbed (rather than 'disturbing') and people seen as 'alien' to polite society were assumed to be 'alienated' in mind. Meanwhile, Europeans involved in the Atlantic slave trade justified slavery on the basis that black people were subhuman (see Chapter 1) and so, not only were social deviants in Europe considered 'outsiders', but similar or more disparaging epithets were applied to any one perceived as non-European. The 'natural' superiority of Europe – seen in racial terms – was by then an article of faith and the term 'primitive' was applied indiscriminately to 'coloured' people all over the world (Worsley, 1972).

The early psychiatrists were called Alienists because they decided who was alien to society and who was not, who was mentally 'ill', 'deficient', etc.; they set the boundary between the mentally 'normal' and the insane. As 'illness' of the mind became the basic model for understanding people regarded by society as 'mad', the ethos of the alienist approach became as one with the medical approach of psychiatry. Socially undesirable behaviour was equated with symptoms of 'illness'. Various theoretical concepts about such illness (of the mind) were developed, initially drawing upon Greek Hippocratic traditions (Simon, 1978) but later from various other sources. 'Pathologies' of emotion, intellect, beliefs, feelings, thinking etc. were identified and elaborated. As illnesses were named, modern psychiatry came into being.

Treatment

During the early years of psychiatry, the approach towards people incarcerated in institutions for 'lunatics' was largely custodial. However, according to Porter (1987), psychiatry began to show 'a new faith in therapy' (1987: 17) from the mid-eighteenth century onwards. The early models of treatment were primarily organic based on drugs 'to sedate maniacs, others to stimulate melancholics, and many designed to purge the constitution of its poisons through sweats, vomits and laxatives' (1987: 18). Electric shocks, hot baths, cold showers and various forms of physical restraints, from special chairs to manacles, were used supposedly for therapeutic purposes. Then, in the late eighteenth century, 'moral management' (also called 'moral therapy') came into fashion in some centres, such as the York Retreat in England, where patients were expected to undergo moral re-awakenings through the kindling of their own 'desire of esteem' and improve their behaviour by learning to 'restrain themselves' (Porter, 1990: 224). Although the advent of moral therapy meant that the insane were subjected to less physical abuse than previously, Foucault (1967) saw moral therapy as the imposition of internalised control of patients' conscious life through creating guilt and replacing repression with authority – a 'gigantic moral imprisonment' (1967: 278).

Moral therapies and physical treatments existed side by side in the asylums during the nineteenth century but, in spite of all the therapies, few patients were actually discharged. Meanwhile, the great confinement continued unabated. The seemingly incessant rise of insanity gave rise to pessimism about any 'cure' for madness, leading to the two theoretical formulations (about mental illness) that emerged in the nineteenth century and underpinned the development of the concept of schizophrenia – Morel's (1852) concept of degeneration and Lombroso's (1911) ideas about physical stigmata of illness and criminality. According to Pick (1989) the theory of degeneration 'served as a convenient method of explaining away the failure of psychiatry to "cure" very many of its patients . . . [and] . . . the function of the asylum was re-defined not as "cure" but as humane segregation of the degenerate and the dangerous' (1989: 54).

Modern nosology

The terminology of modern psychiatry includes under (what is now called) 'mental disorder', three broad categories of 'mental illness' – psychoses, neuroses and personality disorders. It is now generally accepted that the category 'psychoses' includes 'those disorders traditionally regarded as madness, in which strange beliefs and perceptions, often accompanied by violent and destructive behaviour, at one time resulted in incarceration in mental asylums' (Goldberg *et al.*, 1994: 46). Also, under 'mental disorder' psychiatry has a system for diagnosing (what is now called) 'learning disabilities', formerly designated 'mental deficiency' – a system closely linked to definitions of 'intelligence' that the discipline of psychology has fashioned. It was customary at one time to subdivide mental deficiency into feeblemindedness, imbecility and idiocy (Slater and Roth, 1969), but these pejorative terms were dropped in the 1970s. The terms 'mental subnormality' and 'severe mental subnormality' are still used for legal purposes in the UK but people with learning disabilities are seldom delineated into 'types' in the way those with mental health problems are still classified.

Since the Second World War, the World Health Organisation (WHO) has attempted to standardise the nomenclature for 'mental illness' in the International Classification of Diseases (ICD), but largely continues the Kraepelinian tradition of defining two basic forms of madness (or insanity), i.e. the categories of 'schizophrenia' and 'mood disorder' (or manic depression) in the latest version, *The Classification of Mental Disorder and Behavioural Disorders* (ICD-10) (World Health Organisation, 1992). The American Psychiatric Association has taken a similar approach in their *Diagnostic and Statistical Manual of Mental Disorders* (DSM) since DSM-III (1980) – the latest being DSM-IV (1994). However, some odd events have occurred in this essentially political process of achieving agreement between important people from various countries, mainly from Europe but latterly including Japan and India. For example, homosexuality was an illness until 1973 but excluded from DSM in 1974 after a majority vote of the American Psychiatric Association (Bayer, 1981) and ICD followed suit. During most of this century, depression has been reported as rare in both Asia and Africa and among black people in the USA, and this was attributed to their 'irresponsible' and 'unthinking' nature (Green, 1914), or 'absence of a sense of responsibility' (Carothers, 1953). Recently, the term 'somatoform disorder' has appeared in DSM as a result (it seems) of Japanese and Chinese pressure and China is developing its own variation of DSM.

Through all these changes in diagnostic fashion, the type of 'illness' known as schizophrenia has maintained its position almost untouched. Ever since Kraepelin constructed it in 1896 as dementia præcox, schizophrenia has occupied pride of place in the annals of psychiatry but, even more importantly, schizophrenia is the mainstay of the psychiatric order in a political sense because its diagnosis is central to the 'expertise' of the psychiatrist, especially that of the forensic psychiatrist.

EMERGENCE OF SCHIZOPHRENIA

An important – if not the most important – part of the business of psychiatry as it developed as a medical discipline was the analysis of madness as 'illness' leading to the delineation of illnesses of the mind and their classification. And each institution developed its own system of diagnosis based on little if any systematic observation. In 1889 the International Congress of Mental Science in Paris agreed upon a classification drawn up by Morel (Tuke, 1890) but it seems without much success in having it accepted across Europe (Kendell, 1975). The classifications of illness used in Europe were reflected in North America but with variations. For example, diagnoses among black slaves included illnesses, such as 'drapetomania', the disease causing slaves to 'run away' (Cartwright, 1851: 318) and 'Dysaesthesia Aethiopis' in which slaves 'break, waste, and destroy everything they handle . . . raise disturbances with their overseers' and generally refused to work (Cartwright, 1851: 321). However, throughout the nineteenth century and the early part of the twentieth, Germany was the centre of psychiatric thinking; the first chair of psychological medicine established in Europe was at Leipzig, Germany, in 1811 (Hunter and MacAlpine, 1963). The focus of interest was the large mass of people incarcerated in asylums.

As European psychiatry was elaborated, various forms of insanity were described and, towards the end of the nineteenth century, the German psychiatrist Emil Kraepelin (1896) presented his observations on bizarre behaviours among asylum inmates. In the fifth edition of his textbook *Psychiatrie*, Kraepelin (1896) revived an idea put forward by Morel (1852) (whose general theory of degeneration as an explanation for a range of social problems will be described later) to use the term dementia præcox to cover 'hebephrenia', 'catatonia', 'dementia paranoides' and, in the eighth edition (1913), 'simple dementia'. Dementia præcox was renamed schizophrenia in 1911 (Bleuler, 1950) as a subgroup of insanity distinct from mania, melancholia, idiocy and senile dementia, on the basis that it was caused by a split between one part of the mind and another (intellect and emotions). As Kraepelin and Bleuler were eminent psychiatrists, their ideas were rapidly accepted across Europe and North America and form the basis of the current system of classification of mental disorders.

Around the turn of the century, Kraepelin seemed to have divided a unitary concept of insanity into two major illnesses, manic depression and schizophrenia. But, both mania and depression (as melancholia) had been recognised as 'illness' since Greek times, and what Kraepelin *actually* did was construct (in a nineteenth-century European context) a new 'illness', schizophrenia, based on observing people who had been incarcerated in asylums. When Kraepelin (1913) described this 'illness', 'dementia præcox', he stated that 'the disease is probably extremely old' (1913: 232), although he did so without any apparent evidence. Unfortunately, psychiatry accepted this contention without examining its validity. Recently, however, the historical accuracy of the belief that schizophrenia is an 'old' disease has been questioned (Torrey, 1980; Hare, 1988, Gottesman, 1991) and the usefulness of schizophrenia as a concept for either research or clinical work is dubious (see Chapter 3).

Historian R. Porter (1987) has noted that, from its very beginning up to the present, psychiatry has endorsed 'medical materialism' – 'that is expecting to find insanity in organic, neurological or biochemical disorders' (1987: 18). This approach has been particularly evident in the case of schizophrenia but with entirely negative results (see Chapter 3). Taking together the lack of history (before psychiatry described it) and the failure to find any material leads in identifying an organic cause for schizophrenia, the likelihood is that the construction of schizophrenia was intimately related to the social and political forces that were active in Europe in the late nineteenth century – especially those appertaining to Germany where schizophrenia was brought into the psychiatric world by Kraepelin and his followers. So, the context in which this took place is important for an understanding of its power and persistence.

'DEGENERATION', CRIMINALITY AND RACISM

Psychiatric and psychological thinking in Western Europe during the nineteenth century was strongly influenced by two main concepts – 'degeneration' as a basis for understanding poverty, lunacy and racial inferiority, and the idea of the 'born criminal' derived from the science of crime (scientific criminology), bound up with concepts of backwardness and the 'primitive' (as seen through white European eyes). Pick (1989) writes that *dégénérescence* (proposed by Morel in the *Traite des mentales* (1857) 'was the name for a process of pathological change from one condition to another in society and in the body. . . . Madness for Morel and many of his colleagues could not necessarily be seen or heard, but it lurked in the body, incubated by the parents and visited upon the children' (Pick, 1989: 50–1). However, degeneration was not primarily a theory of madness alone. It linked crime, insanity and race (Pick, 1989).

But, where did the ideology of degeneracy come from? By the start of the nineteenth century, Europe had experienced 'progress' for two-hundred years largely through the slave trade and booty from genocide in Europe's 'new world' representing 'four-hundred years of European imperialism' (Thomson, 1966). Colonial ventures in South Asia were yielding considerable amounts of loot but its unequal distribution among white European nations was causing tensions between them. The first half of the century was a 'time of endemic civil war' in Europe (Thomson, 1966: 129) and later in that century nearly all Western European countries were involved in the unsavoury and murderous 'scramble for Africa' (Pakenham, 1992). By the end of the nineteenth century, Germany, having lost time to other European countries in the quest for riches outside Europe, was flexing its economic and military muscle (Carr, 1991), extending aggressive trade routes into Turkey and supporting with force of arms the occupation by German immigrants of land belonging to the Herero people in southwest Africa.

But in spite of European 'progress' and the fact that its military power was establishing colonies in Asia, Africa and America, there was a sense of insecurity in Europe itself with concern about increasing crime rates and the apparent failure to contain the dangers to society from what was seen as criminality and insanity. Political and social anxiety was high, especially in France, which had suffered military defeats, and in Germany, which was established as the German Confederation in 1815 to become the German Empire in 1871 (Carr, 1991). Race thinking – thinking of people as naturally divided into 'races' based on physical appearance (especially skin colour) – was the norm, and the dogma of racism had become well established within European cultures as a result of slavery and colonialism (Chapter 1). Pick writes: 'Evolutionary scientists, criminal anthropologists and medical psychiatrists confronted themselves with the apparent paradox that civilisation, science and economic progress might be the catalyst of, as much as the defence against, physical and social pathology' (1989: 11). Biological ideas of Lamarck and Darwin had become influential and the concept of degeneration, involving race thinking, attempted to explain the other side of what was seen as 'progress': it represented an 'impossible endeavour to "scientise", objectify and cast off whole underworlds of political and social anxiety' (1989: 10). Lurking in the background was the fear of the unknown, the dark forces that threatened Europeans – geographically located in Africa and Asia (America having become an extension of Europe through conquest and genocide) and represented by the 'coloured races'.

During the nineteenth century, Lombroso. an Italian psychiatrist, combined a new doctrine of 'atavism' – reversion to primitive stages of evolution – with the more complex French theory of degeneration. After studying physical features of animals, social deviants and others, as well as conducting anthropometric researches on ethnic diversity of Italians, Lombroso produced tables of photographs pinpointing physical features that identified criminality and insanity. According to Pick (1989), 'Criminality for Lombroso was not "unnatural" sin, nor an act of free will, but the sign of a primitive form of nature within an advancing society' (1989: 125–6). His 'science' of criminal anthropology attempted to provide means of detecting delinquency 'by revealing the true criminal in advance of any particular action' (1989: 128). Lombroso correlated mental and physical characteristics to prove that degenerates were evolutionary throwbacks. Lombroso (1911) found it difficult to analyse the association of race and crime among Africans, Asians and Native Americans because (to him) 'the notion of crime existing in the mind of the savage is so vague that we are often led to doubt its existence in the primitive man altogether' (1911: 21). However, he associated differences in crime rates among groups of Europeans with their 'race': 'In our civilized world, to note the proof of the influence of race upon crime is both easy and more certain. We know that a large number of thieves of London are of Irish parentage, or are natives of Lancashire. . . . In Germany, the districts in which there are colonies of gypsies are recognized as those where the women are most inclined to steal' (1911: 22–3). He went on to conclude that the 'predominance of crime in certain countries is certainly due to race' (1911: 23).

The ideology of degeneration became of 'undisputed importance in clinical psychiatry' (Pick, 1989: 50) from the 1870s onwards and the natural consequence was that the mental hygiene movement, aimed at cleansing society of unwanted elements, was taken up by mainstream psychiatry at the turn of the twentieth century. The idea of degeneration led directly to the eugenic policies for the resolution of social problems enacted in Germany in the early twentieth century, supported (in that country) by both left- and right-wing politics (Weindling, 1989: 337). In 1918 Kraepelin set up the German Psychiatric Research Institute in Munich with his pupil, Ernst Rüdin, as the head of the genealogical department (Weindling, 1989: 336). As Rüdin led its research with money from the US Rockefeller Foundation, the institute's main research thrust was to investigate the genetic patterns of what were assumed to be inherited diseases, including schizophrenia. This Institute stressed its aim of protecting the public from dangerous and burdensome mentally ill people and much of its early work consisted of establishing a data bank of people seen in these terms (Weindling, 1989: 384). The end result was the sterilisation campaigns of the 1930s and finally the actual medical killing of people diagnosed by psychiatrists as incurably 'schizophrenic'.

The link between theories of degeneracy and Lombrosian criminology on the one hand, and the Nazi holocaust on the other, are epitomised in a speech in 1938 by veteran Nazi Hans Frank:

> National Socialism regards degeneracy as an immensely important source of criminal activity . . . in an individual, degeneracy signifies exclusion from the normal 'genus' of the decent nation. This state of being degenerate or egenerate, this different or alien quality, tends to be rooted in miscegenation between a decent representative of his race and an individual of inferior racial stock. To us National Socialists, criminal biology, or the theory of congenital criminality, connotes a link between racial decadence and criminal manifestations.
>
> (in Pick, 1989: 27–8)

It is not clear just how important the ideology of degeneration was in British psychiatric thought in the nineteenth century. It was certainly implicated in the conclusions of John Langdon Down (1866) after he surveyed so-called 'idiots' and 'imbeciles' resident in institutions around London. In hypothesising the aetiology of what he saw as their pathology, Down identified them as 'racial throwbacks' to Ethiopian, Malay and Mongolian racial types – mostly, he said, they were 'Mongols'. According to Pick (1989), the eminent British psychiatrist, Henry Maudsley, discussed degeneration in his book *The Physiology and Pathology of Mind* (1867). In *Responsibility in Mental Disease* (1874) Maudsley referred to 'a distinct criminal class of beings who herd together in our large cities . . . propagating a criminal population of degenerate beings' (1874: 31). According to Pick (1989), Maudsley had preached that criminals were underdeveloped, representing the primitive past of the race rather than the pathological cast offs of civilisation (1989: 208).

Degeneration really took off in England when, combined with the racist eugenics of Francis Galton, 'there was a slide into biological idealism . . . into a conception of degeneration as the imagined subject, cause and force of history' (Pick, 1989: 199). From the 1880s through to 1900, psychologists, psychiatrists, anthropologists and lawyers elaborated the language of degeneration and eugenically orientated academics, journalists and doctors were involved in its promotion. The mathematician Karl Pearson (1901), then a professor at London University and a Fellow of the Royal Society, justified the extermination of 'inferior races' as being a way of improving human stock. Indeed, the influence of a group centred around Pearson, his journal *Biometrika* and his academic department at University College, London, led, by 1912, to London University hosting the first International Congress of Eugenics, with Lord Darwin as president and Winston Churchill as vice-president (Pick, 1989: 199). So, racist ideology became as much a part of British psychiatry as schizophrenia – the two being closely linked in psychiatric thinking.

In the USA, psychiatry had been used in the nineteenth century to legitimise slavery; for example, epidemiological studies based on the US Census of 1840 were quoted in claiming that black people were relatively free of madness in a state of slavery, 'but that the black man becomes prey to mental disturbance when he is set free' (Thomas and Sillen, 1972: 16). During the 1890s eugenic concepts gained wide support in the USA. Laws against marriages between black and white people were widespread (J. Rogers, 1942) and in 1896 Connecticut passed legislation regulating marriages (between whites) for eugenic purposes and other states soon followed (Grob, 1983). Immigration was blamed for an apparent 'increase in insanity and other forms of degeneracy that threatened the biological wellbeing of the [white] American people' (1983: 168).

In addition to the powerful ideas of degeneration, criminology and eugenics that influenced the development of psychiatry in the nineteenth century, this century saw the emergence of psychoanalysis. In their book *Zen Buddhism and Psychoanalysis*, Erich Fromm *et al.* (1960) postulated that Freudian psychoanalysis was an attempt to find a solution to 'Western man's spiritual crisis' (1960: 80) – a crisis attributed by them to Europe's 'abandonment of theistic ideas in the nineteenth century' with 'a big plunge into objectivity' (1960: 79). Cultures in Asia and Africa did not undergo this change – at least not at that time – and although undoubtedly influenced later by Western ideas, appear to have maintained a spiritual dimension to their thinking in many ways until the present. Thus, the psychologies of Asia and Africa have within them a spiritual tradition, and people who derive their cultural background from these traditions tend to value spirituality wherever they live.

Racism and eugenics

Pick (1989: 37) believes that the concept of degeneration must primarily be understood within the language of nineteenth-century racist imperialism – the time when colonialism and slavery were feeding the ethos of racism into European culture. The underlying thesis inherent in the concept of degeneration was that social conflict, aggression, insanity and criminality were all signs of individual pathology representing reversal (throwback) to a racially primitive stage of development, either mentally or physically or both. In parallel with theories about madness among Europeans, there was considerable speculation in the nineteenth century about the nature of the minds of black people and the universality of madness across racial groups. Two distinct views were discernible: Daniel Tuke (1858) and Maudsley (1867, 1879) in England, Esquirol (cited by Jarvis, 1852) in France and Rush (cited by Rosen, 1968) in the USA voiced views similar to Rousseau's mid-eighteenth century concept of the 'Noble Savage', i.e. that 'savages' who lacked the civilising influence of Western culture were free of mental disorder. This idea was expressed most firmly by J. C. Prichard (1835) in his *A Treatise on Insanity and Other Disorders Affecting the Mind*: 'In savage countries, I mean among such tribes as the negroes of Africa and the Native Americans, insanity is stated by all . . . to be extremely rare' (1835: 349). But, according to Aubrey Lewis (1965) a second somewhat different stance was also evident in Europe about that time, namely the view that non-Europeans (black people) were mentally degenerate because they lacked Western culture. In other words, black people already had the quality of degeneration inherent in them – blackness was equivalent to criminality and madness.

Although the 'Noble Savage' viewpoint idealised non-European culture in some ways and the notion that black people were 'degenerate' vilified it, both approaches sprang from the same source – a racist perception of people and their cultures. Almost into the twentieth century, Babcock, a psychiatrist from South Carolina, was to use pro-slavery arguments to develop the theme that Africans were inherently incapable of coping with civilised life. In a paper, 'The colored insane' (1895), Babcock juxtaposed the idea that mental disease was 'almost unknown among savage tribes of Africa', with the alleged 'rapid increase of insanity in the negro since emancipation', forecasting 'a constant accumulation of [black] lunatics' in the years to come (1895: 423–7).

Racism inherent in the theories of Lombroso's work is even more obvious than in the case of the theory of degeneration. Lombroso believed that the white races represented the triumph of the human species, 'but inside the triumphant whiteness, there remained a certain blackness' (Pick, 1989: 136). Thus, the signs of criminality and madness that Lombroso identified in white people were really features of blackness (inherent in black people). In *White Man and the Coloured Man* (quoted in Pick, 1989), Lombroso (1871) gave free expression to his own views of black people: 'Only we White people [*Noi soli Bianchi*] have reached the most perfect symmetry of bodily form. . . . Only we [have bestowed] . . . the human right to life, respect for old age, women, and the weak. . . . Only we have created true nationalism . . . [and] freedom of thought' (Pick, 1989: 126).

Meanwhile, the ideas of de Gobineau emphasising 'scientific racism', 'Social Darwinism' and the work of Galton on the inheritance of human psychology were having a major impact on European thinking when eugenic psychiatry came on the scene (Weindling, 1989: 85). By the late nineteenth century, the ideas of degeneration and Lombroso's criminology had reached the wider public through popular writings (Weindling, 1989; Pick, 1989) and a type of biology with a strong racist message became part of the public discourse on social reform. Eugenic solutions to psychiatric problems were proposed in Germany in the mid-1880s (Weindling, 1989) and the biological control of deviant behaviour impressed Kraepelin so much that he 'accepted that patients with existing mental problems should be advised against marriage' (1989: 86). During the 1890s Forel (in Germany) began to castrate patients as a means of controlling aggression – even then associated with mental problems.

Proctor (1988) has described how German eugenics became 'racial hygiene' – the basic thesis of which was that 'traditional medical care . . . helps the individual but engenders the race' (1988: 15). In 1905 Ploetz together with psychiatrist Rüdin founded the 'Society for Racial Hygiene' (1988: 17) and its chairman, Dr Gruber, proposed the creation of a state institute for heredity and (state-controlled) 'health passports' (Weindling, 1989: 238). In 1908, when Germany occupied southwest Africa (now Namibia), all existing 'mixed' (black–white) marriages were annulled and such marriages forbidden in the future (Muller-Hill, 1988). In the 1920s, there were calls in Germany for the sterilisation of 'Rhineland bastards', the result of the occupation of the Rhinelands by black French troops after the defeat of Germany in 1918 (Weindling, 1989). Racism and eugenics became central to German political thinking as ideas about degeneration and schizophrenia became central to thinking about madness and crime – and politics and psychiatry were never far apart.

Black races

The idea that black people, in comparison to white people, had smaller (i.e. less developed) brains was popular in scientific circles in the nineteenth century, being based on a large body of 'scientific' studies reviewed by Cobb (1942). An assumption of mental under-development naturally followed and when, early this century, Kraepelin (1904) observed that guilt was not seen in Javanese people who became depressed, he concluded that they (the Javanese) were 'a psychically underdeveloped population' akin to 'immature European youth' (Kraepelin, 1921). The belief that the minds of black people were equivalent to those of under-developed white people was openly voiced in an important book on the psychology of adolescence by G. S. Hall (1904), founder of the *American Journal of Psychology* and first president of the American Psychological Association (Thomas and Sillen, 1972: 7), in which he described Asians, Chinese, Africans and Native Americans as psychologically 'adolescent races' because their mental functioning resembled that of adolescent white people.

In the 1920s the Swiss psychologist Carl Jung suggested that the negro 'has probably a whole historical layer less' in the brain (Thomas and Sillen, 1972: 14), referring to psychological 'layers' analogous to the anatomical layers of the brain cortex. Indeed the ideology of degeneration also may well have influenced Jung much more deeply (without apparent insight). In a critical analysis of Jung's ideas about psychological functioning of black people, Dalal (1988) concludes that Jung equated the white unconscious with the black conscious, and then assumed that what he could discern of his own conscious life represented the symbolism used by black people. 'His error was in assuming that because the blacks symbolises the primitive to himself, therefore they were primitive' (1988: 13).

The thesis that black people are essentially underdeveloped white people surfaces in modern theories such as the proposal by Carothers (1951) of a 'striking resemblance between African thinking and that of leucotomized Europeans' (1951: 12) and the conclusion, drawn by Leff (1973, 1981) after analysing observations across the world, that people from Africa and Asia as well as Black Americans (the politically 'Black') have a less developed ability to differentiate emotions when compared with Europeans and white Americans – a finding seen by Leff (1981) as representing the 'historical development of emotional differentiation', an 'evolutionary process' (1981: 65 – 6). These ideas are in line with recurring ideas about intelligence and race – essentially that black people are intellectually under-developed. It seems that African and Asian blackness represent inferiority to most white people – at least at a subconscious level – but deeper down there is a fear of Asia and Africa. This is evident in some of Carl Jung's writings (Dalal, 1988) and is reflected in segregationist policies of the Jim Crow era in the USA which was accompanied by vicious violence well into the twentieth century, and more recently in the policies of the European Community designed to keep black people out of 'Fortress Europe' (Gordon, 1991).

CRIME AND PSYCHIATRY

The punishment of crime in Western Europe until the mid-eighteenth century was largely on an *ad hoc* basis characterised by eclecticism inequality and barbarity. In France, the ordinance of 1670 laid down the following hierarchy of penalties: 'Death, Judicial torture pending proof, penal servitude, flogging, *amende honorable* [a term meaning literally public or open apology with some form of reparation but applied to a punishment involving public humiliation frequently followed by execution (Pearsall and Trumble, 1995)], banishment' (Foucault, 1979: 32). Following *Dei delitti e delle pene* (Crime and Punishment) by Beccaria (1764), and the work of Bentham (1789) in England, the punishment of crime was structured in terms of a fixed exchange rate – every infraction of the law would receive a given punishment in excess of the benefits of the crime (Pick, 1989: 136). Criminality was seen as 'natural' but unacceptable – and the punishment was meant to fit the crime. Essentially, people were responsible for their actions. And in England and most of the Western world, the prison system emerged at the end of the eighteenth century.

Prior to the nineteenth century, lunatics found guilty of a criminal offence were occasionally pardoned by decree of the King instead of being punished (Walker and McCabe, 1968), and later in the case of minor offences by 'ambiguous measures of internment' (Foucault, 1988). In eighteenth-century England magistrates had the power to commit lunatics who were 'dangerous' to workhouses, madhouses and gaols (Porter, 1987: 118). However, in the nineteenth century, psychiatry began to play a significant part in the administration of punishment to criminals, leading to the emergence of the modern concept of forensic psychiatry in Europe.

According to Foucault (1988), 'until the end of the eighteenth century, the question of insanity was raised under penal law only in cases where it was also raised in the civil code or in canon law, that is when it appeared either in the form of *dementia* and of imbecility, or in the form of *furor*' (1988: 130). Whatever it was insanity was easily recognised and a doctor was not really needed to authenticate its existence. In the early 1800s there were a series of cases where questions about insanity were raised in the case of particularly serious crimes with a similar pattern that occurred in England, Scotland, France and America. They were all highlighted as 'crimes against nature' (1988: 131) although not accompanied by any traditional visible symptoms of insanity. In this context, psychiatry began to intervene in a new way at a time when penal reforms were being applied across Western Europe and North America (Foucault, 1988). Thus, the idea developed in the nineteenth century that some crimes were inherently *pathological*, against human nature – irrational crimes (Foucault, 1988). 'The offender becomes an individual to know' (1988: 251). The concept of criminal insanity was born, an insanity manifested as crime, without any other traditional signs of insanity.

At first psychiatry became involved with instances of serious crimes, but gradually other, less serious types of behaviour that appeared to threaten society in some way were taken over into the psychiatric domain – necrophilia around 1840, kleptomania around 1860, exhibitionism in 1876 and then sadism, homosexuality and so on (Foucault, 1988). With increasing medical and psychological intervention in criminality, the system of power moved from an emphasis on the body (for torture and punishment) to the mind (for control and correction). In Europe, crime became an important area of study for psychiatrists and psychologists, 'not simply because it applied a new medical rationality to mental or behavioural disorders, it was also because it functioned as a sort of public hygiene' (1988: 134). And the whole system of dispensing justice changed too.

In *Discipline and Punish* Foucault (1977) described the change that took place in the nineteenth century from an 'inquisitorial' justice (of judging the offence) to an 'examinatory' justice of judging the person (1977: 305). When sent to prison, control over the offender was no longer merely deprivation of liberty, but of domination over his/her entire being, implemented by *knowledge* – not of the offence but of the person. This knowledge fed into the power of the state to control. The prison became not just a place for incarceration, but 'a place for the constitution of a body of knowledge that would regulate the exercise of penitentiary practice' (1977: 250); judges developed an 'immense "appetite for medicine" . . . from their appeal to psychiatric experts, to their attention to the chatter of criminology' (1977: 304).

Sim (1990) has described the history of medical involvement in the British prison system. In the late eighteenth century, concern about general health of prisoners led to doctors, and (later) psychologists and psychiatrists, becoming involved (employed by the Prison Medical Service) in the 'care' of people in prison. But, they were no more than an extension of the system of control and discipline: 'Prison doctors not only were caught up in, but also contributed to the debates about the philosophy and practice of punishment. The disciplinary strategies which lay at the heart of penalty were legitimized by the interventions which Medical Officers made' (1990: 40). In 1816 British law was amended to enable the transfer from prison to asylums of prisoners who became insane during a penal sentence and in 1867 a new act permitted such transfers in the case of idiots and imbeciles (Forshaw and Rollin, 1990).

The development of forensic psychiatry in the nineteenth century meant that an increasing number of people in British prisons and asylums were designated as criminally insane. The initial institutional response to this was the opening of two purpose-built criminal wings attached to the Bethlem Hospital in 1816 (Forshaw and Rollin, 1990). In 1860 an Act was passed for the better provision of custody and care of 'criminal lunatics' which resulted in the building of Broadmoor Hospital in 1863, Rampton in 1910 and Moss Side in 1914 (Gostin, 1986). As it developed, forensic psychiatry functioned by examining the psychological and social meaning of whatever constituted 'criminal behaviour' (in a legal sense) rather than the intrinsic nature of the behaviour itself. And the social meaning increasingly centred around dangerousness to society, irrespective of the nature of the society. In other words, psychiatry (and forensic psychiatry) did not take an ethical position on what constituted criminality – it merely accepted the definition proposed by the state: this is still the position. Foucault (1988) saw in the so-called abuse of psychiatry in the Soviet Union of the 1960s a logical extension of this intrusion of psychiatry into the legal system. For psychiatrists:

> their job was to supervise whatever was in a state of disorder, whatever presented a *danger*. In the end, it is this notion of 'danger', which was introduced at that time, theorized in psychiatry and criminology in the nineteenth century, that you find again in Soviet legislation. This legislation may say: you're claiming that a patient is being put in prison (or a prisoner put in hospital), but that's not at all the case! Someone is being confined because he has been 'dangerous'. They even reached a point of describing *as an offense* in the penal code the fact of being perceived *as dangerous*.
>
> (original emphasis, 1988: 188)

This approach was not unique to the psychiatry practised in the Soviet Union; it has been used wherever forensic psychiatry is practised. Today, assumptions about criminality and dangerousness to society are often made on the basis of 'clinical judgements' which are wide open to permeation by all sorts of influences that are active in society at large, including racism. So, just as in the Soviet Union being a dissident was perceived as 'dangerous' and sometimes a signs of insanity (usually schizophrenia), in the UK being black is conducive to being seen as both dangerous and 'schizophrenic'.

Foucault and racism

According to Sim (1990) Foucault's analysis of the shift in the exercise of state power (in the nineteenth century) from punishment of the 'body' to control over the 'mind' (or more correctly the whole person), may have been too narrow because 'while displays of torture, violence and execution may have disappeared from the public domain they still exist and operate in the various institutions that have developed since the late eighteenth century' (1990: 179).

Another major criticism of Foucault's writings on criminality and psychiatry is that he failed to address issues of race and incorporate in his (otherwise) brilliant analyses an understanding of how racism penetrated both these areas of European thought. This deficiency in Foucault's analysis may have arisen because he ignored the activities of Europeans outside Europe and their attitudes to black people. While recourse to physical punishment may have dropped off in Europe in the nineteenth century, in the USA, India and Africa physical violence and punishment of the body continued as a means of control of black people. The shift in the exercise of power in the field of law enforcement in Europe did not occur in the case of black people in European colonies. In European adventures outside the continent (as much a part of European history as activity within Europe), psychiatry and psychology were not used in the exercise of imperial power; instead (for example) homicide, lynching, looting of property and rape were common imperial activities that were hardly questioned as to their criminal or psychiatric content, quite apart from being both (as it might have been seen in Europe). Following the American Civil War when slavery was officially forbidden, 'the institution of lynching [of black men], in turn, complemented by the continued rape of black women, became an essential ingredient of the postwar strategy of racist terror' (Davis, 1982: 185) – a terror that continued well into the twentieth century.

CONCLUSIONS

Psychiatry as we know it today arose about 300 years ago from two main sources. First, the need to control and put away 'lunatics' who were disturbing the social order in European cities. Second, from a growing interest in matters to do with the 'mind' in European medical circles. Naturally, the culture in which it developed played an important part in the ways of working and thinking that emerged – psychiatry was ethnocentric to European culture. Since both psychology and psychiatry developed together at a time when the powerful myths of racism were being refined and integrated into European culture, racist thinking became an integral part of the system of psychiatry that Europe developed and then exported around the globe.

Psychiatric interest in crime may be seen as the arrival on the European scene of what is now known as forensic psychiatry. From the beginning, this type of psychiatry was associated with control in alliance with whatever forces happened to be powerful in the society concerned. The overt and deliberate combination (within forensic psychiatry) of social control with the practice of a medical discipline resulted inevitably in the confusion of roles for people claiming to be forensic psychiatrists – the confusion of punishment with therapy, judgement about (moral) wrong-doing with (medical) diagnosis and clinical care with custody. However, it should be noted here that, on all these counts, the boundaries between general psychiatry and forensic psychiatry are far from clear and remain unclear to this day.

As psychiatric interest in criminal behaviour increased, Morel's degeneration theory and Lombroso's criminal anthropology worked together in the late nineteenth century in what Pick called the 'new criminological school' (1989: 136). From 1885 onwards, there were regular international congresses of criminal anthropology at which Lombroso's concept of the criminal man was elaborated. The underlying thesis was that criminality and insanity were natural inherited states with racial bases. Criminality and mental pathology had come together and both represented throwbacks to earlier stages of evolution to primitive cultures and peoples. Undoubtedly, European attitudes towards 'primitive people' were determined by the slavery and colonialism going on outside of Europe (see Chapter 1), leading to the incorporation of racism within European culture, psychiatry and forensic psychiatry.

Thus, forensic psychiatry focused on the danger posed to society by individuals; the perception of someone as ‘dangerous’ was seen as an offence symptomatic of madness. The ‘illness’ that naturally became the epitome of madness was schizophrenia. Nineteenth-century ideas of race dominated by racist stereotypes of black people, encountered in Asian and African colonies and the American continent, inevitably fed into building up racist images of criminality and madness, dangerousness and aggressiveness, under-development and primitive cultures. All of these would in the final count become the substance of what goes for clinical judgement and diagnosis in forensic psychiatry – especially the diagnosis of schizophrenia.

Chapter 3

Modern schizophrenia and racism

A standard British textbook on psychiatry (Gelder *et al.*, 1989) states that 'of all the major psychiatric syndromes, schizophrenia is much the most difficult to define and describe' (1989: 268), referring to 'radical differences of opinion' (among psychiatrists) that persist to the present day. The modern definition of schizophrenia refers to first-rank symptoms largely based on work of Kurt Schneider (1959). It is described entirely in terms of behavioural and experiential phenomena. Physical symptoms (prominent in the descriptions by Kraepelin and Bleuler) are hardly mentioned now. 'Insight', which is generally understood to be present when the person concerned agrees with the person making the diagnosis that the 'symptoms' recognised by the latter are alien or strange (i.e. 'abnormal'), is now regarded as rarely present in schizophrenia, although Bleuler had claimed it was always present and Kraepelin too considered his dementia præcox patients to have been capable of recognising their symptoms as abnormal (Boyle, 1990).

Psychologist Mary Boyle (1990) has analysed the change that has taken place in the concept of schizophrenia since it was first described by Kraepelin between 1896 and 1913. In the early part of the twentieth century when the constructs schizophrenia and 'manic depression' were being accepted in Europe, there were very close links between neurology and psychiatry – in Germany the two disciplines were virtually the same. Kraepelin's descriptions of dementia præcox (schizophrenia) specified many physical symptoms but, as psychiatry separated from neurology, the description of schizophrenia changed from a neurological–physical–behavioural concept (envisaged by Kraepelin) to an entirely behavioural–experiential one (about behaviour, beliefs and feelings). The change in the construct schizophrenia has not been accompanied by a change of name (as it should have been) because the process has been interpreted in the psychiatric literature as one of refining and objectifying diagnostic features – as medical progress. By maintaining the original name, the impression has been given that the current description has a relatively long history, that it is (as it were) well established. And psychiatry has managed to keep the basic idea (proposed by Kraepelin) that schizophrenia is essentially an organic state underpinned by a strong hereditary tendency.

AETIOLOGY

Research into aetiology has focused on possible biological explanations of schizophrenia in terms of genetic factors, altered brain dopamine systems, and structural abnormalities in the brain. None of these lines of research have produced definitive answers. One reviewer of the topic (Barnes, 1987) concludes: 'For every point about the biology of schizophrenia there is a counterpoint. Theories about the origin and disease process of schizophrenia are often built on a multitude of empirical observations and a paucity of hard facts' (1987: 433). A review of the research into possible neurochemical and neuroendocrinological causes of schizophrenia by Lieberman and Koreen (1993) found a 'fragmentary body of data which provides neither consistent nor conclusive evidence for any specific etiologic theory' (1993: 371). In reviewing neurobiological research into the topic, Jenner *et al.* (1993) conclude: 'In our opinion, what all these studies appear to indicate is that the finding of (more or less conspicuous) neurobiochemical, psychophysiological, psychoendocrinological, or neurophysiological anomalies (when we proceed to study the working of the human brain) does not necessarily imply the existence of any sort of disease process (which could therefore be the only one capable of producing the anomalies)' (1993: 106).

A theory, which could be called a 'virus theory' for schizophrenia, has been given some prominence recently because it has been used to explain the relatively high rates of schizophrenia being diagnosed among African-Caribbean people in the UK. This theory came about as follows: two studies of the 1957 influenza epidemic (Mednick *et al.*, 1989; O'Callaghan *et al.*, 1991) found an association between maternal viral infection and a diagnosis of schizophrenia in the offspring, but data from other studies (Kendell and Kemp, 1989; Selten and Sleats, 1994; Susser *et al.*, 1994; Torrey *et al.*, 1988) failed to detect such an association. The tenuous evidence from the two positive studies were linked up with the *possibility* (no more) that perinatal virus infection *may* have led to an immunological dysfunction (King and Cooper, 1989) that (in turn) *may* have led to brain damage leading to schizophrenia – all speculations. Then a number of researchers (e.g. Wing, 1989; G. Harrison, 1990; Eagles, 1991; Wessely *et al.*, 1991; Harrison *et al.*, 1997) quoted this immunological virus theory or a variation of it in order to explain away the relatively high likelihood of young British-born black men being diagnosed as 'schizophrenic'. More recently, an association between schizophrenia and the 1957 influenza epidemic has been firmly rejected (Crow and Done, 1992; Cannon *et al.*, 1996), although some psychiatrists (e.g. Adams and Kendell, 1996) try to cling to the (now discredited) hypothesis that was based on such an association – namely that maternal virus infection is a cause of schizophrenia in offspring. The alacrity with which institutional psychiatry, represented by eminent British psychiatrists (including some who obtain support for study of 'racial' groups), grabbed at the virus theory shows the powerful need for psychiatry to protect its current ways of thinking (and hence working), even at the expense of perpetuating the racism it has inherited from the past.

VALIDITY

Western psychology is built upon foundations that incorporate (Western) ideas about the nature of human beings and their minds. Psychiatry too has this same base but also incorporates Western concepts of illness and health. It has been argued elsewhere (Fernando, 1988, 1991) that the modern concept of schizophrenia, as diagnosed on the basis of 'first rank symptoms', has no cross-cultural validity. However, the question arises as to its more general validity even within the culture that produced it. This is an important issue in the current context where the diagnosis of schizophrenia has far reaching consequences, nowhere more so than in forensic psychiatry. However, when one examines this question, what is alarming is that validity studies are virtually non-existent, although there is a general assumption that schizophrenia has a similar usefulness in describing mental health problems as (say) diabetes has in describing problems of sugar metabolism. Even the World Health Organisation (WHO) has used the concept of schizophrenia without verifying its validity in carrying out extensive 'epidemiological' studies – the 'international pilot study of schizophrenia' (IPSS) (World Health Organisation, 1973) and 'determinants of outcome of severe mental disorders' (DOSMD) (in Jablensky *et al.*, 1992).

It is not always important to establish validity at the time that a medical construct is created. The process of making a construct denoting an illness and then building on this as a basis for observation, research and treatment is the way knowledge has advanced using the medical model. However, in continuing to use such a construct it is necessary, at some point, to stop and think about its usefulness, its 'validity' – especially its 'predictive validity', since it is this aspect of validity that is important in the context of clinical psychiatry (Kendell, 1975, 1989). For such validity to be present, the construct must be able to predict, on the one hand, what is called the 'natural history' of the condition represented by the construct, i.e. give some idea of what would happen to the problems subsumed by the construct – a prognosis, in medical language; or better still, on the other hand, the type of intervention that would be useful in alleviating the problems – the treatment that is most likely to succeed. In a recent review of clinical validity of syndromes recognised in contemporary psychiatric classifications, Kendell (1989) concluded: 'Studying populations of schizophrenics or phobics implicitly assumes that schizophrenia and phobic disorders are valid diagnostic categories and I do not believe that we yet have the evidence to justify such an assumption' (1989: 54).

Many constructs designed to subsume human problems have become established before questions about their validity as 'illness'. Their usefulness in many instances may indeed be assumed as beyond question: this applies. for example to diabetes or scurvy, which are undeniably useful as diagnoses of 'illness'. However, in the case of schizophrenia as a construct, such an assumption is not warranted because its validity (usefulness) is being seriously questioned from several angles. Looked at historically and transculturally, there are problems with the concept of schizophrenia. The historical accuracy of Kraepelin's contention that schizophrenia was an 'old' disease has been questioned (Torrey, 1973, 1980, 1983; Hare, 1988; Gottesman, 1991). No reliable ancient descriptions of the sort of 'condition' described by Kraepelin and Bleuler as 'dementia præcox' or schizophrenia have been found. The argument by Bark (1985) that 'Poor Mad Tom' in Shakespeare's

King Lear represents a picture of chronic schizophrenia (including thought disorder, hallucinations and delusions) does not stand up to critical examination and Gottesman (1991) rightly notes that 'no unambiguously schizophrenic character appears in Shakespearean drama, despite the bard's skill as a word-painter of other kinds of behavioral deviances' (1991: 5).

Conditions that amount to mental distress or madness described indigenously in non-Western cultures may resemble what (Western) psychiatry terms mania and depression (usually as a spiritual experience rather than illness). The ancient Hindu works, *Rāmāyaṇaa* and *Māhabhārata*, are reported to contain descriptions of depression (Venkoba Rao, 1969). But, there is no evidence that Kraepelinian schizophrenia has been recognised (apart from its imposition as a result of Western influence) in non-European cultural settings. In a paper that looks for descriptions of (Western) psychiatric illnesses in ancient Indian texts, Bhugra (1992) finds 'descriptions of objectively observable illnesses like alcoholism and epilepsy' (1992: 167), but no clear descriptions of the symptoms of (Western) schizophrenia such as hallucinations, delusions and thought disorder.

There are several objections to the continuing use of the concept of schizophrenia. First, it does not make much sense to many people who use mental health services – especially people whose mental health problems are designated in terms of the diagnosis. Drugs certainly control some unwanted symptoms (of schizophrenia) but cause others and, in any case, no one now believes seriously that they 'cure' anything. In other words, the concept schizophrenia does not appear reasonable or appropriate (i.e. useful) as a medical condition – and this applies particularly in a setting where people given the diagnosis come from African or Asian (cultural) backgrounds. Second, black people often see the schizophrenia diagnosis as being used in ways that do not help them and even work against them. Thus, the lack of sufficient objectivity in the diagnosis of schizophrenia coupled with the ease with which it can be used for political (including racist) reasons has led to its misuse or, even worse, abuse, in certain contexts. Third, it is evident that many years of research using the concept of schizophrenia as indicative of a medical 'condition' has not resulted in any leads towards a consistent biochemical or structural understanding that may justify using the concept schizophrenia as indicative of a specific 'illness'. In fact, the usefulness of the construct for purposes of research is now highly questionable. Finally, experience from outside Europe and transcultural practice within European multi-ethnic societies have questioned the credibility of schizophrenia as a useful concept. Even the results of two major multinational studies, IPSS (Leff *et al.*, 1990) and DOSMD (in Jablensky *et al.*, 1992), both carried out on the assumption that the validity of schizophrenia was beyond question, have not supported the predictive value of the construct; people given this diagnosis in industrially developing countries have a better outcome than that of their counterparts in the developed world where 'treatment' is available more easily and indeed given more thoroughly.

Thus, for all the other reasons discussed above, it is reasonable to conclude that, at present, the concept of schizophrenia, as formulated by Kraepelin and Bleuler and refined by Schneider, is no longer useful for either research purposes or for clinical practice in a multi-ethnic society – or perhaps any society.

GENETIC RESEARCH

If schizophrenia is accepted as an 'illness', popular understanding is that it carries a strong genetic component. Research into this complex and controversial field is beset with the fundamental problem of the validity of the diagnosis (of schizophrenia) itself. However, it is necessary to examine the question of genetics if only because assumptions are rife. Modern techniques such as linkage studies, cytogenetic studies and molecular genetics can be ignored as far as mental illness is concerned because nothing positive has been found as yet. At present, the evidence concerned with genetic factors in 'mental illness' hinge on family studies, twin research and the adoption studies.

Much of the family studies were reported before the Second World War from studies in Germany, mainly by Ernst Rüdin (1916) and Franz Kallman (1938). It was a matter of finding people diagnosed as 'schizophrenic', tracing their relatives and diagnosing them. Early twin studies too were reported by Rudin and these as well as Kallman's observations are still quoted by authoritative text books (e.g. Gelder *et al.*, 1989 – the standard text for trainee psychiatrists in the UK). The method of data collection was to trace anyone who had a diagnosis of schizophrenia who happened to be one of twins and see whether the other twin was diagnosed as schizophrenic too. Results were presented as 'concordance rates' –

i.e. the extent to which the other twin was also diagnosed as 'schizophrenic', comparing identical twins with fraternal twins. The post-war twin studies have been done in various parts of Europe – the main ones being those reported by Slater (1953) in the UK, Tienari (1963) in Finland, Kringlen (1966) in Norway and Gottesman and Shields (1972) from the UK. In the last study, concordance rates were calculated by a novel method ('proband-wise method') not used generally in twin research and were looked on unfavourably when strict methods of data collection were not enforced (Boyle, 1990: 132).

Politics and science of twin research

In the first decade of the twentieth century when schizophrenia was being accepted as an 'illness' in Europe and the USA, racist ideas were stronger than perhaps they had ever been – especially in Germany (see Proctor, 1988; Weindling, 1989) and the USA (see Davis, 1982). At this time the main ideology for understanding madness was that of degeneration – that is, that madness, and indeed many deviations from 'normality' in social and mental functioning, were the manifestations of an inherited degenerative process. This was common sense in Western Europe and soon ideas of degeneration and racism came to together in thinking about racial purity. (The connections between schizophrenia, degeneration, eugenics and racism were discussed in Chapter 2.)

Kraepelin believed in the degeneracy theory of mental illness and had postulated that dementia præcox was inherited in seventy per cent of cases (Weindling, 1989: 545). There was great concern in Germany in the early part of this century (especially after it suffered defeat in the First World War) about social turmoil with a strong feeling that the race (the white Aryan race) was under threat through degeneracy. The mental hygiene movement fostered by psychiatrists grew up, aimed at cleansing society of unwanted elements. This was the context in which research into heredity became popular and, as Weindling (1989) has shown, the main thrust of research at the German Psychiatric Research Institute in Munich (1989: 336) was to investigate the genetic patterns of what was assumed to be the inheritance of schizophrenia (as well as other 'diseases') in order to protect the public from dangerous and burdensome mentally ill people (1989: 384). These policies led to the sterilisation campaigns of the 1930s and finally to the medical killing of people diagnosed by psychiatrists as incurably 'schizophrenic'. Clearly, the work of Rüdin, Kraepelin and others in Germany in the 1920s and 1930s is invalidated by their eugenic zeal. Kallman left Germany in the 1930s and wrote his main report (1938) while he was in the USA, but his zeal for fostering the inheritance of schizophrenia can be deduced from the following quotation from the introduction to his *The Genetics of Schizophrenia*, published in the USA:

> The menace to public health constituted by the traits and unchecked propagation of schizophrenic symptom-carriers makes it imperative to determine exactly those heredito-constitutional elements which are involved in the origin of schizoform abnormalities and to seek reasonable ways of deterring their constant recurrence. We must remember that the prevention of several hundred schizophrenic patients and their tainted descendants, in every state, would save millions of dollars for cultural purposes and would considerably advance the biological qualities of future generations.
>
> (1938: xiii)

Post-war research

Although studies carried out since the defeat of Nazi forces in Europe were in a different context to those in pre-war Germany, these too were flawed. The ways of collecting data about the nature of twins were haphazard (Boyle, 1990: 124). None of the researchers appeared to doubt the validity of schizophrenia as a diagnosis and only the studies by Gottesman and Shields (1972) made any attempt to test the reliability of diagnosis – but did so in a way that was seriously flawed in that the diagnosticians used written material prepared by the researchers who clearly knew details of the twins, i.e. whether they were designated as identical or fraternal. These studies re-presented data from other studies in their own work. These re-evaluated figures often formed the basis of much of the so-called facts presented in many psychiatric texts. Boyle (1990) points out that data were selectively presented and analysed in a way that emphasised support for the 'genetic' argument (1990: 131–3), many methodological flaws in earlier work and in their own work were played down or excused, and the re-analyses of data of other studies used a novel proband-wise method, which is not used generally but gave results that enhanced the genetic argument.

Family studies and twin studies

Family studies into the 'incidence' of a condition do not of course separate genetic from environmental influences. However, because they produced apparently clear figures (in the case of schizophrenia) they have been quoted uncritically as representing genetic risks – a very dangerous habit indeed. In the case of twin studies, validity and reliability of diagnosis were not tested, bias was not controlled adequately, and many studies are suspect because of the context under which they were carried out. Most of the work quoted in text books for concordance rates in schizophrenia refers back to reports by Rüdin and Kallman. In a study from Finland by Tienari (1963), the concordance rates for identical twins was between 0 per cent and 36 per cent compared to that for fraternal twins of 5 per cent to 14 per cent, the variation depending on the criteria used for diagnosing schizophrenia. Concordance rates quoted by Gottesman and Shields (1982), namely 40 per cent–50 per cent *vs.* 9 per cent–19 per cent, get nearer towards providing evidence for a genetic factor, but their reliability is not clear and the method used for calculating concordance rates is questionable.

Adoption studies

A major source of post-war data is contained in the Danish–US collaborative adoption studies by Kety *et al.* (1968, 1976) using the excellent records kept in Denmark. Three types of study were carried out using records for Copenhagen. First, using as 'index cases' people diagnosed as 'schizophrenic' who had been adopted as children, prevalence of schizophrenia diagnosis in their biological relatives was compared to that in their adoptive relatives. Second, using the same index cases as a starting-point, the prevalence of schizophrenia diagnosis (in the adopted people) was compared to its prevalence in people ('controls') without a schizophrenia diagnosis who had been adopted as children. Third, the prevalence of schizophrenia diagnosis among 'adopted away' children of mothers who had been diagnosed as 'schizophrenic' was compared to that among such children who had not been adopted.

Boyle (1990) has carefully analysed the published work based on these studies. A major problem concerned the largely unknown and unassessed biases involved in tracing relatives of people included in them. Also, the researchers used a concept of 'schizophrenia spectrum' which appeared rather arbitrary in that it included within it people with all sorts of problems. The concept was often used on the basis of very little information and was clearly likely to have been open to bias. Another issue not considered by the researchers was the selectivity (of prospective adoptive parents) involved in the actual process of adoption. They seem to have assumed that adoptive parents were chosen at random from the population, which of course was never the case. The likely effects of differential placement of adoptees was confirmed by Steven Rose *et al.* (1984) on examining unpublished data collected by the researchers (and made available by Dr Kety). In twenty-four per cent of the adoptive families of the people diagnosed as schizophrenic (index cases), a parent had been in a mental hospital, compared to zero per cent in the case of controls, suggesting that 'the schizophrenic adoptees, who indeed had been born into shattered and disreputable families, acquired their schizophrenia as a result of the poor adoptive environments into which they had been placed' (1984: 223). Further, the rate of mental hospitalisation among the biological parents of the index cases was *less* than that in the case of controls. The failure by the researchers to publish this important data (which argues against a genetic factor in schizophrenia) is compounded by another finding reported by Rose *et al.*:

> Personal correspondence with the psychiatrist who conducted the interviews with relatives has revealed a few interesting details. The 1975 paper speaks only of 'interviews', but it turns out that, in several cases, when relatives were dead or unavailable, the psychiatrist 'prepared a so called pseudo interview form from the existing hospital record'. That is, the psychiatrist filled out the interview form in the way in which he guessed the relative would have answered.
>
> (1984: 224)

The flaws in data collection and other major drawbacks in the methodologies of the Danish–US studies cast considerable doubt on the authenticity of the results reported by the researchers. More recently Kety *et al.* (1994) have published results of studies covering the whole of Denmark. These new studies have failed to address any of the methodological drawbacks noted in their earlier work.

However, this new work has been taken up by others (e.g. Battaglia and Torgersen, 1996) as a reason for extending the definition of the core illness of schizophrenia to include what DSM-III-R (American Psychiatric Association, 1987) describes as 'schizotypal personality disorder' (SPD): 'Recent twin studies suggest that the affect-constricted and eccentric aspects of SPD are the features that truly belong to the spectrum of schizophrenia, sharing important genetic influences' (1987: 303).

As with other twin studies, the results of studies on children of 'schizophrenic' parents ('adopted away' studies) too do not stand up to close examination and so provide no firm evidence for inherited factors in schizophrenia (Boyle, 1990).

Schizophrenia and other psychiatric diagnoses are essentially constructs which are used as a basis for research and hopefully understanding of certain groups of human problems. They have developed in a particular context and culture and their applicability to people from other contexts and cultural backgrounds is uncertain. Moreover, the very process of coming to a diagnosis – the recognition of what the symptoms are, analysing history and making judgements about people's behaviour and thinking etc. – this very process results in racism becoming involved in the deductions made.

If the concept of schizophrenia is taken as an indication of a specific 'illness', its genetic components need to be examined. The pre-war research, in addition to having been methodologically seriously flawed, was done in a context which make one very suspicious of the findings. And, this is what Mary Boyle (1990), after a thorough critical analysis, concludes generally about the post-war research:

> Severe methodological and conceptual weaknesses have been overlooked . . . while researchers in the twin and adoptive studies have shown a dismaying tendency to omit important procedural details, to define variables in ways which support their hypotheses, to engage in strange statistical practices and to gloss over non-significant results or to report them without comment in papers where they may be overlooked.
>
> (1990: 159)

Kety *et al.*'s published research is often quoted as convincing evidence for schizophrenia, having a large genetic component, but their papers did not always present the whole story. Many of the other such studies were much less comprehensive. On the whole the impression is of a consistent tendency to try and report findings that justify the original contentions about inheritance of schizophrenia set by Kraepelin and Rüdin. So, if schizophrenia is valid as an illness (and this is extremely doubtful), clearly, it is not a genetic disease (in the sense of being carried by a single gene) like Huntingdon's Disease or Cystic Fibrosis. But vulnerability (or susceptibility) to it (or to some aspects of it) may be inherited, perhaps through several genes. Perhaps molecular genetics will identify points on several genes that relate to susceptibility (or 'risk') for heart disease, hypertension and cancer and it is possible that eventually there might emerge similar knowledge for susceptibility to some aspects of (what is called) schizophrenia. If such definite leads are obtained on the 'genetic factors' involved, their importance cannot be judged until much more is known about other factors. For example, genetic factors were assumed as important in tuberculosis for a long time – and certainly the vulnerability to contracting this infection if exposed to the relevant bacteria may well be determined by genetic factors, such as nutrition. Torrey (1994) in a recent book tries to put statistics on twin studies in some sort of context by quoting these for various illnesses, including schizophrenia. The figures for schizophrenia are similar to those for poliomyelitis or multiple sclerosis. Clearly, all we can say from these figures is that the genetic vulnerability to schizophrenia may be similar to that for polio or multiple sclerosis.

Also more recently, twin studies as a basis for studying genetic vulnerability to schizophrenia has been questioned by observations that twins, whether biological or fraternal, may be more liable to develop symptoms that may be interpreted as 'schizophrenic' than are singletons (Klaning *et al.*, 1996). This may have to do with the possibility that peri-natal factors (birth injury and nutritional deficiencies or virus infections in the mother during pregnancy) may be associated with schizophrenia. The position is that the factors involved in what is called schizophrenia may well turn out to be diverse and complex, and until and unless there is much more substantiated information no deductions can be made as to the importance or otherwise of genetic factors. A working hypothesis (if schizophrenia continues to be acceptable as designating an illness) is that there is some evidence of inheritance of the vulnerability to develop tendencies which may lead to problems that may in some societies and under some circumstances be interpreted as schizophrenia. Perhaps the chances of such inheritance are similar to the inheritance of vulnerability to multiple sclerosis or tuberculosis, but with the limitation resulting from the importance of social and cultural context which affects all assessments of mental health.

RACISM IN DIAGNOSIS

Questions about the use of schizophrenia as diagnosis raised by black people in the UK have led to theories about the racist nature of the diagnosis itself. The history of racism in psychiatry and the way racism affects diagnosis are complex topics (see Fernando, 1988). Perceptions of people and ideologies about their cultures, personalities etc. influence the deductions made in the process of diagnosing mental health problems as illness. Concepts, such as schizophrenia, carry their own special images of alienness, and dangerousness, etc., all of which get mixed up and compounded with cultural misunderstandings and mistakes. In the UK, as in the USA, but not in Jamaica, black people are being diagnosed as 'schizophrenic' or 'psychotic' to a disproportionately excessive extent, the latest reports using a standard (Western) diagnostic inventory – the present state examination (PSE) (Wing *et al.*, 1974) – being studies from Nottingham (G. Harrison, *et al.*, 1988; G. Harrison, *et al.*, 1997) and London (King *et al.*, 1994; Bhugra *et al.*, 1997). In the former, white psychiatrists alone were involved; in the latter both black and white psychiatrists participated in the diagnostic process.

When Western psychiatry developed about two- or three-hundred years ago in a cultural context where matters of the mind were distinguished from matters of the body (see Chapter 2), the concept of mental illness arose as an extension, or imitation of the concept of physical illness. Naturally, the art of identifying mental symptoms became a basic tenet of the way of working in psychiatry, and schizophrenia was the name given to a particular grouping of these symptoms identified as 'illnesses'. But, psychiatry did not develop, nor does it function today, in a social and political vacuum. Influences from various sources inform the process of diagnosing mental illness, but the forces that permeated psychiatry play a large part in defining the result. And in a racist society, racism has been, and continues to be, one of these forces.

During recent years, the diagnostic process for identifying

schizophrenia has become increasingly refined and standardised, with operationally defined criteria for diagnosing illnesses and structured ways of eliciting and recording symptoms. However, this superstructure continues to be based on the art of making judgements about people's thinking, behaviour, beliefs, perceptions, feelings, emotional states etc.: judgements inevitably made from a particular cultural standpoint (broadly termed Western culture) and which we incorrectly call 'phenomena' (Berrios and Chen, 1993), thereby implying that they are objective facts. But, in day-to-day practice, symptom identification and illness recognition are not independent processes, the former following the latter, but occur together. Decisions about diagnosis are made early in a clinical interview, before the judgements about the presence or absence of symptoms have been arrived at (Kendell, 1975). Images in the mind of the person making the diagnosis inevitably affect the way the judgmental process goes. In research, structured ways of eliciting and recording symptoms and operationally defined criteria for diagnosing the illness are common. The present state examination (PSE) is one such structured interview schedule described by one of its founders (Wing, 1978) as 'a special technique of interviewing patients . . . which is simply a standardized form of the psychiatric diagnostic interview ordinarily used in Western Europe, based on a detailed glossary of differential definitions of symptoms' (1978: 103).

The permeation of racist and other undesirable perceptions into the current diagnostic system is almost inevitable unless very careful measures are taken to counteract them. Recently, the author had the following experience:

> Not long ago, I had the opportunity of seeing psychiatric reports on two patients prepared by the same psychiatrist within a few days of each other. The former, a young black man, was described (in the report) as not admitting to any of the first rank symptoms of schizophrenia but (the psychiatrist wrote) since the young man had a history of treatment in a psychiatric unit and was judged (by the psychiatrist) to be exhibiting thought disorder as well as appearing to be hallucinating, the likely diagnosis was schizophrenia. In the case of the other patient, a white woman, her claims to hear voices in the third person and to feel influenced by external forces etc. were discounted on the basis that the psychiatrist did not believe her and the diagnosis given was

neurotic disorder. In both instances, in keeping with good psychiatric practice, the psychiatrist was interpreting what the patient told him in deciding whether (in *his* judgement) symptoms (i.e. 'phenomena') were present or absent.

Western categories of illness and their imposition in other cultures during the diagnostic process has been seriously questioned by many people, the best known being Arthur Kleinman (1977), who has proposed the term 'category fallacy' for the well known error of imposing constructions (of illness) derived in one culture in a very different cultural context. The fact that nearly all research into schizophrenia continues to make this error ignoring questions of validity says something about the power exercised by researchers almost unwittingly – a sort of cultural arrogance akin to, if not identical to, institutional racism. The use of operational criteria for identifying schizophrenia as an illness (now a standard procedure in research) may help to overcome idiosyncratic diagnostic habits and increase reliability of diagnosis but, as the researchers admit (Wessely *et al.*, 1991), on reporting a study of the Camberwell Case Register, their use 'brings us closer to committing Kleinman's "category-error"'.

But racism enters the diagnostic process at other levels too. After all, diagnosis is always based on a personal interaction involving at least two persons. In such an interaction in the context of institutional racism, images of black people must play a large part in the conclusions drawn about diagnosis – and such conclusions inevitably affect interpretations that get classified as symptoms. And of course particular diagnoses carry particular images: the images of illness get confounded with images of people. The alienist tradition of psychiatry dies hard. So, if alienness is perceived as an attribute of people considered to be 'aliens' (often because they are black), that impression would play into the judgements made during diagnosis. But alienness is also linked to images of the mad, the people who cannot be understood, the 'schizophrenic'. And, as suggested earlier in Chapter 2, schizophrenia is already constructed to reflect racist ideas of degeneration evoking images of primitiveness and racial impurity. Add to this a view of schizophrenia as being caused by a 'bad' gene (a Kraepelinian tradition firmly held by psychiatry), and a high level of schizophrenia being diagnosed in black people becomes natural. It is not really a question of 'misdiagnosis'; the diagnosis itself is within the tradition of psychiatry and so understandable if the meaning of diagnosis in psychiatric practice is appreciated, but yet it appears to be inappropriate and unhelpful – perhaps even destructive.

CONCLUSIONS

It is generally believed that psychiatry has 'progressed' in developing complicated systems of classification as represented by repeated revisions of the ICD and DSM. However, the original Kraepelinian ideas about schizophrenia, involving concepts of racial degeneration and inherited propensity, appear to have survived almost untouched into modern thinking. Indeed, as modern scientific thinking has moved away from Cartesian mind–body divisions and Newtonian mechanical physics, psychiatry and psychology have embraced these concepts even more firmly than they did a hundred years ago.

Schizophrenia was associated at its birth in the late nineteenth century with ideas of racial degeneration, hygiene and eugenics at a time when the dogma of skin-colour racism was being incorporated into European thinking. Schizophrenia was constructed in the late nineteenth century at a time when social conflict, violence and fear of unknown 'dark' forces were rife in Europe; it represented and reflected those very fears. Outside Europe, in the colonies and in the large numbers of ex-slaves in North America, white Europeans were beginning to see (and fear) the large masses of black people with alien cultures representing (psychologically) the 'dark' forces feared by Europe.

In the latter half of the twentieth century, Europe itself has become multiracial and multicultural. Black people within Europe, black Europeans, Europeans with 'alien' cultures, now represent those dark forces. As stresses and strains arising from black–white racial interaction affect Europe, the construct schizophrenia is again being implicated. As black people attempt to grapple with racism in the 1990s, just as when Soviet dissidents grappled with totalitarianism in the 1960s, forensic psychiatry gets drawn in to assist the state in social control. As in the Soviet Union, controlling people that society sees as 'dangerous' becomes the province of forensic psychiatry. And schizophrenia, – or just generalised 'psychosis' is the diagnosis that is naturally used to medicalise black protest, despair and anger.

Chapter 4

Anger, criminality and dangerousness

It is the purpose of this chapter to explore the background to connections between anger and criminality in the context of racism on the one hand, and, on the other, the issues around 'race' that are involved in judgements about dangerousness in the field of forensic psychiatry. This chapter focuses on situations and conditions in the UK, but also in the wider context of Europe and North America. Analyses of race and criminality, mainly in US literature, lead on to discussions of stereotypes, images and assumptions with racial connotations that feed into assessments of dangerousness in the field of forensic psychiatry.

BLACK RAGE

The high rates of violence among African-American communities in the USA are well documented (see Wilson, 1990; Hacker, 1995). The 'rage', erupting in violence, that characterises black communities in the USA have been analysed in terms of their (for example) pent-up anger and frustration (Cloward and Ohlin, 1965), powerlessness against white domination (May, 1972), criminalisation by psychopolitically engineered processes designed to maintain dependency and powerlessness (Wilson, 1990) etc. But, bell hooks (1995) argues that, far from being pathological, the rage, or 'killing rage', of black people in the USA is 'an appropriate response to injustice' (1995: 26). Patricia Williams (1991), professor of law at Harvard states, after describing in her book *The Alchemy of Race and Rights* several high profile cases involving black–white conflict given much publicity in the USA, that: 'To discount as much violence as we do must mean that we have a very angry population, suppressing explosive rage. Most white Americans, in urban areas at least, have seen the muttering "lunatic" black person who beats the air with his fists and curses aloud: most people cross the street; they don't choose him to satisfy their need to know the time of day. Yet for generations, and particularly in the wake of the foaming public response to incidents like Howard Beach, the Goetz shooting, and Forsythe County, that is precisely how white America has looked to many a black American' (1991: 78).

In *Black-on-Black Violence* (1990), a book that attempts to analyse the forces that compel black criminal behaviour in the USA, Amos Wilson, professor of psychology, argues that the crimes of white USA (an extension of white Europe) 'infinitely outweigh the alleged crimes of African-American men . . . [and] . . . the White male, in order to enhance and protect his self-image, enjoy the material wealth, power, and political advantages of his criminality, must deny truth and reality; he must not experience the guilty conscience which would result from an acknowledgement and acceptance of his own criminality and psychopathy' (1990: 10). Not only does the domination of white USA (as a sociopolitical system implemented at a personal level) restrict, frustrate and abuse black people, but 'white America's need to dominate black America creates the need to perceive the African male as criminal, and to actualize African male criminality by socializing or ritualizing him into it by dint of judicial witchcraft' (1990: 9). These are the colour-blind legal processes within the US (legal) system that institutes subtle racism described so vividly by Patricia Williams (1991).

Amos Wilson (1990) describes the 'criminogenic' effects of US society thus: 'Black criminality is not accidental, coincidental or aberrant, but speaks to an apparent need in the White American community to induce criminality in a significant proportion of the Black American community, as well as its need to perceive African-Americans as innately criminal, just as it exhibits the related need to perceive the average African-American as innately intellectually inferior' (1990: 34). The combination of the power of stereotyping, myth creation and identification with the aggressor results in internalisation of white racism by some black people leading to low self-image, self-hatred and self-alienation, further aggravating their problems and re-enforcing the status quo: 'In the context of White American domination there is no innocent black male, just black male criminals who have not yet been detected, apprehended or convicted' (1990: 8).

In *Understanding Black Adolescent Male Violence* (1991) which concentrates on finding ways of preventing black violence, Amos Wilson focuses on the personal psychology of young black adolescent men who resort to violence, although Wilson identifies many social and political factors which are important contextual issues (Box 4.1). The factors recorded by Wilson 'which characteristically and generally define adolescence in America and which, when represented in the collective personality of Black adolescents, interact with factors related to "being Black in White America"' (1991: 16) are listed in Box 4.2.

So far, there has been very little interest in the UK – and even less in the rest of Europe – in analysing issues of race in connection with anger and criminal behaviour of black people. The relevance of analyses of the US scene to that in the UK (and Europe) is problematic. There are clear differences between the history of African-Americans (in the USA) and that of British black populations but there are similarities too. The black population in the USA is largely derived from formerly segregated ex-slave population where the memories of direct vicious persecution are very recent. Although British black African-Caribbeans trace their origins in the

Box 4.1: Issues for black adolescents in the USA: sociopolitical context

High levels of unemployment, overcrowding, and poverty
Inadequate pre-school education and job-training
Segregated urban existence
Post-modern/industrial/de-industrialised world
Advertising designed to evoke consumatory desires
Rising expectations at a time of increasing poverty of means to fulfil them
Family dissolution
Conservative governments
Changes of power and economic changes in the world
Inner city world characterised by the absence of sociocultural, socioeconomic institutions which can deal with current demands
A world of armed violence and criminally inclined gangs
Urban world flooded with addictive drugs
Markets which provide little room for Black manufacturing etc.

(Wilson, 1991: 19–20)

Box 4.2: Issues for black adolescents in the USA: psychological problems

The effort to resolve critical issues concerning self-identity (including ethnic identity), sexual, gender and social identities

Efforts to establish and maintain self-esteem (for males – masculinity); efforts to deal with issues revolving around the acceptance and rejection of social norms, adult and parental values and demands, adult authority and control

Body image; self-consciousness and self-confidence

Emotional liability, i.e. moodiness; boredom; confusion about life, its meaningfulness and purposes and a sense of direction

Social acceptance and popularity relative to the peer group

General feeling of alienation; anomie; powerlesness; need for attention

Vocational and career choices and possibilities

Intellectual, cognitive/behavioral development and prowess

Issues revolving around status symbols – clothing; hair styles; body adornments; automobiles; money and invidious comparisons of the self with others' race and nationality

(Wilson, 1991: 19–20)

UK in the main to immigration from the West Indies within the past fifty years, British slavery, followed by racial segregation (in the West Indies), was indeed the context these immigrants inherited. The black population of Asian origin is derived largely from immigrants whose forefathers lived under colonialism, facing attacks on their psyches and cultures which may have been less overt when compared to the aggression against Africans during slavery, but perhaps are no less damaging in the long run. There are differences between the current lifestyles *vis-à-vis* black-white interaction between the UK and the USA, represented (for example) by the fact that inter-marriage between African-Caribbeans and whites runs at forty per cent in the UK compared to one to two per cent in the USA (Karpf, 1997). But the reality of racism based on an ideology of white supremacy applies as much in the UK and the rest of Europe as it does in the USA (Bowser, 1995). Thus, in the absence of direct evidence from the UK and other European countries on how exactly racism is connected to issues of violence, the lessons of the US experience must be accepted at least as a working hypothesis for the present. And this highlights the importance of 'rage' – justified rage – of black people.

PSYCHIATRIC ASSESSMENT

A major function of the forensic system is to make assessments based on a body of information obtained from various sources and an evaluation of 'mental state'. The importance of racist stereotypes and myths that become incorporated in the diagnoses ascribed to black people was described in Chapter 3. An earlier book (Fernando, 1988) had summarised the process in quoting from Rendon (1984):

> Thus, psychiatry is comfortable in dealing with, and in, stereotypes; the result is that stereotypes present in society – such as racial stereotypes of black people – are incorporated into its 'machine' with no difficulty. Further by being incorporated into a supposedly scientific body of knowledge, beliefs based on stereotypes become 'facts'. They, in turn, become institutionalised to become myths. In reality, much of what passes for 'facts' in psychiatry are myths – and a major drawback of myths, from a scientific angle, is that they serve to close the circle that science has necessarily to leave open.
>
> (1988: 46)

Psychiatry has not addressed the problem that, both in practice and theory, myths are confused with (scientific) facts and categories with stereotypes. Myths persist for both social and psychological reasons. Rendon (1984) notes that social forces opposing assimilation of human groups and equality of human beings, tend to present social facts, such as poverty, famine and oppression, as natural phenomena in order to stress the lack of equality and the alienness of certain human beings designated as 'barbarian', 'primitive' or 'underdeveloped'. The causes of justified anger arising from racism in society are often not recognised during psychiatric assessments because the black experience in society is not given credence, even if the existence of personal discrimination is recognised in a theoretical sort of way. The alienation felt by most black people is usually seen as *their* problem (and this often leads to 'treatment' aimed at getting people to recognise 'reality'), rather than a problem for society as a whole. And when the experiences and feelings of black people are recognised as significant, a disease or criminal model is used to conceptualise them because society promotes this and needs this.

In the 1960s 'West Indians' were perceived by white psychiatrists as presenting mental health problems in the style of 'primitive psychosis' rather than clear-cut illnesses in the European mould (personal recollection). Many of the stereotypes that feed into diagnoses connect up with a racist ideology that associates skin colour with primitiveness, dangerousness and madness; hence the psychiatric perception in the 1960s could be understood as a slippage of meaning of the term 'primitive' applied to both illness and to people. In the 1980s, 'primitive psychosis' gave way to 'cannabis psychosis' found to have been given to eight to sixteen per cent of West Indian migrants and a diagnosis not given to white or Asian patients in Birmingham (McGovern and Cope, 1987a). At the time, the image of the dangerous black person intoxicated on cannabis was a popular one and a reason often given for any apparently deviant behaviour by black ('West Indian') people; for example, excitement caused by consumption of cannabis was blamed for riots in Birmingham in the early 1980s (Imlah, 1985). As schizophrenia itself has become increasingly perceived in Kraepelinian terms as inherited madness representing degeneration and primitiveness, 'race-specific' diagnoses, such as 'cannabis psychosis' and 'primitive psychosis', have gradually become absorbed into the general schizophrenia type.

A further change appears to be taking place in the 1990s: a generalised undifferentiated 'psychosis' carrying all the hallmarks of Kraepelinian schizophrenia but with a stronger implication of madness, is being attributed to black people. For example, the report comparing diagnoses given to various ethnic groups in Haringey in London (King *et al.*, 1994), concluded: 'Members of all ethnic minority groups are more likely to develop a psychosis but not necessarily schizophrenia' (1994: 1118–9); and the latest report from Nottingham (Harrison *et al.*, 1997) also refers to the 'increased risk of psychosis' (1997: 805), rather than to schizophrenia as such. And today, the sort of dynamics that led to some US psychiatrists diagnosing runaway black slaves as 'drapetomanic' (Chapter 2) is resulting in European psychiatry categorising as 'psychotic', angry 'aliens' perceived as 'dangerous' (Figure 4.1).

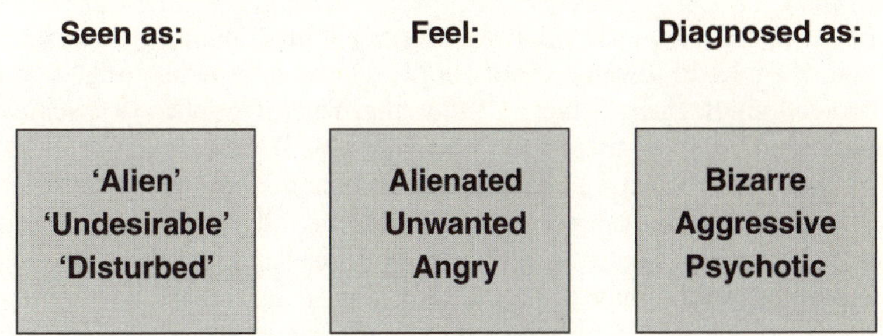

Figure 4.1 The construction of psychosis

The arguments presented above are not designed to suggest simply that feelings and behaviour presented by black people are being misunderstood or misinterpreted when they are given a schizophrenia or 'psychosis' designation, although some misunderstanding and misinterpretation undoubtedly occurs, nor do they suggest that symptoms of schizophrenia are explicable in terms of 'rage' alone. What is proposed is that, in a context of racism and the history of psychiatry, professionals (usually psychiatrists), oblivious of the effects of stereotypes and prejudiced attitudes on the judgements they make during assessment (or, if they do appreciate such effects they are unable to do anything to counteract them), using a narrow medical approach that gives diagnosis considerable importance if not pride of place during assessment, fit into the category of 'psychosis' people they cannot understand in any way (other than by 'diagnosing' them). Thus, given the impetus (to diagnose) and the mind-sets involved during the process, the so-called phenomena of 'psychosis' or 'schizophrenia' follow naturally, partly because they (professionals) expect to 'find' them and partly because the disempowered objects of their diagnoses (namely black people presenting as 'patients') are conditioned to express their problems through feelings and behaviour that lend themselves to the diagnosis (or 'psychosis'). In simple – perhaps simplistic – terms, professionals see black people with problems as 'mad' connecting with (some) black people who 'act mad'.

DANGEROUSNESS

The concept of 'dangerousness' plays a crucial part in the evaluations of people that are specifically 'forensic' as distinct from (generally) 'psychiatric'. It relates largely – predominantly – to the risk of violence towards other people. Hence it generally relates to protection of these 'others', either the general public or specific persons. Criminologist, Cyril Greenland (1985), has observed: 'It is obvious that the expression "violent and dangerous" in the context of mental disorder represents a sociopolitical judgement rather than a psychiatric diagnosis. Because violence and aggression are promoted rather than condemned in our society, the tendency to behave violently in violence-prone situations cannot be regarded as necessarily abnormal' (1985: 27).

There are two related sets of issues involved in the perception of a person as 'dangerous'. First, the concept of dangerousness as a fixed personality trait is of doubtful validity – people may pose a risk at certain times and in response to certain situations but not in others (Gostin, 1986). Yet, forensic psychiatry functions as if such a trait exists; and the search for this elusive 'dangerousness' trait is usually researched in colour-blind, culture-blind ways, and more seriously for 'patients' of the forensic psychiatric system, judgements are made as if established methods for detecting this trait are already available. Second, since objective criteria for recognising 'dangerousness' are not available, dangerousness is very likely to be associated with images and myths about people derived from impressions, misconceptions and ordinary 'common sense'.

Chapter 3 showed how European thinking has historically associated blackness with danger and developed images of black people as dangerous people and at the same time established ways of thinking that connected race with degeneration and schizophrenia. The images connecting schizophrenia and criminality have persisted almost unchanged but (as pointed out in Chapter 1) modern racism is no longer articulated with references to overt racial characteristics; terms such as 'underclass' or 'inner city' and concepts such as immigration or citizenship are used to transmit racial messages about 'dangerous' black people. Kenan Malik states:

> The parallels between the debate on immigration and that on the underclass should already be apparent. Both immigrants and the underclass are regarded as alien to the body of the nation, as groups whose difference imperils the cohesion of the nation and its sense of community. And just as the supposed difference of immigrants helps retrospectively establish the mythical homo-

> geneity of the national community, so the difference of the underclass helps define the supposed meaning of citizenship.
>
> (1996: 199)

RISK ASSESSMENT

In a context of forensic psychiatric practice and the criminal justice system, interest in issues of dangerousness focuses on risk assessment – in the sense of the risk of harm to the public. If the risk is high, prolonged custodial care (in the case of the psychiatric system) or prolonged imprisonment (in the case of the criminal justice system) may be contemplated by forensic psychiatrists or judges. However, risk assessment is itself a risky business fraught with many drawbacks – not least the likelihood of being a self-fulfilling prophecy. This uncertainty applies to people convicted of an offence irrespective of whether they have been diagnosed as 'mentally ill'. The position with regard to the psychiatric system has been well put by Estroff and Zimmer (1994):

> The nature and incidence of violence involving psychiatric patients in community and family settings is a controversial subject, difficult to inform with data. Unreported incidents, different versions of who did what to whom, and other logistic obstacles to data collection make any assessment of the extent of such violence tentative at best.
>
> (1994: 270)

A complex study carried out by these authors illustrates the difficulties involved in coming to any conclusions that may be useful. In a study of 169 individuals with diagnosis of 'severe, persistent mental illness', they interviewed significant people in the community using a mixture of qualitative and quantitative methods of analysis. When examining sociodemographic data, they found that African-American race (the researchers called the category 'social-race') was associated with violent acts but other findings showed that: schizophrenia was diagnosed disproportionately among men designated as African-American and interviews with people confined because of 'dangerousness' revealed that 'many patients in the study, particularly men, did not perceive themselves to be threatening or violent, expressing surprise and bewilderment at the response of others, and contesting their confinement for being dangerous' (1994: 272). The authors concluded:

> We think it is a mistake to categorize people as violent or not, to conceptualize violence as a characteristic of a person without giving equal attention to the underlying or concurrent interpersonal and clinical processes and contexts. These are experienced over time and vary in their contributions to violence. For example, other family and social network members clearly engage in behaviors as menacing as those of diagnosed patients, but responses other than diagnosis and civil commitment are made. It is also possible that family and social network members reinterpret the meaning and gravity of threatening and assaultive behavior once a diagnosis of mental illness has been applied to their relative and may alter their tolerance for and responses to violence accordingly. Thus, while the patients under investigation may not have changed their behaviors after being diagnosed, those who define violence and the limits of tolerable behavior may have altered their views – initiating commitments or criminal charges at a lower threshold and higher frequency.
>
> (1994: 289)

Two eminent US researchers of violence, Monahan and Steadman (1994) suggest that researching risk assessment for 'dangerousness' should address: (1) 'risk factors' – the variables that are used to predict violence; (2) 'harm' – the amount and type of violence being predicted; and (3) 'risk level' – the probability that harm will occur. They recommend that 'harm' should be scaled in terms of seriousness, and 'risk level' should be seen as a continuous probability statement and one that fluctuates over time and context, and that 'risk management' should always follow 'risk assessment'. Attempts to objectify the process of risk assessment are limited by the lack of objective data and (more importantly) the nature of the concept of dangerousness (discussed above). In practice – and forensic psychiatry is, after all, a practical affair – the role of 'clinical judgement' is crucial, perhaps all important. Although clinical judgement (of dangerousness) by psychiatrists is no better than judgement by a lay person (Bowden, 1985), psychiatrists are taught to make such judgements and most psychiatrists – especially forensic psychiatrists – have little compunction about acting upon them or persuading courts to do so. And, there is little doubt that stereotypes (e.g. of race and size) influence all such judgements, that is, unless specific strategies are employed to deal with their effect.

CLINICAL JUDGEMENT

In many situations in general medicine, clinical judgement may well be a necessary correction to 'objective facts' based on impersonal tests, i.e. tests that do not involve personal judgements. In psychiatry, however, there are no such tests, and everything that goes into a 'mental state examination' and into making a diagnosis, is 'clinical judgement'. So clinical judgement is the expertise of psychiatry; the basic training that psychiatrists get is to exercise clinical judgement. Yet, clinical judgement is beset with many problems, not least the fact that its 'correctness' cannot be checked one way or the other. In other words, clinical judgement is not evidence based, but based on intuition and experience; and the concept of 'correctness' is inapplicable in the case of clinical judgement (in psychiatry).

Clinical judgement is exercised within a framework, the psychiatric system of identifying pathological states within the mind, identifying 'illness' of the mind and making a diagnosis (see Fernando, 1988, 1991). This framework is determined by cultural pre-conditions allowing the fairly free permeation into it of ideas and impressions about the person being judged, however much the person making the judgement may try to be 'objective'. For example, clinical judgement is used to sift information given as history – excluding some bits and expanding on others – so that what gets recorded as 'history' will be affected by images and stereotypes associated with the person who provides the alleged information. Clinical judgement is used to devise whether (for example) someone is pretending to be hallucinated or is *really* experiencing hallucinations, and so on. The extent to which culturally induced distortions and racist ideologies determine the result of clinical judgement is immense – unless of course the person making the judgement is trained to allow for them and is able to do so.

The list in Box 4.3 represents the 'factors' commonly used by psychiatrists for making their 'clinical judgement' of dangerousness. After reviewing research into the accuracy of clinical judgements of psychiatrists and psychologists at predicting violent behaviour towards others, Monahan (1981) concluded that these professional groups are accurate in no more than one out of three predictions of violent behaviour over a period of several years among institutionalised populations that had both committed violence in the past (and thus had high base rates for it) and who were diagnosed as mentally ill. An update on recent research in this field (Monahan

Box 4.3: Clinical judgements of dangerousness

History

Previous episodes of violence
Repeated impulsive behaviour
Difficulty in coping with stress
Unwillingness to delay gratification
Sadistic or paranoid traits

Offences

Bizarre violence
Unprovoked violence
Lack of regret
Continual denial

Mental state

Morbid jealousy
Paranoid beliefs plus wish to harm others
Deceptiveness
Lack of self-control
Threats to repeat violence
Attitude to treatment

Circumstances

Provocation or precipitation likely to occur
Alcohol or drug abuse
Social difficulties and lack of support

(Gelder *et al.*, 1989)

and Steadman, 1994) found that correlation between clinical predictions and actual violence remains low or non-significant and that, in a study of people presenting at an emergency room, the accuracy of clinical prediction of community violence (Lidz *et al.*, 1993) substantially exceeded chance levels in the case of male violence, but not in the case of female violence, while clinical prediction was not affected by race or age (of people assessed) – although the meaning of this last statement was not clear.

The poor reliability of clinical judgements of dangerousness taken together with the clear likelihood that they are bound to be influenced by stereotypes connecting race and dangerousness, raises serious issues about the list given in Box 4.3. In practice, recorded past episodes of violence or aggression play a crucial role in determining a positive risk of similar behaviour in the future but seldom, if ever, are the circumstances of what is recorded as 'violence' or 'aggression' examined. Clearly, the current approaches to risk assessment leaves a great deal to be desired generally and, in view of the extent to which such assessments would depend on impressions and 'common sense', the serious likelihood of assessments being racist, thereby perpetuating myths and injustices.

CONCLUSIONS

This chapter presents the psycho-social background for understanding some of the issues behind the over-representation of black people in both prison and custodial sections of in-patient psychiatry including forensic psychiatry. US writers analysing the high levels of violence in black communities take as their starting-point the violently oppressive nature of current racism across the USA. From there they trace its effect on the black psyche, the undermining of self-confidence sometimes to the extent of instilling self-hatred but nearly always a sense of frustration and rage. There are cogent reasons for applying this thesis to the UK and the rest of Europe, although the histories of black people in Europe are not identical with that of African-Americans. In short continuous anger amounting to rage – 'killing rage' – leads to a generalised aggression reflected in crime. The justice system in the USA has been called 'criminogenic' to black people in the sense that the implementation of laws in a racist context results in criminalising black people.

Forensic psychiatry works closely with the criminal justice system in the field of 'social control' – in a general sense maintaining law and order. In doing so, forensic psychiatry uses the tools it has inherited, mainly the process of diagnosing 'illness'. It was shown in previous chapters that, not only is psychiatry (including forensic psychiatry) Eurocentric and therefore likely to be inappropriate for a multicultural society, but by practising in a racist fashion (often racialising cultural difference), it colludes fully with racism in society in general. The concept of schizophrenia, or the more generalised 'psychosis', is well suited for operating in a racist framework for historical reasons (see Chapters 2 and 3) with the result that the mixture of rage, alienation and (what is seen as) bizarre behaviour gets psychiatrised in ways analogous to the psychiatrisation of 'running away' of black slaves in the diagnosis of 'drapetomania' (see Chapter 2). So, in a sense, forensic psychiatry does the dirty work for the criminal justice system so that, up to a point, the 'justice' bit is given credence by using a medical cover-up.

Forensic psychiatry does its work using diagnosis mainly, but claims to want to identify the 'dangerousness' that gives it status because, by doing so, it provides valuable service to society. So, although there is an obvious lack of dependable criteria for identifying 'dangerousness', there are strong political reasons for forensic psychiatry to continue to hold on to this function and present 'clinical judgement' (based on intuition and experience) in this area as dependable. However, when this expertise of psychiatrists is examined, any semblance of objectivity disappears.

The current situation is that forensic psychiatry is an expanding field and risk assessment is a growing industry. This is unlikely to change because it appears to be in line with the general direction of wider changes in society. There is a swing across the Western world into biological thinking and a tendency to look for individual pathology rather than social reasons for issues such as criminality and mental health problems. The blaming (of individuals) is given greater precedence over understanding; and the impact of racism broadens and deepens this blame – represented in psychiatric language as diagnosis.

Part II

Clinical issues

David Ndegwa

Chapter 5

Introduction

Forensic psychiatry is one of the newest clinical subspecialities in British psychiatry and most developments in staff training, recruitment and service provision occurred in the 1970s and 1980s. The (British) Mental Health Act, within which forensic psychiatry functions in England and Wales, was revised in 1959 (Her Majesty's Stationery Office, 1959) to set the scene for what was intended to be an enlightened approach to people designated as 'mentally handicapped' and 'mentally ill'; it was further revised in 1983 by the current Mental Health Act (Her Majesty's Stationery Office, 1983). The key reports setting the style for services in forensic psychiatry are those by Butler (Home Office and Department of Health and Social Security, 1975) and Glancy (Department of Health and Social Security, 1974). There have been a number of other reports and circulars giving guidance on service provision and multi-agency working. These reflect research in the area of prevalence of mental abnormality in prison populations, serious incident enquiries, e.g. suicide, homicide and prison inspections. A recent report, *Review of Health and Social Services for Mentally Disordered Offenders and Others Requiring Similar Services* (Department of Health and Home Office, 1992a), commonly called the 'Reed Report', makes a number of recommendations for the style and type of services, research, staff recruitment and training. Also, the 'Reed Report' made recommendations about the need to involve black people in the commissioning and provision of services.

The product champions and catalysts for better forensic psychiatric services have been reformers and campaigners calling for improvement in prison conditions with an understanding of the vulnerability of people going through the criminal justice system and the need to protect their civil and human rights. In pursuit of these objectives, they have reminded the public of the best traditions of the medical profession – a humane approach to patients and advocating their rights to treatment and care. Forensic psychiatrists deal with those people with mental health problems who are caught up in the criminal justice system but they have also developed areas of interest in psychiatric intensive care, the management of people thought to have violent or dangerous propensities, challenging behaviours and some types of 'personality disorders'.

Psychiatrists are largely drawn from the middle classes: in the main they did not attend multicultural, multiracial urban schools, or grow up in racially mixed neighbourhoods. Black people do not feature in the cultural, philosophical and historic interests and education of the white middle class, apart from in popular music and sports. The first intimate contact with black people may be in situations where judgements and decisions have to be made about a black person who is in a vulnerable position in terms of power relationships.

FORENSIC SERVICES

Hospitals serving forensic psychiatry within the National Health Service (NHS) can be classified in terms of the security they provide. A simple and common classification uses terms like 'low security', 'medium security' and 'maximum security'. Low security characterises the sort of treatment setting that exists in most general psychiatric hospitals. Maximum security describes the environments to be found in the special hospitals (where security approximates those of maximum security prisons), catering for people who would pose a grave and immediate danger to the public in relation to their mental health problems. Forensic settings of medium security are meant for patients with violent or dangerous propensities requiring more than 'low' security but not requiring the level of security that special hospitals provide. The bulk of practising forensic psychiatrists in England and Wales work in medium secure units – generally called 'regional secure units' or RSUs. The majority of patients coming into RSUs are transferred from prisons, either on remand or serving sentences. In the early 1990s there was a massive increase in the numbers of persons transferred from prison to hospital, leading to serious bed shortages. Indeed it appears that the only reason the increase was not even larger is the lack of beds in RSUs.

The special hospitals have been the subject of much criticism not least on account of their failure to address issues of human rights, racial discrimination and mistreatment of women. The issues have been highlighted in reports available in the public arena and will be dealt with in Part 3 of this book.

A major practical problem faced by RSUs at present is a result of the continued stay of large number of patients in medium security (although RSUs were planned for relatively short stays). One reason is the unmet demand for low security services and supervised specialist hostels. The urban and inner city areas with the highest admission rates to medium security are also likely to have the poorest infrastructure in general psychiatric hospitals and community. Thus, a considerable number of patients who enter and remain within medium security would have shorter in-patient stays if infrastructure at the lower levels of security was better. Increasingly, a large number of patients admitted to medium security, particularly in urban areas, are admitted on 'restriction orders' which remove the doctors' power to discharge patients or to grant leave for patients to visit the community. (When a 'restriction order' is imposed by a Court under Section 41 of the Mental Health Act, the powers referred to are held by the Home Office, except that a Mental Health Review Tribunal has the power to discharge.) Clinical issues are just one of the many factors that are included in an assessment of risk made by the Home Office and there may be differences of opinion between doctors and the Home Office. Although there has been no published ethnic statistics on the use of restriction orders by courts, it is obvious (and verified by unpublished research) that black people (as compared to white people) are disproportionately over-represented. In other words, black people are much more likely than are white people to be the recipients of psychiatric evaluations that support the courts in imposing Section 41. The tendency (as it were) to protect the public from black people through the legal instrument of a restriction order, with its quasi-medical basis raises serious concerns for justice and social harmony in a multi-ethnic society.

The current situation within the NHS is that, with an increase in demand for beds, accommodation for NHS patients is being purchased (by the NHS) in the independent and private sectors. With the exception of those parts of the country with enough capacity, NHS based forensic psychiatrists act as gatekeepers for patients going into the private or independent sector who are usually paid for on an extra-contractual or case-by-case basis. Thus, the NHS uses units in the private and independent sectors as extensions of their wards, although they are often located a considerable distance from the urban areas which provide most of the forensic clients.

The private/independent sector

Private and independent hospitals have a range of services particularly in areas where the NHS has always been deficient, e.g. specialist provision for challenging behaviours and head injury patients. Although not designated as forensic psychiatry services as such, many private hospitals do in effect provide such services. The private sector has the advantage of being able to move into a 'market gap' quickly, they can conceptualise and build facilities quickly or change the use of existing facilities from medium secure to serve new needs.

There is little research comparing the care and outcomes of patients managed by the NHS or the private sector but there are some clear differences between them. Private hospitals are usually located in rural surroundings far away from city centres. They have larger wards than NHS hospitals, e.g. wards with more than fifteen beds. Directions issued to NHS hospitals, such as the instruction to carry out ethnic monitoring, do not apply to these private institutions. Private hospitals that provide services for patients detained under the Mental Health Act receive regular visits from the Mental Health Act Commission, but such visits merely provide 'snapshot' impressions that seldom detect the sort of serious issues that affect black patients.

Since the private sector takes no responsibility for the training of psychiatric medical staff – or indeed any other staff such as nurses, social workers, medical students, or occupational therapists – private hospitals are not subject to scrutiny by accreditation bodies established (for example) by the Royal College of Psychiatrists interested in the training of psychiatrists. And, most private hospitals do not usually employ junior trainee doctors such as senior house officers, registrars or senior registrars. It is possible to conduct research in the private sector but there is not much expenditure in this area. Staff working in the private sector are not involved in community activities, e.g. the aftercare of patients discharged from medium secure units, or working as product champions/catalysts for developments in the community for other mentally disordered offenders. It appears that most medical and nursing staff wish to work in NHS services in preference to private forensic facilities. Consequently, the private sector has recruitment problems and it is not clear to what extent the private sector is able to offer more attractive financial packages than the NHS to overcome recruitment problems, given the need to make a profit.

There is very little information available (in the public domain) about the sort of forensic psychiatry that is practised within private hospitals. Private hospitals providing forensic services are not subject to the sort of auditing and monitoring of their services that are established in the NHS. It appears that the private sector has been slow to develop advocacy services for patients and to adopt measures designed to bring about services that address issues of race and culture; it lags far behind the NHS in ethnic monitoring of its users and staff. People from black and other ethnic minority communities often feel isolated when detained in private hospitals because the units are usually located in parts of the country where the general population contains few ethnic minorities.

Purchasers and providers

The relationship with health authorities and commissioning (or purchasing) bodies (which buy in services for the NHS and so are supposed to ensure quality standards), is in most cases ambiguous and unsatisfactory. Health authorities differ in their sophistication and ability to determine appropriate quality standards or to develop measures for monitoring or enforcing those standards. Health authorities are in some cases so ignorant of what is involved that they typically compare costs of services in the private sector with costs in the NHS, insisting that costs in the NHS should approximate those in the private sector despite clear differences in the two types of providers.

The relationship between commissioning agencies (purchasers) and providers of services is often driven by costs rather than considerations of quality. Currently, the standards of clinical care within the NHS are being threatened as the NHS comes to approximate private provision. The most recent governmental directive to encourage private involvement in the NHS (the so-called 'Private

Finance Initiative') is likely to give some companies in the private sector, with no particular interest in the welfare of vulnerable patients, actual ownership of health care facilities. The private sector is likely to use this opportunity to cater for inner city or other urban populations where the demand for medium secure facilities is high – the very areas with large black populations. Some of the negative speculation about what goes on in private sector facilities could be reduced if more auditing and research were carried out in private sector facilities by the private sector themselves, independent agencies or collaboratively with the NHS or academic institutions. The private sector clearly provides better hotel and recreational services than the NHS and if the private sector were to move into urban areas, some of the problems generated by geographical isolation of current facilities might be reduced.

The future

In the current climate it is important that there is a clear way forward for forensic services which, after all, work with extremely vulnerable people. The ethos within the NHS during the past few years appears to demand cost effectiveness with little regard to quality, justice and equity. If this continues, the likely future for forensic services is that custodial care will predominate over therapeutic care with greater use of large doses of tranquillising medication. Inevitably, services will be based in parts of the country where it is easy to build and so they will be poorly integrated to local services. Patients entering such services would be alienated from their families, relatives and normal environments. Increasingly, forensic hospitals will be owned by the private sector, probably by construction companies, and core NHS services will be tenants. The NHS might itself be priced out of the market if all elements of the service were open to privatisation. However, it should be noted that this 'doomsday scenario' may be averted if a new ethos affects planning and development in the NHS – something that may be possible as a result of the election in May 1997 of a Labour government.

BLACK PEOPLE AND FORENSIC PSYCHIATRY

Black people have a relationship with psychiatric services similar in many respects to their relationship with other institutions. These include institutions in environments where black people are majorities (e.g. ex-European colonies in Africa). This can be understood partially by examining the history of legislation (in criminal and mental health) and the history, education and traditions of the professions who administer regulations arising from the legislation. In stable progressive democratic countries one would expect a situation where the public respects doctors and freely accesses them expecting (a) to be treated with respect; (b) that communications with their doctors will be privileged and confidential; and (c) doctors, in the main, provide the best care available, defending their rights and respecting their wishes.

Psychiatry, and especially forensic psychiatry, provides an institutional structure and culture that promotes a different relationship between the doctor (psychiatrist) and the public because psychiatrists are vested with powers other doctors either do not have or do not routinely exercise. Cochrane and Sashidharan (1996) write that psychiatry as a medical speciality is unique in having the legal authority to detain and treat people against their will on the basis that they have 'illnesses' that require treatment. Indeed the power vested in psychiatrists under the Mental Health Act (Her Majesty's Stationery Office, HMSO, 1983) and recent changes in community care legislation in the Mental Health (Patients in the Community) Act (HMSO, 1995), exceed even those available to police officers and any one else in British society. Cochrane and Sashidharan (1996) also note that the raw material of clinical practice in forensic psychiatry is concerned with people's behaviour, which is often received by second hand accounts, and deductions about emotional states and cognitive processes that are not backed up by objective scientific tests. Consequently, the validity of diagnoses and effectiveness of treatment cannot be measured objectively. Essentially, black and other ethnic minorities in the UK do not see psychiatry as benign and there is a long history of interpreting psychiatry as a way of legitimising the suppression of non-normative and subversive behaviour by applying labels of madness to activities which threaten the status quo or even just embarrass the respectable white middle classes. There is a common assumption that behaviours (and problems) in the white population are normative and that deviation from the white pattern shown by another ethnic group in either direction indicates 'pathology' (see Fernando, 1988).

Sociologist Paul Gilroy (1987) describes law as a national institution and popular politics as having infused legality with the capacity to define the very core of national identity. Smith (1994) points out that neither current law nor the corresponding sense of identity grew out of a tradition that included present day ethnic minorities. Yet the law seeks to impose a universal framework on more or less diverse groups which may differ in their perceptions and definitions of deviance, in the methods they use to control it and the readiness to appeal to the formal legal process. Forensic psychiatrists, as medical specialists, have entered this legal field with unique access to power in the criminal justice system; they are often seen as 'expert witnesses' invited to comment on areas even where their expertise is questionable. Thus, by participating in the criminal justice system wearing as it were a medical hat (rather than a judicial one) the possibility exists that they may add to any injustice that may be inherent in the system. In a multi-ethnic setting, forensic psychiatrists, by presenting their views as 'clinical' judgements, can unwittingly give credence and some legal force to myths about the pathological nature of cultural differences, to stereotypes about (for example) dangerousness associated with racial difference, and to prejudices held by the public.

Forensic psychiatry clearly exercises power and is in the process of expanding. In such a situation, its practitioners need to reflect on its ideologies ranging from the best to the worst as found in the general population. Whatever their personal attributes and whatever their initial motivations as a group (for example as a reforming group concerned with the welfare of vulnerable and powerless people), forensic psychiatrists as a body can be hijacked by various forms of thought. In recent years, there has been the rise in what can be described as 'hard' thinking within the profession. The 'hard' man or woman within the psychiatric profession takes pride in being strong on law and order, being highly aware of danger to society posed by 'mental illness', overpredicting dangerousness in assessments, complaining of public interference and scrutiny in their activities, feeling that they are doing such an important job that they should be left unregulated and unaudited, and finally, believing that psychiatrists lack sufficient powers to do their job properly. It is inevitable that people who, as patients, come across these hard men and women (in comparison to those who come across psychiatrists with different attitudes to their professional roles) will receive longer prison sentences, longer periods of stay in hospital, more coercive management, higher levels of physical treatments, etc. In such situations, the expression of legitimate concerns is likely to be stifled and patients are left wondering whether there are any differences between psychiatrists and those people that black people have had to fight against in other walks of life.

Practical issues

Most black people caught up in the forensic psychiatric system in the UK were either born in, or have parents who come from, English speaking West African and Caribbean countries. The plight of black people caught up in the criminal justice systems of these countries is in most respects worse than it is in the UK. Most of these countries have been colonies of the UK and have legal, judicial and administrative systems developed by the British which were adopted with few modifications by the incoming African or Caribbean governments. Most of these countries are frequently cited for repeated abuses of the human and civil rights of their populations and in some countries governments of the day live by intimidating the powerless. Repressive legislation enacted in colonial times has been found useful by such black governments who have added on to it and modified it to make it even more encompassing.

Mental health legislation in many African and Caribbean countries borrows heavily from British Mental health legislation, but the countries have not kept pace with changes in the UK, e.g. the 1959 or 1983 Mental Health Acts. Despite this, it is possible to access psychiatric services on an informal basis particularly for those with the financial resources to buy them: old fashioned legislation is not usually a barrier and sometimes those working in hospitals or private psychiatry are unaware of such mental health legislation. When it comes to those who are in the process of passing through the criminal justice system or have been through parts of it this archaic legislation becomes a serious barrier. It seems there is little understanding of the need to have good services for people designated as mentally ill *and* caught up in the criminal justice system, of barriers put up by existing legislation, of the contribution of mental health factors to behaviour or vulnerabilities of individuals at any stage of the criminal justice system.

Although mental health legislation in the UK is often regarded as 'progressive', the practical situation in the UK gives little cause for complacency. For one thing, there are relatively few black practitioners working within the British forensic psychiatric services – at least very few who carry much power or influence. And, even more importantly, issues of race and culture within the systems generally termed 'forensic', whether within the purview of 'criminal justice' or 'psychiatry', are patently obvious but seldom grasped or even thought about in any depth. The succeeding chapters in this part of the book will examine in some depth aspects of forensic psychiatry that may be crucial to an understanding of what is going wrong in clinical (forensic) practice and where the remedies may lie. The discussion will focus on the UK but refer elsewhere where necessary. In particular, US literature will be cited (although the US forensic scene is often very different to that in the UK) because the themes that emerge from US literature on decision-making, social psychology and epidemiology indicate directions for future research in the UK and offer tentative understanding for some of the observations in the UK. Moreover, US studies and commentaries on issues of race and crime hold lessons for the UK and Europe in general.

Most research in forensic psychiatry is at the building blocks stage with a concentration on descriptive studies of out-patient/in-patient characteristics, prevalence of 'mental disorder' in specific offender groups or in the remand and sentenced prison population. The question of diagnosis looms large in forensic psychiatry and the problems associated with this will be discussed, referring to both US and UK literature. Forensic psychiatry is institutionally and historically a part of general psychiatry. Therefore, the issues in clinical practice in forensic psychiatry are very similar to those in general psychiatry; indeed, one cannot describe practices in forensic psychiatry without reference to general psychiatry. Psychiatrists in the former have a general training but in addition have taken an interest in violence, offenders and management of patients in conditions of security. Their knowledge base is the same as that of generalists and justification for practices is sought within mainstream general psychiatry. The criticism on practice and research in this book thus applies to both general and specialist practice.

Chapter 6

Race and crime

THE BRITISH SCENE

There is little direct information on the ethnic breakdown of the processing of 'mentally disordered offenders' (people designated as 'mentally ill' in the criminal justice system). There is however a large body of general criminological literature from which inference can be drawn on the relationship between black people, the police and the courts. The *British Crime Survey* (Home Office, 1994) offers some ethnic statistics about fear of crime and victimisation. Compared to whites, black people fear crime more, and are more worried about burglary, mugging and racial attacks. Among car owners, black people (compared to white counterparts) are more worried about theft of or from a car. Black households (compared to white ones) are more likely to have reported household offences of vandalism, thefts, burglary and all household offences. And a greater proportion of black people (compared to white) aged sixteen and over, who have been victims of crime, show victimisation for assaults, threats, robbery and theft from person, personal theft and all personal offences.

The *Youth Lifestyle Survey* (Home Office, 1993a) provides information on self-reported crime for youngsters between the age of fourteen and twenty-five. Both black and white young people showed similar rates of offending with the lowest rates recorded among the Bangladeshi youth. Property offences were the most common type among all ethnic groups – two-fifths of black and white compared to one-eighth of Bangladeshis. Violent offences were most common among the black group – one-quarter of black youths in the survey, one-fifth of Pakistanis and whites and one-tenth of Bangladeshis admitted to violent offences. Pakistani and white youths were more likely to have committed acts of vandalism. Of interest too was that young black women were more likely to have committed any offence than had young women from other ethnic groups.

Black people are over-represented in the prison population according to the statistical bulletin of the Judicial Studies Board (Home Office, 1996b). In mid-1995, there were 8,300 males from minority ethnic groups in prison in England and Wales; 17 per cent of male prisoners were from ethnic minority groups, compared with 6 per cent of the male general population. Among prisoners aged fifteen to sixty-four years of age whose ethnic origin were known (and excluding foreign nationals), British minority ethnic groups accounted for 13 per cent of the male prison population although they formed merely 5 per cent of the male general population of the corresponding age groups. Excluding foreign nationals, the rates of imprisonment per 100,000 in 1995 were: 1,048 for blacks, 134 for whites, 104 for south Asians and 280 for Chinese and other Asians. One reason given for the relatively high rate for blacks was that they received longer sentences than others did: 51 per cent of black prisoners over the age of twenty-one as opposed to 35 per cent of their white compatriots, were serving sentences of over four years (excluding life sentences).

In reviewing research on race, crime and processing in the criminal justice system, Smith (1994) finds evidence of bias against black people at various stages in law enforcement, such as the decision to prosecute juveniles and in sentencing by the Crown Court. He believes that, where there is bias, this amount to direct discrimination as defined in the *Guide to the Race Relations Act* (Home Office and Central Office of Information, 1977) and so decisions in the criminal justice system should be covered by this Act. But then Smith goes on to argue that since the magnitude of biases is small, compared with the stark contrast (between black and white people) in the rates of arrest and imprisonment, there is a real difference in the rate of actual offending. However, this conclusion cannot be taken at face value; much more sophisticated and targeted research is required. For example, according to the studies by Hood (1992) the over-representation of black people (when compared to whites) receiving custodial sentences was attributable to their over-representation among people brought before courts, the tendency of black offenders to have pleaded not guilty (and so to have received longer sentences on conviction than white offenders did) and harsher treatment (for which there was no adequate explanation within the parameters of his study).

Most of the bias elicited by research, such as that by Hood, is a result of direct discrimination. Therefore, changes of policy and training (of police officers, judges and magistrates) should not be too difficult to devise and implement. Clearly, the areas to focus on should include ways in which charges are formulated, suspects are dealt with, risk of re-offending and the 'seriousness' with which the alleged crimes are viewed, legal representation is arranged, the decision to prosecute is taken, and decisions about sentencing are arrived at. The Criminal Justice Consultative Council (see Home Office, 1996a) has already made a number of recommendations that should be taken up. They include the ethnic monitoring of police activity at various levels – cautioning, admitting of offences by suspects, informal disposals short of cautioning, decisions about granting of bail, sentencing at magistrates courts, decisions about commitment to Crown Court, etc. In fact, since 1 April 1996, police forces have been required to monitor arrests, cautions, stop and search and homicide. Also, the Consultative Council has recommended that the Crown Prosecution Service (CPS) monitors bail and remand recommendations, the lowering of charges, the allocation of prosecution work to lawyers, discontinuance and the division of discontinuance into evidential and public interests in order to show the role of evidential and public interest decisions. And it has recommended that the Law Society surveys the nature and quality of legal advice given to black defendants. Clearly, assumptions about (what appears to be) high crime rates by black people cannot be taken as given until recommendations such as those referred to above have been implemented.

Forensic psychiatry

In the case of black people coming into the hospital forensic psychiatric system, their numbers are either a reflection of the high numbers of black people in the prison system or there are factors in their offending which made them prone to ending in secure psychiatric settings. These factors might include a relationship between offending and mental distress amounting to 'mental illness' or the offending being particularly 'severe', measured in terms of gravity of offences, frequency of offending or escalation patterns in offending. Other factors might be that their offending histories or the information they give suggest that they show a high risk of re-offending, a particularly high risk of violent re-offending, or that their offending or predicted re-offending is associated with particularly serious risks to the public. The possibility of such associations need to be studied because other explanations for crime, violence or violent offending do not seem to explain the relatively high admission rates of black people into the forensic psychiatry system.

Hospital admission rates for black people in forensic services do not appear to be predicted by social and economic deprivation indices. Ethnicity, particularly the number of black people (African or African-Caribbean descent) in the population seem to have an independent effect on admission rates to forensic services which cannot be easily discerned from assessments of economic disparity. For example, the London Boroughs of Tower Hamlets and Hackney have roughly similar rates of recorded crime but different rates of admission to forensic psychiatry services (the latter being greater than that for the former), although it is the former that is more socially deprived on several indices. This situation may be related to the difference in the ethnic structure of their populations – Hackney has a larger black population of West African or African-Caribbean descent. Endeavours to research explanations for these differences may be productive in elucidating the interplay between 'ethnic' factors, forensic psychiatry and crime.

Black people designated as 'mentally ill' who interact with the criminal justice system before admission to secure psychiatric hospitals are likely to be victims of the same or more bias as their 'mentally well' counterparts. There is a possibility that (compared to their white counterparts) black people may be more 'vulnerable' (through perhaps the effects of 'labelling') and therefore, more likely to be arrested, more likely to be recommended for prosecution, more likely to be convicted, more likely to be perceived as dangerous, more likely to be perceived as people the public needs protection from, particularly if they have a history of past psychiatric contact – as around seventy per cent of them seem to (Cope and Ndegwa, 1990). They are likely to be particularly perceived as dangerous or needing to be locked away if their previous contact with psychiatric services was adversarial because they were non-compliant with prescribed treatments or disagreed with their psychiatrists.

THE CRIMINAL JUSTICE SYSTEM IN THE USA

The USA has one of the biggest prison expansion programmes in the world. It is also one of the few countries with accessible records. A report by Human Rights Watch (1991) estimated that out of every 100,000 persons 426 were currently confined, with 3,109 out of every 100,000 African-American males being confined. The USA imprisons more than 1,000,000 of its citizens at any given time (India with a population that is three times more than that of the USA's has only an estimated quarter of a million prisoners). There are more African-American men between the ages twenty and twenty-nine years under the control of the criminal justice system (in prison, jail or on probation or on parole) than there are in college. Black people are over-represented in prisons among people who are considered difficult, dangerous, those serving long sentences, those on death row and on those people who are victims of the brutality of the system. Human rights reports cite deteriorating conditions, lack of medical care, use of physical restraint, denial of access to family, correspondence, communication with friends and relatives, brutality by other inmates and prison officials. Human Rights Watch report that the most staggering aspect of the human rights situation in US prisons is a trend towards the creation of super-maximum security institutions. Increasing numbers of prisoners are confined to these segregation/punishment units without independent supervision and adequate safeguards for any of their rights.

Racial discrimination within various aspects of the US criminal justice system has been described over the centuries. Hawkins and Thomas (1991), in reviewing the history of race and social control in the USA, describe a white policing syndrome caused by the need to maintain racial dominance during slavery in the seventeenth century and up to the establishment and consolidation of black ghetttoism in nineteenth and twentieth centuries. The movement of slaves and free blacks into towns and villages had to be controlled with elaborate systems being developed to police black people. And the system continued post-slavery. There was a long established pattern of policing by arresting blacks in urban areas for minor misdemeanours such as vagrancy, petty larceny, disorderly conduct, etc. and arrests were used as a method of social control and a means of generating extra income for police officers. Moreover, policing was characterised by intimidation, non-protection and brutality. More recently, the appointment of black mayors, police chiefs and aggressive recruitment of black police officers has helped to improve black–police relationships to some extent. However, black defendants continue to receive harsher treatment from white juries than white defendants do; jurors' perceptions and interpretations of trial testimony are significantly influenced by defendant race (e.g. Gray and Ashmore, 1976; Pfeiffer and Ogloff, 1991; Sunnafrank and Fontes, 1983).

There is a considerable US literature on racial disparity in sentencing decisions: (Hagan and Bumiller, 1983; Kleck, 1981; Spohn *et al.*, 1981–2; Zatz, 1987; Blumstein, 1982; Langan, 1985); most of the literature agrees that black defendants, when compared to white defendants, receive heavier sentences, although some of the studies have been criticised by Klein *et al.* (1990) and Kleck (1981) for not controlling offenders' prior records and victims injuries. However, studies by Petersilia (1983) and Klein (1990) did controls for these factors: the former found that courts imposed heavier sentences on blacks (compared with those imposed on whites) while the latter found that this was not the case. Albonetti (1990), in a study of race and probability of pleading guilty in 464 cases in Virginia between 1977–8, found that the effect of marital status, prior record of felony convictions, type of counsel, number of charges and use of a weapon on the probability of pleading guilty varied in accordance with defendants' race, with black defendants less likely to plead guilty than go to trial. For black defendants, retaining private counsel seems to increase probability of not pleading guilty. This may be related to black perceptions of injustice or the need to have a more rigorous testing of the facts of the case, and opportunity to have independent judicial review of procedures leading to conviction. J. F. Nelson (1994), in a study of minor offences in New York, found that after controlling for differences in arrest charges, prior criminal records, conviction charges, and county of processing, whites were sentenced to pay fines more often than minorities. Beck (1994) summarises US literature showing that when charged with similar crimes, blacks more often than whites are imprisoned before trial, when convicted receive longer sentences, and when incarcerated spend a larger proportion of the sentence in prison. In states where murder is a capital crime, the murder of blacks is punished less often by death than the murder of whites.

Surprising results come from a study of sentencing decisions of black judges and another which examined the views of black prison officers. Spohn (1990) found that black and white judges were similar in that both sentenced black offenders more severely than white offenders. And J. A. Arthur (1994) found black correctional officers supported rehabilitation, retribution and deterrence, and also agreed with the need for harsher and longer sentences and supported capital punishment.

FORENSIC PSYCHIATRY IN THE USA

The USA does not have a well developed health care system for its prison population. There is no forensic psychiatry service equivalent to the systems in Western Europe and no uniform standards for training and caring for prisoners with psychiatric problems across the various prison systems and states. Money still dictates the quality of legal representation and the psychiatric assessment a defendant gets. There are large numbers of prisoners with mental health problems who receive no psychiatric treatment and have no access to care of the quality offered (for example) by the British National Health Service (NHS) (Beck, 1996; Brakel and Cavanaugh, 1996).

UK psychiatrist Gunn (1996) points out that the worst aspect of US psychiatry is its involvement with the death penalty, i.e. its involvement in assessing competency (for prisoners) to be executed or/and treating people to make them competent to be executed. He writes that all other ethical problems pale into insignificance compared with this one; and the USA should not be immune from international professional pressure to change its ways since the current practice there has an adverse effect on forensic psychiatry everywhere.

Black people continue to be disadvantaged at every point of their processing through the US criminal justice system. This ranges from the violence at the investigation and arrest stage, lack of respect for suspects, biased formulation of charges, poor legal representation, the brutality of court disposals which is compounded by the lack of public interest in the rights of offenders and a political consensus which calls for even more brutality. The USA implements the death sentence even when the person concerned is a juvenile, mentally or physically handicapped or 'mentally ill' (Hood, 1990; Amnesty International, 1997). Forensic psychiatry in the European sense cannot function in such an environment. In fact, the US system for dealing with people with mental health problems who come up against the criminal justice system is very different to that in Western European countries. In some ways, it resembles that in some African countries where human rights abuses (in the shape of corporal punishment, forced labour, capital punishment and extra-judicial killings by police) are common.

VIOLENCE IN US BLACK COMMUNITIES

So-called 'black on black violence' is probably one of the biggest public social and health problems in the USA but its causes are poorly understood. A number of theories from correlative studies have been put forward and a number of strategies for intervening with vulnerable groups suggested (see Chapter 4). Adult black males are at the highest risk of becoming homicide victims and homicide is the leading cause of death in the age group fifteen to thirty-five (Centres for Disease Control, 1985). In a study of 15,005 deaths in Jefferson County, Alabama, between 1978 and 1989, Fine *et al.* (1994) found that the average annual homicide rate among blacks was about six times the rate among whites; black males in the twenty-five to thirty-five-year-old age group had the highest rate. During the twelve-year study period, homicide rates declined with the rate of black homicides decreasing at twice the rate of whites, but the rates *increased* in the age groups between ten and forty-four – the greatest increase being in the fifteen to twenty-four-year-old age group accounted for by an increase in the rate among black males. In the case of black male victims, they were most likely to have been killed by other black males (74 per cent) or black females (21.6 per cent).

In the study noted above, interpersonal arguments were the most common underlying reason for homicides in both black and white males. In comparing deaths of black men and women, while such arguments accounted for a significantly greater proportion of deaths among black males, domestic disputes were the most frequent underlying reason for homicide among females. Firearms were implicated in seventy-two per cent of homicides with their use being reported more often in homicides involving black male victims than white male victims. In their discussion of the results, the researchers emphasised the higher rates of black on black male violence, the fact that the victim and the perpetrator knew each other and the importance of argument as an inciting event.

American *Uniform Crime Reports* (Federal Bureau of

Investigation, 1981) define 'justifiable homicide' as the killing of a felon by a police officer in the line of duty or the killing during the commission of a felony of a felon by a private citizen. Alvarez (1992) studied trends and patterns of justifiable homicide between 1976 and 1987, to find that having declined at first, they had started to climb again to a high point in 1980 then declined for the next seven years. Although they detected a considerable under-reporting of the figures, in the 8,354 cases of homicide recorded as 'justifiable homicide', 4,348 (52 per cent) involved the police as perpetrators and 4,006 (48 per cent) ordinary citizens. Forty-five per cent of the police victims and 61 per cent of the others were African-Americans. The calculated rates of police victimisation in the case of white people was 1.2 per 100,000 and citizen victimisation was 0.8 per 100,000, while the corresponding rates for African-Americans were 7 per 100,000 and 8.9 per 100,000. Thus, almost six times as many African-Americans (as compared to whites) are killed by police – 'justifiably'. And 86 per cent of the police officers who use deadly force in this study were white and only 14 per cent were African-American. Fifty-three per cent of the citizens who committed so called justifiable homicide were white, while 45 per cent were African-American. There was a significant lack of African-Americans perpetrating 'justifiable homicide' with white victims; a likely explanation was that white perpetrators (compared to black people) were likely to have been successful in having inter-racial killings ruled 'justifiable'.

Onwuachi-Saunders and Hawkins (1993), using national data, examined death rates due to four types of injuries that contribute most of the black/white mortality gap. The age adjusted death rates from residential fires, drownings and pedestrian mishaps in US black people are higher than for white people: black men being particularly over-represented among injury victims. Black men were at high risk of both intentional (e.g. homicide) deaths and unintentional injuries and the death rates from unintentional injuries were stable and increasing. They proposed prevention efforts targeted at the causes and the consequences of socioeconomic inequality. Greenberg and Schneider (1994), examining violent deaths in three medium-sized New Jersey cities, found high death rates for all ethnic groups among people residing in 'marginal landscapes', i.e. areas that were near abandoned derelict sites and generally least sought after. They concluded that progress cannot be made in preventing urban violence unless some action is taken on the location of housing.

A number of theories have been advanced for explaining the high rates of homicide and violent crime in black populations. They range from the blatantly racist ideas put forward by Rushton (1995) to theories which suggest targeted pragmatic interventions that can be experimentally tested. Rushton uses suspect data sets (such as international crime statistics published by Interpol) and unscientific assumptions about 'race' to develop theories about genetic differences between black and white people. As Cernovsky (1994) points out, Rushton's approach falls within type one error (misleading rejection of the null hypothesis); his theories resemble the pseudo-scientific argument put up doing the Nazi era. Blau and Blau (1982) hypothesised that racial inequality as measured by socioeconomic inequality is related to rates of violent crime committed by blacks and whites in urban areas. The causal process that underlines this hypothesis can be summarised as racial inequality leading to economic inequality, to lower class status, to blocked opportunity, and finally to frustration, aggression and violence.

Harer and Steffensmeir (1992) have criticised the racial inequality hypotheses, pointing to conflicting results in studies using this hypothesis due (according to them) to variations in sampling and in the use of controls. They contend that the measures of group inequality and of violent crime had not adequately corresponded to the concepts supposedly being measured and they argue that race specific measures should be used. These researchers attempt to disaggregate inequality and crime issues by race to provide what they consider would be a rigorous assessment of the evidence on economic inequality and violent crime for standard metropolitan statistical areas (SMSA). In their study on 125 of the largest SMSAs in the USA, using arrest data drawn from 1980 FBI *Uniform Crime Reports,* they found that the effects of inequality differed sharply for blacks and whites. Inequality strongly affected white violence rates (i.e. high inequality was associated with high white arrest rates for violent crimes) but had a weak effect on black violence rates. They concluded that the effects of economic inequality on arrest rates for violent crime varied by race and they argued for a sociological inquiry to shift attention away from inequality and poverty to other structural or community sources of variation in black rates of violence.

In view of the increase in rates of violence and homicide in younger age groups considerable attention has focused on this group. Durant *et al.* (1994) studied 225 adolescents aged eleven to nineteen years old living in or around nine housing projects in an urban area. Self-reported use of violence was associated with exposure to violence and personal victimisation, hopelessness, depression, family conflict, previous corporal punishment, purpose in life, self-assessment of the probability of being alive at age twenty-five. The strongest predictor of use of violence was previous exposure to violence and victimisation. Callahan and Rivara (1992) in a study of eleventh grade students in Seattle found that 6 per cent of males reported having carried a handgun to school; 27 per cent of males and 22 per cent of females reported easy access to handguns; and around 11 per cent of males reported owning a handgun. Among the young gun-owners 78 per cent reported gang membership, involvement in drug sales, a history of school suspension or a history of assaultative behaviour. One-third of the gun-owners reported firing their handgun at somebody.

In reviewing the literature on drug trafficking among African-American adolescents, Stanton and Galbraith (1994) found such activity was associated with increased mortality accounting for one-third to one-half of homicide related deaths in some studies. Also, the practice was associated with other health risk behaviours including non-fatal violence, substance abuse and incarceration. Perceived social pressures by family members and/or peers to engage in drug trafficking and the belief that a wage earning potential is limited to drug trafficking were highly correlated with involvement in this activity. In a study of 600 youths, Whitehead *et al.* (1994) found pursuit of non-mainstream activities such as drug trafficking was perceived as offering an opportunity for economic advancement and for establishing a power base for individuals who had been denied access to mainstream opportunities. Ricardo (1994), looking at perceptions of youth to messages in the environment found that youths who were able to identify alternative activities from which they can derive positive experiences were less likely to become involved in drug trafficking. Black and Ricardo (1994), in their study of 192 youths in a low income community, found that most boys (73 per cent) were not involved in either drug activities or weapon carrying. Boys who were involved in drug activities or weapon carrying were often involved in other high risk activities, e.g. cigarette and alcohol use, school failure and expulsion and had low rates of adaptive communication with their parents.

The boys reported high rates of drug involvement by their families, friends and community. However, psychological and interpersonal factors were better predictors of individual risk activities than community or family variables.

Fitzpatrick and Boldizar (1993) looked at the prevalence and consequences of exposure to violence in a non-random sample of 220 low income African-American youths between the ages of seven and eighteen. Males were more likely than females to be victims of and witness to violent acts. Post-traumatic stress disorder (PTSD) symptom reporting was moderately high for the sample of youths with 27 per cent meeting all the PTSD diagnostic criteria considered. Regression analysis revealed that being victimised and witnessing violence were significantly related to the reporting of PTSD symptoms and that these were more extreme among victimised females and youths who had no primary males living with them in the household, e.g. fathers and/or brothers.

Rates of head injury in the black population are high possibly because of the high rates (in this population) of accidents in the home and at work, and of being assaulted. The implications of this can be seen from some rather sad observations. Lewis *et al.* (1986) found that the fifteen people on death row studied for psychiatric, neurological and psycho-educational characteristics had extensive histories and evidence of head injuries. Black people appear to experience high rates of coma (Bell *et al.*, 1985): in a retrospective survey of 108 research subjects who were asked whether they had experienced states of consciousness defined as 'coma', 45 per cent reported having experienced at least one state of coma, trauma having accounted for thirty-seven of the forty-nine reported episodes, while infection, drug overdose, near drowning, diabetic coma and sickle cell crisis accounted for eleven episodes.

Stark (1990) has reviewed literature on violence, race and gender, focusing on instances where no other crime was involved. She argued that homicide should be conceptualised as a by-product of interpersonal violence, a broad category of social entrapment rooted in the politics of gender inequality and including wife abuse, child abuse and assaults by friends and acquaintances. According to Stark, blacks were no more violent than whites though they were arrested and died more often as a consequence of violence; the majority of homicides were between social partners or involved gender stereotypes; and homicide was often preceded by a series of assaults that were known to service providers and had grown out of intense social engagements or issues of male control and independence.

In an interesting psychoanalytic analysis, Schoenfeld (1988) argues that the crippling and devastating psychological effects of slavery on black Americans has led to black aggression as a result of a weakening of the 'superego'. He considers that these difficulties have persisted among poor uneducated lower class blacks who populated (what he describes as) the 'rotting core' of many US cities. He then argues that, unlike their parents and grandparents, no longer fearing imminent bodily harm or death at the hands of violent whites, these blacks now turn their aggression upon themselves resulting in periodic riots and violent crime. Schoenfeld suggests drastic measures to reinforce the black super-ego arguing that punitive solutions are justified. The underlying themes in Schoenfeld's arguments and solutions may well reflect fears of white people (rather than the needs of black people) and the rationalisation of their need to control and subjugate black people (rather than a wish to help them).

Shakoor and Chalmers (1991), in a study of violence among adolescents, suggest that adolescents who were frustrated by witnessing a large number of crimes tended to act out their frustration by committing violent acts. They concluded that derogatory statements, belligerent gestures, television violence and interpersonal violence aroused and stimulated violent behaviour among adolescents. Stack *et al.* (1983) argued that those who depict an underclass of broken families and hedonistic males forget that these images are consumed by young black people. However romantic to some the myth might be of a subculture of violence, drugs and promiscuity feeding hopelessness and cynicism back to the younger generation, reinforcing the law of the street which he feels hardly originated among black people, a fast buck and cheating people are nevertheless the bottom lines.

Harrison *et al.* (1984) contrasts traditional African societies and modern US society. He argues that members of traditional African societies feel their unity and perceive their common interests in symbols and that their attachment to these symbols gives their societies cohesion and persistence. These symbols are in the form of myths, fictions, dogmas, rituals, sacred places etc. – symbols which are considered superstitious (and so irrelevant) in US society and so black people cannot call on traditional African ways of bonding. He argues that black people in low income communities have little or no sense of unity with the rest of US society and blacks who are upwardly mobile too feel alienated from them. (He described the upwardly mobile black as having lost touch with traditional black cultural patterns or caught between the traditional pattern and white cultural patterns, but low income blacks are being left to flounder.) Black Muslims form the only group that offers a system that bonds people together however poor or even criminal they might be.

Oliver (1989) controversially argued that some specific patterns of black on black violence occurred as a result of lower class black male adherence to norms that emphasised the sexual conquest. This was a result of racially induced structural pressures and dysfunctional cultural adaptations to those pressures. He also adds that high rates of social problems among blacks were a direct result of the imposition of Eurocentric worldview on African-Americans. Afrocentric socialisation would encourage blacks to define self- and group-destructive behaviours, e.g. drug abuse, drug dealing, exploitation of other blacks, violence, etc. as being anti-black and imposed on their African worldview. Karenga (1986) described the problematic conditions that exist among blacks as having emerged from the cultural crisis brought on by enslavement and oppression as well as the acceptance of popular cultural values from the dominant society. Central to the cultural crisis of blacks was their loss of historical memory regarding their African heritage and the adoption of deprecating attitudes towards Africa and blackness. Failure of blacks to develop an Afrocentric cultural ideology and worldview has made them vulnerable to structural pressures that promulgate definitions of blacks as innately inferior to whites, ignorant, lazy, dependent, promiscuous and violent. In addition to the failure to develop an appropriate cultural ideology he identified another dysfunctional cultural adaptation which was the tendency of blacks especially lower class blacks to tolerate the tough guy and the player of women images as acceptable alternatives to traditional definitions of manhood.

CONCLUSIONS

There has been a large amount of research on so-called 'black on black violence' in the USA and sometimes this has led to community violence prevention interventions. However, the state of the criminal justice system (CJS) itself is seriously flawed – so much so that the USA should be encouraged to respect the human and civil rights of people who come into contact with its CJS. Although there may be lessons to be learned for the UK from the US experience, there are many differences between the USA and the UK, the most obvious being that, in the latter (compared to the former), black people are more integrated into the rest of society in housing and patterns of intimate relations and firearms and illicit drugs are less extensively available to the general public.

The UK has recently seen a rapid increase in its prison populations and the need for secure hospital provision within the forensic psychiatry services is likely to parallel this increase. There is an urgent need to tackle some of the issues in the criminal justice system (around sentencing for example) and to understand the connections between race and crime in order to prevent the problems around it spilling over into the forensic psychiatry system – which has enough problems of its own. The number of offences which attract a prison sentence should be drastically reduced. Variability in magistrate court behaviour should be reduced by having trained, easily monitored magistrates, e.g. trained lawyers acting as magistrates. Prison should be reserved for those offenders who are clearly a danger to the public and there is more that can be done to make the environments and regimes in prison humane, liberal and progressive.

Chapter 7

Problems with research

Issues of bias

THE QUESTION OF NUMBERS

A number of studies (Castle *et al.*, 1991; Harrison *et al.*, 1991) suggest that variations in admission rates between urban districts and the rest of the country are accounted for by the large numbers of immigrants and descendants of immigrants in the former, particularly black patients of African-Caribbean origin. While there is a trend towards a decline in the administrative 'incidence' of schizophrenia in non-urban areas, in urban areas rates are stable or increasing. A large number of studies (Hemsi, 1967; Rwegellera, 1977; Hitch and Clegg, 1980; Bebbington *et al.*, 1981; Littlewood and Lipsedge, 1981; McGovern and Cope, 1987b; Harrison *et al.*, 1984; Wessely *et al.*, 1991; Castle *et al.*, 1991) have claimed that the 'incidence' of schizophrenia is high in persons of African-Caribbean origin. On average these studies indicate that people of African-Caribbean origin (compared to the native white population) are three to seventeen times more likely to attract a diagnosis of schizophrenia. They also suggest that hospital diagnosis of schizophrenia accounts for 40 per cent to 52 per cent of all admissions for the Caribbean born in England (compared to 12 per cent to 14 per cent for the British born) and over one-third (33 per cent to 35 per cent of first admissions) compared to one-tenth (7 per cent to 10 per cent for British born) (Sashidharan and Francis, 1991). Most of these studies can be criticised on the basis of being retrospective and their use of 'diagnosis' uncritical even where standardised diagnostic instruments or operationalised criteria are used (Fernando, 1991, 1995).

Kendell *et al.* (1993) review the problems of detecting changes in the 'incidence' of schizophrenia using case registers. When there are differential pathways to care among black and white patients (McGovern and Cope, 1987b; Cope, 1989) and when diagnosis is an issue, problems of using case register information are particularly relevant. Studies in Jamaica (Hickling, 1991; Hickling and Rodgers-Johnson, 1995) show that admission rates for people diagnosed as suffering from schizophrenia in Jamaica are in keeping with corresponding rates reported for the general population in the UK. These studies lend some credence to the argument that reported variations in rates of diagnosing schizophrenia in the UK and in Jamaica might be due to the high rate of misdiagnosis in the former or some other anomaly whereby schizophrenia is over-diagnosed among black people by British psychiatrists. The problem is that none of the so-called epidemiological studies address the crucial question of validity of diagnosis or the possibility of diagnostic bias resulting from the effects of stereotyping etc. on the diagnostic process.

A high 'incidence' of schizophrenia, the disturbed picture of illness and perceived uncooperativeness are often given as reasons for black people being subject to restrictive measures when admitted to hospital, high rates of compulsory admissions and to over-representation in locked ward environments, medium secure units and special hospitals (Bolton, 1984; McGovern and Cope, 1987b; Cope 1989; Noble and Roger, 1989; Harrison *et al.*, 1984; Hitch and Clegg, 1980; Rack, 1982). A number of studies suggest poor outcomes for those diagnosed as suffering from schizophrenia (McGovern and Cope, 1991; Birchwood *et al.*, 1992; McGovern *et al.*, 1994), an increased risk of re-admission, increased periods spent in hospital, poor social status and treatment resistance. McKenzie *et al.* (1995) describe these studies as having had limited power because of small numbers of patients, retrospective study designs and short follow-up periods and the failure to allow for differences in social class and the age of onset of illness. In their longitudinal study, they identified African-Caribbean patients with a better prognosis of psychosis than their white counterparts who were less likely to have a continuous psychotic illness in the early course of their illness and a lower risk of self-harm. While there are no differences in hospital use between these patients, the African-Caribbean group had more involuntary admissions and more imprisonments over a four-year follow up period. They speculate that the better prognosis in African-Caribbean patients may be due to a higher prevalence of the illness with social precipitants. Patients of the African-Caribbean group were less likely to have received psychotherapy and anti-depressant treatment in the follow up period.

Given the unique UK picture (referred to above) and the confidence with which it is described, it is important to examine the methodologies used in arriving at the figures that have been quoted. If the figures (for schizophrenia as an illness) were confirmed, they would be truly important, as epidemiologists would then be close to an understanding of the causes of schizophrenia or some of the variants of schizophrenia. In criticising the methodology a number of approaches can be adopted. They include an examination of the ideology behind the research, the nature of instruments that are used and their relevance to cross-cultural studies, bias in decision-making, the adequacy of demographic information on which the calculation of rates are based, and the context in which the research takes place.

Many of the early studies that claimed an excess of black people diagnosed as 'schizophrenic' were based on hospital admissions. In such studies, there was an assumption that patients diagnosed as suffering from schizophrenia from the African-Caribbean and white groups have equal chances of being admitted to psychiatric hospitals. This was patently not the case and factors affecting admission were often not allowed for in studies that use hospital samples.

More recent studies have used community samples. Sashidharan (1993) discusses the problems that result from calculating a rate of incidence and prevalence when either the numerator or the denominator (or both) used in the calculation is uncertain. The numerator – the number of cases in any given group – depends on case identification and case definition; the denominator depends on estimating the size of the average population from previous census data, electoral rolls, local authority lists, head of household surveys etc. These problems are unlikely to have been overcome by the inclusion of an ethnic item in the 1991 census since different ethnic groups may well have responded differently to the questions asked in the census. Sashidharan also describes problems in assessing at-risk populations in areas with transient and highly mobile populations of urban catchment areas (in which most studies are based). He wonders whether there is an ethnic bias in population shifts in and out of inner cities which would have a differential effect on local hospital utilisation. Whereas most studies take into account the skewed age distribution within the minority groups, there is no similar correction for other demographic factors such as social class, which affect hospital utilisation and illness onset.

Another major problem in studies that compare 'incidence' of a particular 'illness' in one ethnic group with that in another, is that, before assuming that inception rates are indicative of true incidence rates it has to be established that all true cases of schizophrenia from both groups are likely to be represented equally within the sampling frame, i.e. contact with specialist facilities or hospital admissions. Such hospital based rates can only be perceived as administrative morbidity. Variations in professional practice, availability of alternative provision and perception of illness and satisfaction with the services available could all influence hospital utilisation and disease rates based on this. Sashidharan (1993) points out that recognition of psychiatric illness among black people and the subsequent referrals to specialist services involves more multiple agencies such as social workers, the police, the courts than is the case with white patients. Any of these agencies can introduce various biases leading to different probabilities of admission. Problems with case definition would also undermine the magnitude of risk ratios derived on the basis of current studies. Poor reliability of psychiatric diagnoses or variability in diagnostic criteria and the use of secondary data such as case note diagnoses or those based on case registries would bring further bias in case definition. He indicates there is good evidence to suggest that diagnosis of schizophrenia is over-inclusive in the case of black patients.

It could be argued that if British studies were as good as the US epidemiological catchment area (ECA) survey which examined the prevalence of mental disorders in the general population (Robins and Regier, 1991), differences between various groups would be modest. It is likely that with proper community services which avoid some of these pitfalls the peculiar findings in the UK will disappear. After data from the ECA were collected for age, sex, socioeconomic status and marital status no differences between blacks and whites in prevalence of schizophrenia were found. There were no statistically significant differences between blacks and whites in prevalence rates of anti-social personality disorder, affective disorder, drug dependency and panic disorder. Race related differences were found in rates of alcoholism, generalised anxiety disorder and somatisation disorder which were more frequent among blacks than obsessive compulsive disorder which was less frequent. The ECA data showed that racial differences prevalent in the general population were not as wide as differences in the treated population.

US studies

Adebimpe (1994) reviews reasons for ethnic differences in US studies of 'mental illness'. He believes that one reason may be related to racial differences in help seeking behaviour; for example, the ECA study (noted above) found that few blacks meeting diagnostic criteria for depression had sought professional help in the previous six months, especially if the depression was mild. Blacks were more likely to have discussed mental health problems exclusively with friends and relatives and they may have used religious forms of self-help, herbalists, fortune tellers and root doctors more than whites. Another reason identified by Adebimpe was racial differences in commitment status. He cites a study by Lindsey and Paul (1989), which showed that blacks were more frequently involuntarily committed than whites during the data collection periods and in all regions of the country. Reasons given for this are similar to those in the UK. Blacks were under-represented in private facilities and in facilities that admit only voluntary patients. A third reasons for ethnic differences concerned selectivity in obtaining research samples. Very few blacks tend to be used on research reports because of a combination of staff attitudes, patient attitudes and institutional factors (Weiss and Kupfer, 1974). Also, blacks were thought to be poor candidates for research because they resisted research procedures or were perceived as physically dangerous, perhaps sexually threatening to female staff and as creating extra work for staff on the ward and blacks may have feared and distrusted researchers.

A fourth factor suggested by Adebimpe as a possible reason for ethnic differences in research findings was racial differences in psychopathology. These included subtle differences between the two racial groups in the presentation of psychiatric symptoms which often cause clinicians to interpret the symptoms differently (Adebimpe, 1981; Adebimpe *et al.*, 1982a), such as ignorance of black patients' belief systems which may lead to a diagnosis of psychosis instead of a less severe diagnosis (Gray *et al.*, 1985) and difficulties in diagnosing schizophrenia and affective disorder in black patients (Jones and Gray, 1986). An interesting study by Loring and Powell (1988) using vignettes, showed clearly that gender and race influenced diagnosis. Another reason suggested by Adebimpe (1994), quoting an extensive tract, was that racial differences in the accuracy of psychological tests influenced findings. Finally, he referred to the problem of racial differences in treatment, e.g. the excessive use of physical seclusion and restraint, the use of emergency medication, differences in prescription of medication in out-patient settings, particularly the use of long acting anti-psychotic medication, perceptions about black compliance and non-compliance with treatment related to social distance between clinicians and patients. Adebimpe suggested standards for conducting epidemiological surveys to try and overcome the above problems.

World Health Organization studies

Kleinman (1987) views the analysis of data from the WHO Report of the International Pilot Study of Schizophrenia (IPSS) (World Health Organisation, 1973) and the 'Determinant of Outcome Study' (Sartorious *et al.*, 1986). He finds impressive evidence of cross-cultural differences, but notes that the researchers chose to de-emphasise this, highlighting evidence of broad similarities. In the data of annual incidence of schizophrenia there are differences in the incidence rates of the broad diagnostic definition of schizophrenia which include virtually all cases sampled compared to the more restrictive definition based on the Catego computer programme S+ class. In the centres studied, Kleinman points out that the broad sample from an anthropological viewpoint is the more interesting and valid one, the restricted sample being a constructed sample which places a template on the heterogeneous population. The restrictive sample he argues leaves out precisely those cases which show the greatest cross-centre and cross-cultural differences and therefore the ones that disclose that the pattern incidence is not uniform. In the description of differing causes and outcomes across different centres there is a report of better outcomes in developing countries: a difference that holds even when the mode of onset is controlled. However, he feels there is no detailed investigation of this. In his view, this was arguably the single most important finding of this study which received very scant attention compared to that devoted to the findings of cross-cultural similarities. In the same light, findings of cultural differences in mode of onset and symptomatology and help seeking behaviour are de-emphasised. He feels that this is a case of interpretative bias in cross-cultural psychiatric research which is a reflection of the dominant interpretative paradigm in cross-cultural psychiatry. Kleinman criticises the fact that most cross-cultural psychiatric research exaggerates the biological dimensions of disease and de-emphasises the cultural dimensions of illness.

INSTRUMENTS AND INTERPRETATION

An area which has received little study is that of psychometric properties of instruments used in cross-cultural studies and whether there are better methods of doing such studies. Marsella and Kameoka (1989) stress that in making valid and reliable assessments of psychopathology across cultures there are four cultural considerations that must be recognised and attended to by any clinician or researcher engaged in psychiatric research. All these considerations centre around the concept of equivalence. They describe four types of equivalence, i.e. linguistic, conceptual, scale and norm-equivalence. Unless the assessment instruments applied to a particular subject of a study are 'equivalent' for his/her ethnocultural background and experience it is doubtful that conclusions will be valid and reliable. 'Linguistic equivalence' refers to the extent to which the content and grammar have a similar connotative and denotative meaning across cultures. Conceptual equivalence refers to similarities in the meaning of the concepts used in assessment. Scale equivalence must be considered even after linguistic and conceptual equivalence have been obtained and it requires that the scales used are culturally relevant and applicable. Norm-equivalence ensures that normative standards developed for one cultural group are not applied indiscriminately to another culture. They emphasise that statistical solutions do not address the fundamental problem regarding data gathering methods themselves and what is questionable is the common practice of transporting assessment tools across ethnocultural groups ignoring indigenous meanings and perspectives of psychopathology that are inextricably embedded in a sociocultural system that differs from the system from which the assessment was originally developed.

Marsella and Kameoka believe that a study of subjective experiences of subjects constitute a necessary first step in the development of culturally appropriate assessment tools. They suggest ways in which emically derived assessment instruments could be used in cross-cultural comparisons. Hui and Triandis (1985) believe that clear demarcation of equivalents is not easy and that there were no methods available (at the time they wrote) for testing and demonstrating the four kinds of equivalence at the same time. These authors emphasise the importance of researchers admitting the limitations of their methods of validating a particular form of equivalence and the need to avoid making inferences or decisions regarding other types of equivalence.

Poortings and Van de Vijner (1987) make suggestions on bias analysis and Irwin *et al.* (1977) describe ways of establishing cross-cultural validity of instruments used in research, borrowing on three types of approaches to cross-cultural research identified by Berry (1969). These are, 'imposed etic', 'emic' and 'derived etic'. Imposed etic investigations impose imported constructs in attempting to describe behaviour in the host culture. Imposed etic constructs or the emic approach is appropriate where an investigator wishes to understand the structural behaviour from the point of view of the host culture. The researcher's task in such an investigation involves not only transcending empirical observations, but also one's conceptual networks, i.e. the researcher moves like a child through the conceptual realm of the host culture always doubting his/her own conceptions and heavily dependent upon the guidance of local informants. Derived etic validity is a derivative procedure that cannot be undertaken until imposed etic and emic validity have been established. One method of identifying derived etics consists of identifying those aspects of measured constructs that have proven to possess both imposed etic and emic validity, i.e. the conceptual units represent an empirical convergence of home and host culture ways of organising the world.

Zarin and Earls (1993) believe that uncertainty in psychiatric diagnoses is inevitable because of the overlapping characteristics of test results between populations with and without 'psychiatric disorder' and the lack of a single correct method of identifying cases and non-cases (i.e. 'case definition'). They recommend the use of principles of decision analysis in research and express concern that the results of structured interviews are being accepted as valid without explicit consideration of the consequences of choosing specific case definition strategies based on these instruments. In many research reports, the choice of an external validity is either not mentioned or poorly justified and the separator that is frequently used is a 'standard' instrument whose published validity and reliability may not be related to the task at hand. Further, where several instruments are used, the methods used for combining them is either not explained or if explained not justified. Also, the choice of categories is almost always based on the distribution of scores in a mixed population of 'disordered' and 'non-disordered' subjects and since the prevalence of 'disorder' in the study population and the separate distribution in the disordered and the non-disordered groups are not reported, the rates of false positives and negatives cannot be determined. Zarin and Earls make a number of recommendations for improving the quality of cross-cultural research including the need for explicit recording of each step of the case definition process and for the reporting of data in an uncategorised fashion so that information is not lost. They believe that data should be reported in such a way as to allow other researchers to analyse the research data (possibly using different case definition strategies or certain cut-offs) so that studies can be compared.

British studies tend to use versions of the Present State Examination (PSE) (Wing *et al.*, 1974) and its associated tools, as well as the more recently developed Schedule for Clinical Assessment in Neuropsychiatry (SCAN) (Wing, 1996), for classifying symptoms. Wing, the main author of these instruments, has noted that an unexpected problem appreciated after long use was a tendency to regard the computerised output from the ninth version of PSE (PSE9) only in terms of a single diagnosis, rather than a rich and varied psychometric profile, although the author of the PSE did intend that it should be used in this way. He adds that a central principle of the PSE and SCAN was that the system could not make a diagnosis in the straightforward clinical sense and that people who use these instruments were responsible for interpreting the results according to their judgement on the adequacy of the interview, the quality of the data recorded, and the choice of outputs from the computer analysis. He points out that the PSE was not originally designed as a diagnostic instrument but in the course of its development as a comprehensive clinical tool it came to provide a database capable of expanding to exploit the more exacting algorithms presented in the *Diagnostic and Statistical Manual III of Mental Disorders* (DSM III-R) (American Psychiatric Association, 1987).

INFORMATION PROCESSING BIAS

The justification for management of patients in secure environments depends on the assessment of behaviours or patient attributes and characteristics which are open to various forms of bias. The behavioural associations of mental illness, which lead to a person being described as disturbed, are particularly open to bias. Bias operates at different points in the criminal justice system where decisions have to be made and it affects/shapes the raw material used by the forensic psychiatrist. If a person is apprehended by the police and charged, his/her outcome is affected by decisions about bail, remand in custody, referral to a psychiatrist, especially a forensic psychiatrist, etc. If a person is admitted to hospital without the involvement of the police or a court, his/her outcome is affected by decisions about 'treatment', dosages of medication (including emergency medication), control and restraint within hospital, seclusion, restrictiveness of ward environment and discharge. Bias can occur at each and every stage but is most likely to occur during the decision-making process which involves judgements about 'risk' and dangerousness. As noted elsewhere, professional judgements in these areas are seriously flawed and often merely reflect perceptions generally held by the public.

There is little research on biases in the UK and most research in this field has been carried out in the USA particularly by social psychologists. In English literature there is mention made of stereotypes entering into decision-making, but not much exploration of how this happens. US research has demonstrated that heuristic judgement strategies are more likely to be used by decision-makers when the task confronting them is relatively complex (Nisbett and Ross, 1980). Decision-makers may use judgement relevant ethnic stereotypes as a heuristic in making judgements when these stereotypes are available. The use of stereotypes may be a routine phenomenon by normal individuals when faced with complex situations. Stereotypes arise from information processing biases. The stereotypes are used as a way of simplifying judgements. Stereotypes enter into social perceptions of others probably as a result of encoding bias and an attribution bias in information processing mechanisms (Miller and Turnbull, 1986). In the case of an encoding bias, hypotheses, and activation of stereotypic concepts leads to selective attention towards stereotyped consistent information, which can easily be organised around a central stereotypic theme. Inconsistent information is likely to be overlooked or poorly integrated into the mental representation being formed. The content of the mental representation will be biased towards category consistent information. When this representation is later used to make judgements they should reflect this bias. In a judgement task inconsistent information receives relatively little processing and is uninfluential in the judgement process for this reason. In the case of attribution bias hypotheses, the activation of a stereotype results in additional attributional processing of information in an effort to discount it or reinterpret it in a way that reconciles with initial stereotypic expectancies. In a judgement task stereotype inconsistent information is discounted or construed in a manner more consistent with initial expectations.

Nisbett and Ross (1980) and Chidester (1986) write that cognitive and interpersonal processes that serve to aid formation or maintenance of stereotypes include illusory correlation (the persistence of associations in the face of validation studies which show these presumed associations to have no empirical bases), paired distinctiveness (a heuristic inferred from the resemblance of a person to a characteristic thought to be common to his originating group), perseverance of theory (where subjects find studies supporting their own position to be significantly more convincing and better conducted than ones that oppose their views) and a preference for confirming rather than disconfirming information.

Chidester (1986) describes three perspectives or lines of research that have focused on interpersonal processes. These perspectives include hypotheses testing, compensation strategies and repressed affect models of interracial interaction. In the case of a hypotheses testing perspective in an interaction, the perceivers' questions and behaviours would be directed towards eliciting evidence confirming the stereotype. Targets seem to confirm perceivers' expectancies in their behaviour. In relation to compensation strategy, Ickes *et al.* (1982) described an experiment where perceivers who believed they would interact with an unfriendly target initiated more conversation, sat closer to target and verbalised more than the perceivers in the control group. Perceivers of unfriendly targets adopt a compensation strategy whereas perceivers of friendly targets adopted a reciprocity strategy. The most interesting aspect of this study lay in the self-reports of perceivers. Perceivers of 'unfriendly targets' rated them as less friendly and reported that they liked them less than they did perceivers of 'friendly' targets. Perceivers act in a positive manner, but leave the interaction with negative expectancies intact. The targets themselves perceive nothing but positive treatment from their perceiver and leave the interaction unchallenged even when the expectancy is incompatible with the targets' self-concept.

In the case of a repressed affect model (Weitz, 1972), the situation is similar to that in which a perceiver adopts a compensation strategy: the distinction offered lies in the communication of mixed message. This is due to the negative affect associated with racial stereotypes where white perceivers of black targets are unable to communicate only positive feelings or evaluations to black targets. Negative evaluations leak out through the non-verbal or paraverbal channels and the compensation strategy fails. These lines had not been fully tested at the time because of differing paradigms associated with supporting research.

In the UK, research on perceptions has been important in understanding the processing of black school children into special education for those with alleged behavioural problems. Tomlinson (1981) described over-representation of black students in schools catering for children with learning and behavioural disorders. She surveyed the perceptions of head teachers making referrals to ESN schools and found that black children were perceived as having 'natural functional handicaps and behavioural problems'. Tomlinson's other work on black school under-achievement showed low expectations of black students held by teachers and described this as the most important contributory factor to under-achievement. This has only been recently recognised by both major political parties who in their way have promised to provide better education particularly in inner city areas. Discrimination against black children persists as evidenced by recent research on exclusions. Black people are excluded up to six times more frequently than their white counterparts for the same behaviour and this process is fundamentally unfair. Rates are increasing and younger children, e.g. age four, are being excluded (see Parsons, 1996; OFSTED, 1996). The decisions to exclude are made on probably the most vulnerable people in society, children, in a biased way by teachers in local education authorities. Such teachers and education authorities have projected/presented themselves as caring, liberal and broadminded, despite their behaviour. Exclusions are introducing large numbers of black children into a future of hopelessness, unemployment, illiteracy and increased contact with the criminal justice system. This is particularly sinister but seems to have attracted little public attention.

CONCLUSIONS

There are many and varied problems with research in the cross-cultural field, especially where issues of race have to be addressed. There is need for community based studies comparing rates of psychiatric morbidity in different ethnic groups but it is very important that (a) both major and minor psychiatric morbidity are studied and (b) the intruments used have been validated for use in the ethnic groups concerned (so that they are sensitive to the cultural characteristics of the groups) and free of bias. This will entail major studies of psychometric properties of such instruments in cross-cultural studies using acceptable and rigorous methodologies (acceptable in the field of psychometrics, social psychology and anthropology). Further, the effects of racist perceptions on judgements made during research need to be minimised. More generally, experimenter effects in design and execution of studies should be recognised and where possible persons uncontaminated by current clinical or professional bias and mythology should be used to gather data. The decision-making rules need to be explicit and open to testing. The limitations of methodologies need to be openly acknowledged. And the key role of experimenter effects and bias in interpretation of material should be recognised and attempts to remove bias should be a routine part of research activity.

Closer attention needs to be paid to the eliciting, recording and interpretation of clinical research data. The methods of minimising bias in police interviewing could be usefully copied in the field of psychiatric research and indeed clinical practice. Subsequent to the 1984 Police Criminal and Evidence Bill and the exposure of several miscarriages of justice in the UK, audio taping of police interviews (with suspects of crime), in addition to detailed recording of what takes place before, during and after the interview, was introduced. In fact, many British police stations have gone further and installed video taping facilities for recording interviews at police stations. Finally, in the case of any psychiatric research carried out where issues of race and cultural difference are pertinent, the original or transcribed material should be made available in such a form that other researchers can use it for alternative analysis.

Chapter 8

What is the right diagnosis?

The high rates of schizophrenia diagnosed among black people attending psychiatric settings in the UK is now well known. The situation appears to be similar in general practitioner settings too. Lloyd (1992, 1993) reviews some findings on ethnic differences in the UK in general practitioner (GP) consultation rates and diagnoses given by GPs: men of African-Caribbean origin consult GPs more often than their white counterparts, but African-Caribbean and Asian women do not appear to do so (compared to white women). In terms of ethnic difference in diagnoses given by GPs, white women of British origin are more likely to be diagnosed as having a non-psychotic mental illness by a GP and Asian and African-Caribbean women are least likely to be diagnosed as such.

In a recent review of UK literature on mental health and ethnicity, the authors (Cochrane and Sashidharan, 1996) expressed surprise that, given the association between ethnicity and indices of social deprivation known to be associated with increased risk of mental health problems such as depression and anxiety, black people are under-represented in mental hospitals once admissions with a diagnosis of schizophrenia and other psychoses (which are not thought to be associated with adverse social conditions) are set aside. They offer three possible explanations for this phenomenon: (a) black people (compared to whites) are actually less likely to suffer from non-psychotic conditions; (b) black and white people suffer from non-psychotic disorders at similar rates, but the former receive some sort of 'alternative' care; and (c) black and white people suffer these disorders at similar rates but do not gain access to care because they find existing services aversive and/or they are blocked off from receiving services.

US studies show that black people (when compared to whites) in in-patient settings are over-diagnosed as suffering from schizophrenia, but this difference is not evident in general population studies. For example, the ECA catchment area survey (Robins and Regier, 1991) found no statistically significant differences between blacks and whites in prevalence rates of anti-social personality disorder, affective disorder, and drug dependence. Race-related differences were found in rates of alcoholism, generalised anxiety disorder and somatisation disorder, which were more frequent among blacks, and in obsessive compulsive disorder which was less frequent. Others studies have reported the under-diagnoses of depression in black people (Mukherjee *et al.*, 1983; Simon *et al.*, 1973; Lawson *et al.*, 1994; Jones and Gray, 1986; Helzer, 1975; Keisling, 1981).

DEPRESSION OR SCHIZOPHRENIA?

Simon *et al.* (1973) demonstrated that routine hospital diagnosis yielded a higher rate of schizophrenia and a lower rate of depression among black patients, but these differences vanished when a structured mental state examination was used. Adebimpe (1994) has pointed out that in prospective studies the observers' preconceived ideas of the rates of illness in the two racial groups in a study may contaminate their recognition of symptom patterns and the process of making a diagnosis. It can be argued that the training that precedes the application of structured interviews and diagnostic rating instruments builds in a bias in researchers, particularly those with a clinical background. In an environment or arena where professional folklore emphasises an 'epidemic' of schizophrenia in black people the thrust of the training and subsequent research projects constitute an exercise in describing this 'epidemic'.

Adebimpe (1984) has suggested that the retrospective study of data obtained without any research intention (i.e. data obtained for clinical purposes) might be less vulnerable to errors arising from 'misdiagnosis'. Earlier, Adebimpe (1981) suggested that factors – such as problems arising from patient–therapist distance, the influence of stereotypes of pathology, and the misinterpretation of symptoms – that may increase the possibility of misdiagnosis in blacks, may have less influence when the population dealt with is predominantly black than is the case when the population is mainly white. He reviewed the records of 5,493 patients, 71 per cent of whom were black and 23 per cent white, in an area where patients were socioeconomically homogeneous to find few white/black differences in diagnoses. In fact, any difference was towards schizophrenia being diagnosed more frequently among whites compared to blacks in this patient population.

Mukherjee *et al.* (1983) reviewed the records of seventy-six bipolar patients in an out-patient department of an inner city hospital. There were no ethnic differences in mean number of total hospitalisations, nor in hospitalisations during lithium maintenance, but white patients had been on lithium maintenance for longer than either black or Hispanic patients. Sixty-eight per cent of all patients had a previous misdiagnosis of schizophrenia with most patients having received multiple schizophrenia subtype diagnoses during the course of their illness. Ethnicity showed a significant association with misdiagnosis – blacks and Hispanics having been misdiagnosed more often than whites. Blacks were significantly more often misdiagnosed as paranoid schizophrenic than were either whites or Hispanics. There were no significant differences among the ethnic groups on symptoms of anger, irritability, violent or destructive behaviour, bizarre behaviour, ideas of reference, persecutory delusions or bizarre delusions (delusions of control, thought insertion, thought broadcasting). But significantly, more blacks and Hispanics had experienced delusions of any type, grandiose delusions and auditory hallucinations. Such hallucinations correlated strongly with misdiagnosis.

Skilbeck *et al.* (1994) examined ethnic differences among black, Hispanic and white applicants for out-patient psychotherapy using symptoms self-reported on Symptom Checklist 90 Revised (SCL90R). The relationship between self-reported severity of symptoms and therapist-reported severity of psychiatric diagnosis also was examined in order to assess the utility of SCL90R as a predictor of diagnostic severity for these ethnic groups. Significant ethnic difference was found on several symptom dimensions, with black patients less likely to report symptoms than Hispanic or white patients. While overall, the severity rating (of symptoms) assessed by therapists was similar to self-reported assessments, this positive relationship was strongest for white patients. And black patients generally received diagnoses that were more severe than their self-reported symptoms alone would have predicted. Black patients who were diagnosed as psychotic (i.e. in the severe category) reported symptoms that were in the same general range as white and Hispanic patients who were diagnosed in the lowest severity category (i.e. that of neurosis and situational disturbances). The researchers commented that their findings raised the possibility of psychiatric diagnosis having been made on the basis of cues and information that differ from one ethnic group to another and that these differences raise questions for future research on the proper interpretation of self-report measures and psychiatric diagnoses with minority and low income patients.

Adebimpe *et al.* (1982b), using a structured interview to review 273 patients with a diagnosis of schizophrenia, showed that some clinical symptoms appeared more severely among black than among white schizophrenic patients. Black patients tended to be more angry, impulsive, hallucinatory, dysphoric and asocial than their white counterparts. The issue of black/white differences in symptomatology has been studied by others (e.g. Fabrega *et al.*, 1988) who, using structured interview evaluations, found prominent black/white differences in psychopathology. However, their interpretation of results does not do justice to their work. For example, they showed that aggression was noted in blacks with diagnosis of schizophrenia, depression and anxiety. They saw that social aggression was a significant clinical component of disorders otherwise characterised as involving negative or unpleasant effects, i.e. anxiety and depression. They thought this peculiar to black people and speculated that it might be related to under-diagnoses of substances abuse and alcohol abuse disorders, social conflict and maladaptations.

DEPRESSION IN BLACK PEOPLE

There is a growing body of US literature on affective illnesses in blacks, particularly depression. Tonks *et al.* (1970) reported high rates of manic depressive illness among black and low income groups and among white and high income groups. Warheit *et al.* (1973) found high rates of depression among women, blacks, young persons, and those in lower socioeconomic groups. And Jones *et al.* (1981) showed that blacks who belong to lower socioeconomic status suffer from manic depressive illness at a rate of four times higher than the national admission rate. A study of a general population sample show that black men who are young, poor and unemployed and who live in large household units and have considerable conflicts with women, had the highest depression scores (Gray and Berry, 1985). This study also found that demographic variables and variables involving stressful life events were better predictors of the presence of depressive symptoms among black men than were social cultural variables. Jones-Webb and Snowden (1993), using a large national probabilistic sample, showed that both white and black females were at greater risk of depression than males; respondents who were formerly married or separated were at greater risk than those who were currently married. There were differences in the patterns of risk between the races, with blacks of thirty to thirty-nine years of age, belonging to non-Western religious groups and living in the west of the USA being at greater risk than comparable whites. Blacks who were widowed, members of the middle and lower middle class and unemployed were at less risk. Zung *et al.* (1988), using approximate equal numbers of black and white out-patients from primary care settings completing a self-rating depression scale, found that there were no significant differences between the races in prevalence of depressive symptoms or distribution of symptom severity levels. Amato (1991), using a national probability data set to study long-term consequences of parental absence during childhood for adult depression showed that whites and African-American males and females separated from a parent scored higher on measures of depression than those raised in continuously intact families but Hispanic males and females showed no such differences.

A finding which is frequently replicated when looking at non-hospital samples is the failure of blacks, particularly those with minor depression, to have consulted traditional health services. Sussman *et al.* (1987) examined data from a survey of about 3,000 households in St Louis. Significantly fewer blacks meeting psychiatric criteria for diagnosis of depression had sought professional care (meaning medical care). Blacks with major depressive episodes were significantly less likely than whites to have spoken to any professional (including social service workers, clergy and alternative healers) about mental health or emotional problems in the six months prior to interview. This was the case despite the fact that black people had contact with health care professionals during this time almost as frequently as white people. Approximately three-quarters of white people had spoken to someone about emotional problems and about half of the depressed blacks had not spoken to any one about their symptoms. Severity of the problem was significantly related to treatment seeking among black people. It was among those with the least severe problems that the greatest differences were found. Whites did not significantly exceed blacks in seeking care when depressive episodes were long lasting, scarce or frequent. Blacks were more likely to report that fear of treatment and of being hospitalised had prevented them from seeking care.

Jenkins-Hall and Sacco (1991) examined the effect of client race and depression level on global and interpersonal interlocutions by white therapists. Therapists held more negative evaluations of depressed versus non-depressed clients and the combination of black and depression led to the most negative evaluations. Pryor Brown *et al.* (1989), in a study of adolescent medical patients, found a stronger than expected relationship between stress and several types of psychiatric disorders, such as depression, in black adolescent females (compared to their white counterparts). Brown *et al.* (1995) found a one-year prevalence of 3.1 per cent for major depression in a non-institutionalised African-American population. Age, residential mobility, health status and stressful life events were significantly associated with major depression, but none of the possible pathogenic factors in their sociocultural and family backgrounds were implicated. The strongest predictors for major depression in their sample were poor or impaired health and being twenty and twenty-nine years of age. In that study, only 11 per cent of the black people who were depressed actually consulted a mental health professional and 7.4 per cent saw no-one at all for help. The researchers concluded that few African-Americans with major depression actually received clinical treatment for their illness and that being young and/or poor were the major risk factors involved.

CONCLUSIONS

Much of the research in the USA points to serious doubts about diagnoses given to black people both in clinical settings and in research studies. The British scene may well be similar. US findings (quoted earlier) raise the possibility that some of the black people diagnosed as schizophrenic are better designated 'affective psychosis' – on both sides of the Atlantic. It seems highly likely that a considerable number of black people diagnosed as suffering from schizophrenia are more appropriately diagnosed as depression or perhaps as atypical psychotic illnesses. Preoccupation with the political correctness of the labels – that is, being careful about 'correctness' in maintaining the accepted system of diagnosis – has delayed progress in correcting a situation that is harmful and unjust. To avoid new sensitivities to the politics of labels, perhaps a neutral label which emphasises the need for further research (e.g. designating the unknown as 'psychosis X'), should be used.

The conspicuous failure of many black patients to attract diagnoses other than schizophrenia raises the question of whether psychiatric practitioners in the business of diagnostic decision-making are able to describe normal and abnormal feelings or emotions in black people or the range of other behaviours and attributes that define personality. If black people respond to environmental stress by developing a 'condition' that is misdiagnosed or misunderstood (in a psychiatric setting), the conclusion to be drawn is that psychiatrists are unable to detect or describe normal/abnormal mood states in black people – for whatever reason. This raises questions about the appropriateness or relevance of psychiatry to the life of black people in the UK.

Questions about diagnosis may well be best understood in a context where white institutions (such as psychiatry) tend to deny the humanity of black people – humanity in terms of their ability to feel mental pain and intense emotions (such as depression). Such a denial was indeed a key justification for the Atlantic slave trade and colonialism (see Chapter 1) and may explain the continuing strength of stereotypes about black people that have such a strong effect on many aspects of their lives, including their experience of psychiatry. If psychiatry is to overcome the major problems that it faces in its dealings with black people (through diagnoses), it needs to face up to its racist tradition (see Chapter 2) and the limitations of its diagnostic system (see Chapters 3 and 4). In some way psychiatrists have to re-organise their thinking and ways of working in order to understand and empathise with black people in ways not usually associated with traditional European black/white relationships.

In addition to understanding themselves and their discipline, psychiatrists must also appreciate that black people are not oblivious to their history and inheritance, and the experiences of their forebears shape the way they relate to white people today. Given a number of factors which include the history of black/white relationships, biased perceptions about normality and illness among blacks, and bias at most levels of contact between white therapists and black people in the psychiatric system, it is not surprising that black people do not readily discuss their feelings with white people. Moreover, black people may also have different explanatory models and constructions of their difficulties of problems and the most appropriate way of resolving them – explanatory models that are not given serious consideration by UK psychiatrists and are not even referred to within the training of psychiatrists.

Black experience shapes the politics and dynamics in their relationship with white people. They may have come to expect that others are incapable of understanding their feelings or would be destabilised by information on their suffering and experience. They may be wary of offering information or developing relationships in which they are vulnerable and open to exploitation. A discussion on feelings and/or a frank exchange of views would thus be a charged interaction. The language, behaviour and symbolism of such an interaction can be easily misunderstood, particularly by observers with a closed mind. It is impossible for black people in an environment where they are a minority not to be conscious of the fact of their blackness which they are reminded of in all sorts of ways. The frustration, anger, feelings of powerlessness and depression felt – and suffered – by black people need to be acknowledged.

It is clear that the preoccupation with diagnosing schizophrenia blinds researchers and clinicians to the possibility of other ways of understanding the mental health problems of black people. This may be a particular problem for the UK, the USA and some European countries. The Scandinavians and the French, using different classification systems, may be better placed in this respect. The Scandinavians have the concept of psychogenic or reactive psychosis which can have paranoid, depressive or confusional symptoms or sometimes a mixture of all three (Stromgren, 1974). The French classification system, based on the combination of psychopathology and philosophy (Pichot, 1984) has the category *bouffée d'élirants* (the sudden onset of a delusional state with trance-like feelings of short duration and good prognosis), which is seen as a condition that may develop into schizophrenia but is clearly separated from it. In fact, Littlewood and Lipsedge (1981), in their prospective phenomenological study of psychosis in Hackney, referred to patients presenting with a 'religious flavour' to their illness as suffering from such 'acute psychoses'.

There is considerable integration of black and white people in the UK, particularly among the working classes and some sections of the middle classes (Office of National Statistics, 1996). In a way, black people have problems with institutions and those who work in institutions (including those within forensic psychiatry), rather than with white people as such. When power is not an issue, normal human relationships seem to develop easily and naturally. But power is a major issue in the forensic field, and it seems that when white people – and perhaps some black people too – don uniforms or wear badges indicating their authority, and work within the constraints of institutional policies and practices, they soon run into problems with black people caught up in the system. Generally, black people are aware of this and attempt to balance opposing forces in order to survive – many do, but some go under. If psychiatry is to be a discipline that helps black people in trouble, then it needs to establish a credibility that is independent of the institutional forces that oppress black people. Perhaps a useful starting-point would be for psychiatrists, and indeed other mental health workers, to take on some of the basic qualities of a good counselling relationship – empathy, positive regard, sympathy, a non-judgmental approach, patience, open-mindedness, and the ability to listen.

Chapter 9

Clinical practice

Research into issues around psychiatric practice has concentrated on treatments deemed desirable and those felt to be physical or coercive. There is British literature on describing, but not on explaining, modes of entry into hospital and use of medication. US literature covers these areas including issues of psychotherapy, physical or mechanical restraint and seclusion. The latter three areas are not properly described or researched in the UK.

ENTRY INTO INSTITUTIONS

It is well established now (see Preface and Chapter 7) that black people are over-represented in institutions where the mode of entry is compulsion. A likely explanation for this phenomenon is that, in any scenario involving evaluations of negative features/characteristics/attitudes by white judges of black people, blacks would be judged as having these negative attitudes/characteristics/features more frequently and in a more severe form. These negative features would include anything which has featured in European thinking – mythology – about black people during the past five-hundred years. They are features which suggest conflict, disorganisation, threat, malfunction, disruption of social order or de-stabilisation (e.g. violence, aggression, laziness, untrustworthiness, high sex drive, low intelligence, etc.). In institutions catering for people who show these negative conditions, the group which is deemed to show these features to a severe degree would receive the most powerful treatments or interventions available. In the case of psychiatry this would be any treatment which is physical or coercive. In institutions set up for punishment (e.g. prisons), black subjects will be among those receiving the most severe penalties and disciplinary measures.

This behaviour owes little to the real presence of the assessed quality or feature, but more to prejudice. But prejudice need not be based on skin colour alone. Similar phenomena are seen in relation to oppressed groups such as the Romany people in eastern Europe, the Maoris of New Zealand and the Aborigines of Australia.

British studies of in-patient populations have reported hospital staff perceiving black people (compared to whites) as generally showing a more disturbed clinical picture of psychiatric illness (Hitch and Clegg, 1980; Harrison *et al.*, 1984), sometimes accompanied by uncooperativeness (Bolton, 1984; Noble and Roger, 1989). Noble and Roger (1989) also report that black in-patients were involved in more violent incidents than non-black in-patients in a London based retrospective study. Many researchers (Harrison *et al.*, 1984; Ineichen *et al.*, 1984; McGovern and Cope, 1987b; Owens *et al.*, 1991) report higher rates of compulsory hospital admission for black people (compared to whites). Others (Rogers and Faulkner, 1987; Dunn and Fahy, 1990; Pipe *et al.*, 1991) have shown a strong trend for Africans and African-Caribbeans to be over-represented among those apprehended by the police under Section 136 of the Mental Health Act (Her Majesty's Stationery Office, 1983). Pipe *et al.* (1991) in their study in south London found that this over-representation was accounted for by men under the age of thirty who (when compared to their white counterparts) were more likely to have been perceived as threatening, incoherent and disturbed, less clearly diagnosed with a mental illness and more likely to have been living in stable accommodation. Most instances of black people assessed for formal (compulsory) admission invariably get admitted to hospital compulsorily. Dunn and Fahy (1990) found that black men (compared to white men) were more likely to be put on compulsory orders and to be kept in hospital longer and Harrison *et al.* (1984) found that blacks admitted compulsorily tend to be less socially disabled than their white counterparts.

A large number of patients admitted to secure units are admitted through the criminal justice system (CJS) under Part III of the Mental Health Act (Her Majesty's Stationery Office, 1983). In other words, they are people who are or were about to be involved in some criminal proceedings at the time of admission to hospital. Further, a person admitted to a secure unit is someone judged as showing violent or dangerous propensities or posing a grave and immediate danger. So, if over-representation (of black people in secure provision) is to be justified, these 'qualities' should be demonstrable as more common in black patients compared to white patients. It also needs to be shown that black people are either more criminal, violent, aggressive or uncooperative with treatment than their white counterparts so they pass through any filter mechanisms at lower levels of security in large numbers. If black patients are over-represented among patients referred to forensic services from general psychiatric hospitals (on the basis of being more difficult to manage) it is necessary to show that qualities pertaining to being 'difficult to manage' are more frequently seen in black people when compared to whites when they are being cared for as 'patients'.

Most research into violence in in-patient populations is retrospective and there are few studies using objective criteria for assessing violence, dangerousness or imminence of risk to others. Morley *et al.* (1991) looked at the attitudes and experiences of relatives of fifteen patients admitted compulsorily and ten admitted informally. All the patients were African or African-Caribbean and were reported by nursing and medical staff to have been experiencing psychotic symptoms. When severity and pattern of symptoms was assessed using the Present State Examination (PSE) (Wing *et al.*, 1974), there was no evidence that those in the compulsorily detained group were more 'ill'; the informal group had slightly higher total scores on the PSE scores and a higher index of definition. While there was no difference in the reporting of bizarre or anti-social behaviour between the groups twice as many of the relatives of the compulsorily detained group as the informal group felt that the patients were not at all a danger to themselves or others. Further, relatives in the informal group reported significantly higher levels of psychotic symptoms. Thus a substantial proportion of patients were compulsorily detained even though their relatives did not think they were dangerous and there were no differences in the reported/observed disturbed behaviour in an objective measure between the two groups. These findings did not support a hypothesis that the present psychiatric–legal model is consistent with views held by relatives of patients on levels of 'dangerousness'. As the study was a pilot project, further research is required but the indications are clear.

Davies *et al.* (1996) examined ethnic differences in the risk of compulsory psychiatric admission in a sample of 535 patients, 439 of whom had been clinically assessed as suffering from 'psychosis'. Of the whole sample, 229 (51.5 per cent) had at some time in their lives been compulsorily detained under the Mental Health Act (Her

Majesty's Stationery Office, 1983). This rate was significantly higher for black Caribbean and black African patients when compared to that of white patients. The researchers considered a number of risk factors which included social demographic characteristics. They found a high likelihood that black patients (compared to white patients) had previous compulsory admissions (independent of psychiatric diagnoses, age, sex, etc.) and were also more likely to have been admitted to a psychiatric intensive care unit or to prison. Although numbers in the study were relatively small, compulsory detention rates for black patients were significantly higher than those for white patients. The researchers concluded that, in the case of black people, high compulsory admission rates and the differential experience may set up a vicious cycle which further increases the likelihood of future compulsory admissions.

SELECTION FOR SPECIFIC TREATMENT

There is a growing body of literature (mainly from the USA) on the effects of staff perceptions on decisions about treatment. Black women unlike their white counterparts are more likely to be assigned to short-term crisis counselling (Krebs, 1971). Low income blacks are perceived as non-verbal, concrete and lacking in intelligence and therefore ill-suited for psychotherapy (Jones and Segal, 1977). Less preferred modes of treatment of short duration are often used (Bloombaum *et al.*, 1968). Some studies of psychotherapy have shown a higher drop-out rate for blacks (Rosenthal and Frank, 1958), but this rate is reduced by referral to intensive psychotherapy (Leif *et al.*, 1961). In studies in which mental health professionals were presented with research protocols identical except for the race label, blacks were judged less suitable for insight therapy and received the least favourable disposition (Umbenhauer and De Witte, 1978).

Yamamoto *et al.* (1967) studied racial factors in-patient selection. Therapists were interviewed using the Boganda social distance scale and an additional questionnaire designed for the study. The former assessed the degree of physical or social distance that individuals are willing to permit (e.g. whether they would marry into the group or have close friends from that group) and the latter rated therapists' perceptions of their clients in terms of the extent to which they were superstitious, grasped abstract ideas, etc. The study found that therapists with low ethnocentricity (as measured using the Boganda social distance scales) more often treated ethnic minority patients in proportions comparable with white patients, but therapists with greater feelings of ethnocentricity, less often saw ethnic minority patients in treatments lasting six or more visits. On the issue of knowledge about other ethnic groups apart from their own, therapists who were unaware of oppression and discrimination against minority races also showed relatively low ethnocentricity (scoring very low on the Boganda scale). Those with low ethnocentricity who were naive about local patterns of prejudice and discrimination had no difficulties in seeing black people, showing a complex situation being present. Clearly, these findings require replication with large samples.

Stack *et al.* (1983) looked at predictions of re-hospitalisation by therapists in a state community mental health centre asking therapists to estimate the likelihood of future re-hospitalisation. Black patients were considered more likely to be re-hospitalised than white although the opposite occurred – showing the presence of bias based on ethnicity. The researchers noted that clinicians' expectancies were influenced unduly by their perceptions of patients' severity of illness and cooperativeness rather than 'objective' factors such as age, residential area, etc. in estimating prognosis.

MEDICATION

In the 1970s, Littlewood and Cross (1980) found that black psychiatric out-patients (compared to their white counterparts) in Hackney were more likely to have received antipsychotic medication particularly depot medication. Although during the 1980s there was a general impression that medication levels were higher for black patients compared to those for whites, there were no systematic studies of this until Chen *et al.* (1991) published their report. These researchers found that, although the total amount of medication given to black patients was similar to that given to white patients, black patients (compared to equivalent white patients) were more likely to have received depot preparations early on in the course of their admission. And a small subgroup of African-Caribbean patients in their sample had received very high peak doses during their admission. Glover and Malcolm (1988) also reported relatively high use of depot antipsychotic medication among black West Indian patients in London, and from south London, Lloyd and

Moodley (1992) reported that a survey of in-patients showed that more black patients had received antipsychotic medication than had white patients. Another black–white difference in that survey was that black patients were significantly more likely to have received depot antipsychotic medication after being detained compulsorily. Although there were no significant ethnic differences in total dosage equivalents of antipsychotic medication, doses of the depot medication were significantly higher for black patients, compared to those for white patients.

There are no studies using objective measures and measuring medication throughout a patient's admission and no reported research on ethnic differences in the temporal relationship between medication and behavioural manifestations of illness or symptoms of the illness. Subsachs *et al.* (1995) found that black patients (compared to their white counterparts) in Rampton special hospital between 1977 and 1986 received higher doses of antipsychotic medication four weeks after admission to that hospital. They found the medication history in special hospitals similar at one year and three years after admission.

Despite the lack of detailed studies of medication it seems reasonable to conclude that high doses of medication are given in the period judged to represent the most behaviourally disturbed acute phase of illness or time when the symptoms are most severe. In an intensive care environment with a rapid turnover and a tradition for using high doses of neuroleptics this phase may be a matter of days or a few weeks. It is during this phase that patients are likely to experience the most severe side-effects of medication including effects that patients subjectively perceive as life-threatening. Patients may well remember this period after discharge and perceive it as a defining moment in their history of contact with psychiatric services. It is important that research on medication taps into this period of a patient's experience of hospital, if research is to have any meaning. The main factors determining choice of medication and changes of medication also need to be studied but this must be done in an objective way where both behavioural and experiential aspects of 'illness' are examined. Further, the likelihood of bias in clinical practice must be addressed.

Patients who experience side-effects of medication are less likely to comply with subsequent taking of medication in the community (Van Putten, 1974). Non-compliance or dropping out of community follow-up arrangements is likely to increase the risk of future compulsory admission or involvement in the criminal justice system. Large doses of neuroleptic medication may also contaminate assessments of symptoms of psychopathology and make it more difficult to understand other phenomena or illnesses. Strakowski *et al.* (1993), in trying to understand why the use of a diagnosis of schizophrenia in blacks continued to be commonplace despite all the problems this entails (see Chapters 3 and 7), point out that the high doses of antipsychotic medication that black patients receive may alter clinical presentation and contribute to discrepancies in diagnoses. In other words, the diagnosis of schizophrenia if always followed by high dose medication, may well institute a vicious circle. This is much more likely in the case of black people because black people are over-represented on both parts of the circle.

Flaherty and Meagher (1980) looking at racial bias in in-patient treatment, carried out a retrospective audit of charts of 101 patients (sixty-six black and thirty-five white) with a diagnosis of schizophrenia admitted over a six-month period. They collected data on variables including emergency tranquillisation, seclusion, restraints, the ordering of occupational and recreational therapy and the level of privilege over time. Also included in the study was a sample, studied prospectively, of fifteen black and fifteen white patients. The researchers found that, compared to white patients, black patients spent less time in the hospital, gained a lower privilege levels, were given more emergency medications, and were less likely to receive recreational therapy and occupational therapy. Also, seclusion and restraint were more likely to have been used for black patients. The researchers concluded on the basis of their measures that treatment differences were influenced by racial bias, but observed that this bias was not due to hostility or contempt for black patients, but from subtle stereotyping and greater familiarity with and preference for white patients. Feedback of the results of data to the staff was met by an openness to consider racial bias as a possible explanation. The staff also considered measures to reduce bias. The researchers were impressed by staff responses to the feedback and the subsequent steps made to improve conditions. They were also impressed by the willingness of the institution to allow such research to take place and felt that the institution was a sensitive one, concerned about issues of racial bias.

SECLUSION AND RESTRAINT

Most studies on seclusion are descriptive or cross-sectional surveys and studies of ethnic differences in the use of seclusion and restraint are few and far between, and entirely from the USA. Moreover, although it is often assumed in the literature that seclusion is 'effective', this has never been tested in a controlled evaluation with other methods of responding to aggressive or violent incidents (see Brown and Tooke, 1992). There is a considerable body of literature showing that staff have very different views compared to patients (Soliday, 1985; Schmied and Ernst, 1983; Wadeson and Carpenter, 1976; Hammill *et al.*, 1989; Phillips and Rudestan, 1995). Patients fear seclusion, seeing it as punitive and coercive, while staff are often convinced of its efficacy and acceptability. Most discussions by staff about seclusion lead to calls for new guidelines and more training, particularly on restraint techniques. For black patients, particularly in the UK, seclusion and the antecedents and subsequent events, particularly the various staff responses, are loaded with the potential for serious injury or even death.

Soloff and Turner (1981) conducted a prospective study over an eight-month period of two in-patient units and looked at 107 episodes of seclusion. They compared secluded patients with non-secluded controls on a variety of variables. They found a tendency towards greater incidence of seclusion for black patients – a trend that was statistically independent of the effects of chronicity of illness or legal status. Race itself was not related to other variables such as legal status and mental state. Further, since race was not related to the presumptive diagnosis at the time of seclusion or the final discharge diagnosis, this finding could not be attributed to a systematic bias in diagnostic labelling. The researchers felt that a more likely explanation was the failure of communication between predominantly white medical staff and black patients. Attribution of violent traits, cultural prejudice, fear and distrust may also have been factors compromising the quality of understanding between patients and staff and contributing ultimately to a systematic bias in seclusion practice. Their data showed that seclusion was used primarily to contain physical violence and second to establish control over what were described as progressively destructive behaviours, i.e. as a preventive measure.

Wadeson and Carpenter (1976) in a study of unmedicated patients diagnosed as suffering from schizophrenia who had been secluded, found that seclusion room experience was viewed with terror, fear, anger and resentment, and the feeling of bitterness concerning seclusion persisted through a one-year follow up. Carpenter *et al.* (1988) in a study of nineteen New York State hospitals found that when the ethnicity of the sample was compared with that of the hospitals, whites were under-represented in the sample and blacks over-represented. The secluded or restrained blacks or Hispanics were significantly younger than the secluded restrained whites. The variables that made important contributions to seclusion rates for three ethnic groups were sex, age differences and the reference hospital populations. They considered age to be the variable of paramount importance because it could explain sex difference and to a lesser extent diagnostic differences.

The issue of seclusion was highlighted by the Committee of Inquiry into the deaths in Broadmoor (Special) Hospital of several black patients (Special Hospitals Service Authority, 1993); the committee subtitled the report 'Big, Black and Dangerous' to emphasise the commonly held stereotype that may have led to the tragedies. (This report is discussed in Part 3 of the book.) Following a real or imagined violent or aggressive action it appears that an automatic system is set in motion where a patient is restrained, medicated and secluded. Each of these interventions on their own would be successful in containing most situations, but it seems that once there is an incident there is no pause or consideration of any intervention apart from seclusion. Most violence lasts for a short period and is self-limiting and it is possible that without any intervention it would end. The grounds for triggering the automatic response system seem to be wide and include issues of patient and environmental control and use as prophylaxis against certain behaviours or attitudes deemed unacceptable by staff. Staff readings of what constitutes a threat or events that may lead to violence or aggression are key to triggering the sequence. There is a strong staff attachment to the tradition of using an 'intervention that works'.

There have been a number of inquiries into the care of patients in maximum security and there have been concerns repeatedly expressed at the custodial attitude and the anti-therapeutic nature of work in these environments which can be seen as professionally and geographically isolated from the mainstream of NHS practice. Staff attitudes to the generality of patients in maximum security are not particularly positive. These environments are also subject to infiltration by extremist political elements as pointed out by the inquiry into Ashworth (Special) Hospital (Department of Health, 1992b). Clearly, black patients in such environments are particularly vulnerable to abuse.

There are many elements to the management of acute disturbed behaviour. Clearly, space, architectural and staff constraints will affect the most popular mode in a particular area or country. If criteria for the use of each of the interventions were more objective and justifiable to patients (not a blanket response to incidents) and a more rational choice of sequence of events was possible (not the actions of an automatic system, e.g. restraint leading to medication, leading to seclusion, leading to medication) perhaps seclusion/exclusion would be more acceptable. Staff training in non-violent defensive approaches to managing violent incidents, better staff selection – including assessment of staff personality factors, would help in avoiding the non-thinking confrontational approach that patients and the black public are concerned about.

There is urgent need for imaginative research into the use of seclusion. Studies of the management of patients comparing units that do not use seclusion with those that do, may be a start. If it can be shown in a controlled evaluation that safe and effective management is possible without seclusion then serious consideration should be given to phasing out and abolishing seclusion. Seclusion is one of those practices which in the interest of observing human rights can be legislated against particularly if there is no internal momentum or movement for reform within psychiatric practice.

RISK ASSESSMENT

Assessments of risk and dangerousness are a key part of a forensic psychiatric practitioner's work. Forensic psychiatrists are sometimes called upon to provide such assessments before sentence is passed by courts on prisoners released for parole boards and on various players in custody battles, particularly where a parent has a history of previous offences or of mental illness. Also, forensic psychiatrists are often asked to provide opinions about dangerousness of people in general psychiatric settings and in the community. In fact, forensic psychiatrists may be perceived by their colleagues and the courts as experts on dangerousness and, consequently, they may be drawn into areas where they are acting as experts beyond the limits of their competence. Pollock *et al.* (1993) consider that offering a clinical opinion in court about dangerousness is often a matter of balancing between scientific integrity and social responsibility. And scientific literature fails to address the complexity of the realities faced by forensic psychiatrists.

Decisions which result in black people (compared to whites) being over-represented in settings of high security in both the psychiatric system and the criminal justice system (CJS) are often based on their perceived risk or dangerousness. In the psychiatric field, these decisions include the need to be admitted compulsorily, the need to be managed in a locked ward, medium or maximum secure unit, being placed on a restriction order (Section 41 or 49 of the Mental Health Act, 1983), and being supervised in the community. In the CJS, the decisions include the length of the prison sentence and the appropriateness of community disposals for persons found guilty of offences, and those about access and the type of access to family, especially children. The assessment of dangerousness is only partly objective if at all (see Chapter 4). And there is no evidence that judgements made by psychiatrists are better than those made by others – if anything, they are more conservative (Harding and Montandon, 1982). Even in the field of assessing danger or risk in people designated as 'mentally ill', there is no evidence that psychiatrists make better predictions than anyone else does. Psychiatrists and other practitioners within the forensic services are subject to the same biases that affect members of the public.

Prediction of violence is plagued by problems. In a large number of studies offering statistical analysis there is an emphasis on correlating biographical/clinical information, with violence. Most of these associations are based on studies with a cross-sectional or retrospective design. Because of the consequences of receiving a conviction or being identified as violent, most studies focus on institutional populations and this introduces a selection bias. There is a lack of community or controlled studies, poor definition of outcome measures, lack of objectivity in describing the nature, severity and frequency of violence, failure to use multiple sources of data on extent of violent acts and a tendency to use institutional or arrest records which are either unreliable or result in considerable under-reporting.

Wessely and Taylor (1991) reviewed studies which gave sufficient data to enable calculations on the effect of prior criminal record on subsequent offending, and using odds ratios, showed the effect of the magnitude of any increase in the risk of subsequent offending attributable to the pre-admission arrest record. They also pointed out the need to acknowledge the effects of other confounding variables in prediction, e.g. co-morbidity, with alcohol and drug abuse.

Monahan (1988) identified sources of clinical error in prediction, which include lack of specificity in defining a criterion of violence or dangerous behaviour, and tendency for clinicians to ignore the low statistical base rates. In summarising studies before 1988, he concluded that the best demographic predictors of violence among the mentally disordered are the same as those for the non-mentally disordered, namely, age, gender, social class, substance abuse and history of violence; and the poorest predicting factors were personality traits, diagnosis and severity of disorder. Brizer (1989) suggested that clinical and actuarial material should be combined in a way dictated by weight of findings to date, and that predictions should be restricted to short intervals of time in single settings, so as to increase predictive accuracy.

The new generation of research (i.e. research carried out since 1988) has used community samples and multiple sources of information on violence to compare those who are mentally well, and those who are not (Swanson *et al.*, 1990; Link *et al.*, 1992). Using the epidemiological catchment area survey, Swanson *et al.* demonstrated that having a major mental illness, substance abuse alone, or a combination of a mental disorder and substance abuse, were each significantly related to a report of violence in the last year even when a co-variation of demographic variables and the history of institutional involvement were controlled. Link analysing data from a project using the psychiatric epidemiological research interview revealed high rates of violence (measured by self-reports and arrest) in a sample of mental patients when compared to rates among residents from the same community in New York City who had never received psychiatric treatment.

Mulvey (1994) has summarised the current state of knowledge as follows: (a) mental illness appears to be a risk factor for violence in the community because the body of research taken as a whole supports the idea that an association exists between mental illness and violence in the general population; (b) the size of the association between mental illness and violence, while statistically significant, does not appear to be very large and the absolute risk for violence associated with the diagnosis of mental illness is small; (c) the combined diagnoses of serious mental illness and substance abuse disorder probably significantly increases the risk of involvement in a violent act; (d) the association between the diagnoses of mental illness and violence is probably significant even when demographic characteristics are taken into account, but there is no sizeable body of evidence that clearly indicates the relative strength of mental illness as a risk factor for violence compared with other characteristics such as socioeconomic status or history of violence; (e) active symptoms are probably more important as a risk factor than is simply the presence of an identifiable disorder; and (f) no clear information about the causal paths that produce the association between mental illness and violence is available.

Steadman *et al.* (1994) on the basis of developments in decision theory, public health and audits of existing studies suggested seven characteristics for future research. These include: (a) desegregating dangerousness into its component parts – the variables used to predict violence (risk factors), the amount and type of violence being predicted (harm) and the likelihood that harm will occur (risk); (b) choosing a rich array of theoretically chosen risk factors in multiple domains; (c) scaling harm in terms of seriousness and assessing this with multiple measures; (d) treating risk as a probability estimate that changes over time and context; (d) giving priority to actuarial research that establishes a relationship between risk factors and harm; (e) using large and broadly representative samples of patients at multiple coordinated sites; (f) making the management of risk and its assessment the core for research. Link and Steuve (1995) suggest that epidemiological research should examine a comprehensive package of background variables so that violent incidents would be seen against the relative importance of mental illness, social responses to mental illness and other aspects of the social context in generating violence.

People making decisions in the hospital and criminal justice systems which impact on black people need to appreciate the limitations of research knowledge and methods of research, as well as the fact that biased perceptions of black people affect decisions that are presented as clinical opinion. It is the perception of many black people that, whenever there is mention of risk or danger, they are likely to be perceived as more dangerous in contrast to white people of the same background and that any policies designed to supervise or restrict freedom of people who are assessed as 'dangerous' impact more on black people than they do on white people.

It seems that a result of a series of inquiries following serious incidents involving people designated as 'mentally ill' (see Chapter 11) is that psychiatry as an institution has become increasingly defensive. Practitioners in the mental health field, especially psychiatrists, have become more cautious than they used to be in order to limit their liability. This might lead to an improvement in methods of risk assessment, but it might equally well have other consequences. First, patients who are deemed to pose a higher than manageable risk may be excluded from services; second, practitioners may tend to over-predict dangerousness in order to insure themselves against making mistakes. Thus, should there be an incident in a case that has received such an assessment, it would be argued that the danger was predictable and if no incident occurs that it is only a matter of time before one does occur. This tendency to over-predict dangerousness may well be occurring already in the case of black people to judge from the over-representation of black people in restrictive psychiatric environments.

CONCLUSIONS

The reasons behind the under-diagnosis of minor psychiatric morbidity and major affective illness by psychiatrists should be examined from various angles. The inability of psychiatrists to understand or describe normal or abnormal emotions in black people is a matter of serious concern. There needs to be open acknowledgement by psychiatrists as well as others involved in delivering forensic psychiatry that black people are disadvantaged in various ways. There are biases around information processing leading to ethnic differences in pathways into the services; black people appear to be differentially selected for physical treatments as opposed to other forms of therapy (which incidentally they may prefer); and black people seem to be stereotyped as 'dangerous'. Where there are ethnic differences in the uptake of a service or the use of a service, mode of entry into a service, application of a statutory instrument, or application of a control or treatment intervention, objectivity (which must be the aim of every practitioner) should be carefully exercised. Multiple sources of information should be used, including a patient's advocates (voluntary sector, relatives, friends, etc.) and the clinical methods used for assessment should include the traditional as well as an 'emic approach', i.e. where 'illness' is seen as 'a part of a total cultural pattern deriving its meaning from the "culture" [of the person] concerned' (Fernando, 1988: 62).

Part III

Public policy

Melba Wilson

Chapter 10

Public perceptions: the psychology of image

> I am an invisible man. I am a man of substance, of flesh and bone, fiber and liquids – and I might even be said to possess a mind. I am invisible, understand, simply because people refuse to see me. . . . When they approach me they see only my surroundings, themselves, or figments of their imagination – indeed, everything and anything except me.
>
> (Ellison, 1952: 3)

The 'invisibility' of black people must be viewed within the context of racism – racism which is sometimes casual; sometimes unintentional; sometimes vociferous; often deliberate; seldom acknowledged; always damaging to the psyches of those who are at the receiving end. Public perceptions about black people and the corresponding actions and reactions which flow from them are framed within this context of their invisibility. Any discussion about the mental health of black people, whether in a forensic or general sense, therefore, must take as its starting-point the failure of those in the mainstream to see beyond the 'invisible' stereotypical images which determine the experiences of black people.

Dolan *et al.* (1991) argue that 'the fact and effect of racism in British psychiatry are obvious, although the racism itself is often more aversive than active and the racism in psychiatry is frequently played down' (1991: 71). In the mental health system and elsewhere, black people are, by and large, unknown. This is because often, the images have become a replacement for the reality. The stereotypical images which frame black people's existence in Western societies are a by-product of racism. This can be seen in the demonisation of black people in the media, literature and history. Historically, it has suited those in the mainstream to characterise black men as violent and dangerous rapists and to regard black women as aggressively sexual. One outcome of this is the attachment of a spectre of the 'other' or 'alien' to black people.

In mental health terms, the invisibility engendered by the image, when combined with an overall tendency to portray people with mental health problems as outside the bounds of normality (Fernando, 1995a; Perkins and Repper, 1996; Sashidharan, 1994a) compounds the disadvantage experienced by black people in both the mental health and criminal justice systems. This is because perceptions which are based on erroneous information (stereotypical images) set in motion a range of institutional responses to black people, which bear little resemblance to their cultural, social and personal realities. Dolan *et al.* (1991) note:

> Enforced treatment approaches, involving loss of personal liberty, place the recipient in a state of subjugation and powerlessness. In this way the institution of the NHS is adding to the experience of subjugation and alienation received by black people from other aspects of British society. Psychological tests, which are used to 'assess' and 'understand' the client, have usually been developed using the white Anglo-Saxon male as the 'normal group' and discriminate against minority groups both in terms of test construction and the inferences drawn from test results.
>
> (1991: 72)

In this section, we explore first the underlying reasons behind the stereotypical images which govern perceptions of black people; discuss their historical basis in racism; look at the consequences in terms of how such consistent negative imagery affects the mental health of black people and how this is made worse, not better, when they encounter a system which is ill-equipped to meet their needs effectively, because it is grounded in an adherence to perceptions which have little basis in fact.

IMAGES OF SEXUALITY AND VIOLENCE

Angela Davis (1982) discusses the myth of the black rapist as a 'political intervention' (1982: 184) and notes its central role in the shaping of post-slavery racism in the USA. In the thirty years following the Civil War, more than 10,000 African-American men were murdered by lynch mobs. It was the rape charge which proved most effective in mobilising such mobs and justifying the lynching of black men. The rape charge has been indiscriminately aimed at black men, the guilty and innocent alike and has served to perpetuate the myth. Thus, of the 455 men executed between 1930 and 1967 on the basis of rape convictions, 405 of them were black (Davis, 1982).

Black post-Civil War campaigner Ida B. Wells named and denounced the southern social control in 1895. There were, she noted, three excuses given by whites for the lynching of black people (Lorence, 1996). First, was the 'necessity to stamp out race riots; second, to counteract the black man's right to vote'. Even after the lynchings accomplished these two goals:

> Brutality still continues; Negroes were whipped, scourged, exiled, shot and hung whenever and wherever it pleased the white man so to treat them, and as the civilized world with increasing persistency held the white people of the South to account for its outlawry, the murderers invented the third excuse – that Negroes had to be killed to avenge their assaults upon women. There could be framed no possible excuse more harmful to the Negro and more unanswerable if true in its sufficiency for the white man.
>
> (1996: 17)

The institution of lynching, in turn, complemented by the continued rape of black women became an essential ingredient of the post-war strategy of racist terror. The sexual myth promulgated in relation to black women contained the added dimension of loose morals and promiscuousness. So, for example, during the 1920s a well known southern [US] politician could declare that there was no such thing as a 'virtuous colored girl' (Davis, 1982: 182). Black US writer, academic and essayist Audre Lorde (1984) discussed the US propensity to justify the labels that were attached to black people in this way:

> One tool of the Great-American-Double-Think is to blame the victim for victimization: Black people are said to invite lynching by not knowing our place; Black women are said to invite rape and murder and abuse by not being submissive enough, or by being too seductive.
>
> (1984: 61)

These mythical constructs for black women and black men have helped to perpetuate the aura of 'other' assigned to black people and, by implication, the notions of inferiority which are part and parcel of this concept. The legacy of this negative imagery in the forensic sense in modern-day Britain, has been the instilling of fear – transmitted through media images of black men such as Christopher Clunis, Stephen Laudat and Orville Blackwood (see Chapter 12 for details), who stare wide-eyed and 'dangerous' from the pages of newspapers. These images are burned into the public consciousness. So much a part are they of the conceptualisations surrounding black men, that black people must themselves struggle to avoid internalising the negativism associated with their colour. Though the homicides committed by black men, such as Clunis and Laudat, form a tiny minority within a very small number of people designated as 'mentally ill' who commit violent crimes (MIND, 1994a), they are used, by the media in particular, to perpetuate the stereotype, which in turn maintains the justification of the image of the dangerous black man who cannot be let loose onto an unsuspecting, particularly female, public.

The 'market profile' of black people is constantly associated with loaded images of violence or lawlessness, hence a relentless depiction of black males in particular being 'mad, black and dangerous'. This image was evidenced in the case of Christopher Clunis (see Northeast Thames and Southeast Thames Regional Health Authorities, 1994), as it was previously associated with Orville Blackwood (see Special Hospitals Service Authority, 1993) and others. Yet, what the report of the inquiry concerning Clunis demonstrated is the way in which the mental health system has on the one hand subverted the issue of race, while simultaneously pandering to racist fears (Aveleon Associates and the Black Mental Health Professionals Network, 1994: 2).

The perception of African-Caribbean men as violent can result in the police being asked to assist in their hospital admission whatever their behaviour or state of mind. For example, 'police were asked to take Winston Rose, a black man who showed no signs of violence to hospital. One of the police officers involved said 'all I knew was that he was big and coloured'. This skewed response to black men, notably the propensity to label them as dangerous, is in itself dangerous' (MIND, 1996b:11).

> There is a well-established stereotype of the black psychiatric patient as volatile and dangerous. The efforts of the reforming Medical Committee to desegregate the Robben Island lunatic asylum in 1858 failed when the new classification of patients,

> constructed on perceived dangerousness, simply replicated the old system based on skin colour. Although behavioural criteria officially determined allocation within the asylum, in practice skin colour was the decisive factor, with the black patients being automatically located in the most disturbed section. White patients were not only regarded as more tractable but also deemed more susceptible to cure.
>
> (Lipsedge, 1994:14)

Francis (1996) notes that:

> almost every major and heavily-reported case involving lapses in community care has involved young black men. They are the most feared sector of our population and their predicament commands a disproportionate amount of attention by the media. Yet, legitimate concerns such as unemployment, education, housing, family life are barely mentioned. It is race which is the underlying issue in crime, danger and mental illness, though the concern is not explicitly stated.
>
> (1996: 4)

PERCEPTIONS OF BLACK PEOPLE AS 'OTHER'

> Is not whiteness in symbols always ascribed in French to Justice, Truth, Virginity? I knew an Antillean who said of another Antillean, 'His body is black, his language is black, his soul must be black too'. This logic is put into daily practice by the white man. The black man is the symbol of Evil and Ugliness.
>
> (Fanon, 1967: 180)

Black American law professor and Reith lecturer, Patricia Williams is quoted in a recent *Guardian* (1997) newspaper report as saying that: 'Whiteness should start being considered as race and not as benchmark':

> Whiteness is unnamed, suppressed, beyond the realms of race. Race lives 'over there' . . . in black bodies and inner city neighbourhoods. Black children learn early to see their blackness as their mark; white children never learn to see themselves as white.
>
> (1997: 4)

Part and parcel of the effects of racism is the deliberate creation and perpetuation of an alien sense of the 'otherness' of black people. The issue of racial identity in the psycho-social development of black people has been researched in the USA for about twenty-five years, but in reality, it became an issue when 'African people were forcibly removed from their homeland and shipped to a dismal life of servitude in Europe and the Americas almost four-hundred and fifty years ago' (Ferrell, 1995: 24). The result has been that people of African descent have been rendered powerless and open to maltreatment, invalidation, and exploitation (Akbar, 1984). Ferrell (1995) writes:

> Stripping African people of their names was an important tool in the initial subjugation and subsequent oppression of African people in Europe and the Americas. It served to cut Africans off from their roots (i.e., knowledge of themselves and where they came from); to divide them from other African slaves (Negro; Mulatto; Sambo; Quadroon, etc.) as well as from people in Africa (who were deliberately portrayed as 'primitives). Taking away their names also served to degrade Africans and confirmed their status as the property of a white man.
>
> (1995: 24–5)

It can be argued that black people are disadvantaged, not because they are different *per se*, but because of persistent attitudes which equate being different with being bad and being black with being inferior to white. The conjunction, therefore, of being black and suffering from mental ill health and receiving care and treatment within a mental health system where often the first gate of entry is the criminal justice system, places black people in such situations in double jeopardy. W. E. B. Du Bois (1904 [1970]) discusses the 'peculiar sensation' which afflicts the lives of black people, calling it a 'double consciousness – this sense of looking at one's self through the eyes of others, of measuring one's soul by the tape of a world that looks on in amused contempt and pity' ((1904 [1970]): 3).

Racism and 'otherness' combine to place black people at a severe disadvantage in any interface with British institutions:

> Historically, the relationships between black and white people have been influenced by slavery and colonialism, and this continues to influence the perceptions of many white people even today, so that even when black and Asian people have been born

> in the UK, they may still be regarded by some people with suspicion or lack of respect.
>
> (University of Manchester, Department of Health, 1996: 104)

It can further be argued that black people in both Britain and the USA are further disadvantaged because, despite experiencing the worst aspects of slavery and colonialism, their innate sense of humanity and cultural identity led them to expect to survive and eventually to triumph in the face of adversity. Unlike in the situation governing the indentured whites in the USA who could legitimately buy their freedom after a given period and take their equal place as part of the new world structure, history shows that the experience of black slaves was dramatically different. Colour, the great dividing line, was obstinately not crossed (the continuing sexual abuse of black women slaves by slave owners, overseers, etc. being the exception) and black people remained – in economic, social and moral terms (to the extent that black people were considered to be without morality) – the outcasts in the building of British and US colonial empires. In the USA, in spite of its legacy of the great melting pot, once slavery was abolished as an institution, black people continued to be denied their rightful place, despite the fact that they contributed much in terms of skills, diversity and culture to the new US milieu.

Owens (1980a) notes: 'the status of blacks in America did not change significantly as a result of the demise of the slave system. They were accorded freeman status as a result of the Civil War and the Emancipation Proclamation, but this did not mean an upgrading of equal treatment in the justice system. The devaluation of black life continued in America as recorded, most poignantly, in lynching statistics' (1980a: 4–6). These revealed that between 1882 and 1961, 3,442 black people, compared with 1,294 white people, were lynched in the USA – a ratio of nearly three to one' (ibid.).

Marable (1983) discusses the nature of the newly created Black Diaspora in the USA and assesses how it was experienced from the inside. The slaves 'forged a new world culture that was in its origin African, but in its creative forms, something entirely new' (1983: 24). This new worldview, states Marable, was created by a black majority:

> who experienced and hated the lash, who labored in the cane fields of the Carolina coast; who detested the daily exploitation of their parents, spouses and children; who dreamed or plotted

> their flight to freedom, their passage across 'the River Jordan;' who understood that their masters' political struggle system of bourgeois democracy was a lie; who endeavoured to struggle for land and education, once the chains of chattel slavery were smashed; who took pride in their African heritage, their black skin, their uniquely rhythmic language and culture, their special love of God.
>
> (1983: 24)

This black majority was joined by a 'black elite' argues Marable, 'who were often distinguished by color and caste . . . who sought to accumulate petty amounts of capital at the expense of their black sisters and brothers; whose dream of freedom was one of acceptance into the inner sanctum of white economic and political power' (1983: 24). That both groups were racially black, notes Marable, 'escaped no one's attention, least of all the white authorities' (1983: 25).

There is no doubt that the damage done by a worldview which has racism as an inherent part, adversely affects the mental health of black people. The legacy of devaluation and demoralisation engendered by this racist worldview has combined to create a spiritual destitution (whether conscious or unconscious) among black people in the Diaspora. The effects of this deliberate creation of separateness and of being made to feel inferior are responsible for the 'disconnectedness' which is at the root of much of the emotional damage which contributes to the mental ill-health of black people (Stephen, 1996).

> Modern heterogeneous society contains a series of subcultural groups, some of which, like the American Negro, have their total cultural identity with the American scene blocked by a towering barrier of social and economic discrimination. The culture of colored [sic] people is a deeply ingrained American culture, but the opportunity to identify as Americans rather than second-class citizens is denied, of course with psychological results. . . . Psychiatry . . . must treat individuals now and then on whom the mark of oppression has been laid. It cannot do so without noting a subcultural pattern which grows out of the discriminatory pattern.
>
> (Opler, 1959: 6)

According to Gilroy (1993) the physical manifestation of black people's discomfort with self has a historical basis in that 'black people have always grappled with a body type which is regarded as inferior, and have, as a result, striven to achieve a body that is out of keeping with what is right for us as a people' (Wilson, 1993a: 73). The distress caused by slavery has been passed on through generations of black people, and might be regarded as the effects of long-term post-traumatic stress disorder.

CAUSE AND CURE?

In considering the interface between, on the one hand, the suffering of black people and, on the other, the mental health services, especially those around forensic psychiatry, a discussion around causes and cures becomes highly problematic. The suffering derived from discrimination and oppression is compounded when black people are then confronted with having to go to a different arm of the same system for help. The consequence for many black people with mental health problems, particularly those who encounter forensic psychiatry, is that they are at the mercy of a system which neither knows their real needs (because they have remained largely 'invisible'), nor, in the main, understands the importance of or need to explore ways of meeting them in a fundamental way.

Ethically, it should not be possible to attempt to treat black people within the context of forensic psychiatry or any other branch of psychiatry without at the very least: first understanding the context in which they come to use mental health services; second, attempting an understanding of culture and diversity as *positives*; and third, incorporating these perspectives into policy and practice. Yet, more often than not, this does not happen – neither for African-Americans nor for African-Caribbeans:

> Traditional models of mental health cannot be legitimately applied a priori to many black Americans. Numerous mental health workers in recent years have criticized mental health theory and practice because of racism and sexist approaches. . . . The mental health of any black individual must be viewed in the context of his or her socioeconomic and cultural background, particularly as this context is shaped and influenced by a society pervaded to some degree by institutional racism. Mental health

> or illness does not exist in a social-political vacuum that can be analyzed free of the danger of subjectivity and cultural biases.
>
> (Ruiz, 1990: 44)

A dramatic example of the sociopolitical partnership that is both psychologically and politically abusive and repressive was represented during the time of slavery in the work of Dr S. A. Cartwright. Dr Cartwright was a surgeon and psychologist who was summoned to a Louisiana plantation in 1851 to investigate the causes for the high percentage of slave runaways (Cartwright, 1851). After many weeks of study, he wrote a long report which concluded that the slaves who ran away to freedom were suffering from a mental disease he dubbed 'drapetomania', which means literally 'the *manie* (mania) for running away. This illustration is germane to blacks' current predicament because Dr Cartwright, as probably most whites of the time, accepted slavery as 'normal' and considered it an acceptable social system arrangement for African-Americans. Black rejection of this norm was viewed as pathological.

Though different, the reality of the British experience for people from the Caribbean who came to Britain (having been openly and actively recruited in their home countries) was to find a hostile racism which has pretty much remained intact. With images of the Mother Country, God and Queen, and the affinity which colonialism engendered in its British colonies in the Caribbean, African-Caribbeans could be forgiven for expecting to be welcomed with open arms. Instead, 'within a few weeks of arrival, most of us found Britain a bitter disappointment' (Bryan *et al.*, 1985: 24). Isolation, racial resentment and racism in the workplace and in schools combined to make the lives of Caribbeans who came to Britain in the 1950s and 1960s mentally and physically arduous:

> These poor working conditions were compounded by the racism we experienced at the hands of both bosses and workers. British workers felt threatened by our presence and were unable to shake off years of racist and sexist conditioning. Even though our arrival usually ensured their own promotion to less tedious and better paid sections of the industry, the fact that we were there at all was openly resented. The Race Relations Act of 1966, far from outlawing such attitudes, merely entrenched them. The act outlawed individual acts of incitement to racial hatred in places of public resort, but left racism virtually unchallenged in every other area of our lives, such as housing, employment, etc. The

> unions believed that their role was to protect the rights of the indigenous workforce, rather than to take up and defend the rights and working conditions of black workers. . . . The blatant racism of employers only added to our sense of alienation, and in the absence of any union protection, many of us had no choice but to accept daily harassment as a fact of life.
>
> (Bryan *et al.*, 1985: 26–7)

The children of those Caribbeans, encountered a school system which actively disallowed any validation of their cultures or their places within society.

> Rigged scientific theories about race and intelligence combined with the cultural introversion of the school curriculum to ensure that those of us who went through school here in the sixties found it a negative and wounding experience. From the earliest Janet and John readers onwards, we found ourselves either conspicuous by our absence or depicted as a kind of joke humanity, to be ridiculed or pitied but never to be regarded as equals. Right across the curriculum and at every level, the schools' textbooks confirmed that Black people had no valid contribution to make to the society, other than to service its more menial requirements. Children were presented with a worldview in which Blackness represented everything that was ugly, uncivilised and under-developed, and our teachers made little effort to present us or our White classmates with an alternative view.
>
> (ibid.: 66)

The extent of the jolt that racism represented to the psyches of African-Caribbeans is becoming apparent in the nature of the interface of black people with the mental health system in Britain – as the children of those children who absorbed so much negativism have begun to suffer its effects. The very nature of that damage can be found in the disadvantage suffered by black people as a result of 'hitching their horses' wholly to the prevailing wagon of Western thought and practice. For it is a wagon whose axles are greased by the tendency to disallow or discount the independent development of black people as equally contributing to and acknowledging participants in the construction of societal mores and processes. One result of this, is that black people can become vulnerable and prone to being cast adrift:

> Many black people regard racism and its effects as a major contributing factor in the mental ill-health of black people. The tensions associated with living in a society in which some people are racially prejudiced are felt to represent a draining and wearing influence in black people's lives. Second, the view is that the needs of black people can be overlooked. Many black people say this is shown by what they feel is first the reluctance of the mental health system to address issues of culture in psychiatric treatment, and second the tendency to make assumptions about black people based on notions of their racial characteristics.
>
> (Department of Health, 1994a: 23)

Cochrane and Sashidharan (1996) point out that one factor which all generations of non-white ethnic minorities in Britain have in common is exposure to racism:

> Racism, in so far as it is manifested in discrimination and economic disadvantage may well have an effect on physical as well as mental health as poverty and low socioeconomic status are among the best predictors of risk for many forms of morbidity. But unlike for physical conditions the other manifestation of racism, prejudice, will also impact upon psychological wellbeing. It would come as no surprise to discover that the experience of stereotyping and denial of humanity, jokes and other verbal disparagement, the easy assumption that skin colour is associated with a whole range of assumed problems from academic under-achievement to serious criminal activity, as well as explicit social rejection, had very significant influences on self-esteem and mental health.
>
> (1996: 109)

Fernando (1995a) writes that 'although race is a scientific myth, it persists as a social entity for historical, social and psychological reasons – in fact for all the reasons that result in racism (1995a: 24). And Ahmad and Atkin (1996) note:

> Here, the emphasis is on cultural particularity, which highlights the 'otherness' of black people. The continuous reference to the difference and specificity of the needs of black and 'other ethnic minorities' carries an implicit assumption that there is a homogeneous white British culture of which black people are not a part. A further serious implication of this approach is that those responsible for the provision of mental health services in a

> multiracial society may assume that by appointing some 'black or other ethnic minority' workers and providing some interpreting and particular food they are addressing black people's needs without consideration being given to the broader issues of the inequalities and discriminatory practices that may underpin the distinctive experiences of black people in relation to mental health services.
>
> (1996: 111)

The constantly reiterated messages to black people in Britain as being other, inferior, unequal was graphically illustrated in a article in the *Guardian* (Moorhead, 1997). The article, entitled 'The Other Mrs Lawrence', explores the differences in the public approaches to the appalling tragedies suffered by Doreen Lawrence, the mother of the murdered black south London schoolboy Stephen Lawrence, and Frances Lawrence, the wife of the murdered white headteacher Philip Lawrence. Both families were innocent victims of senseless violence, but while the white family was cradled in the bosom of public sympathy and support, the black family's experience was diametrically different. After the trial Frances Lawrence wrote concerning the police: 'Since my husband's murder, they have acted tirelessly, unstintingly and with meticulous application to the truth. They have displayed qualities which go far beyond any textbook notion of duty to support and sustain the children and myself' (1997: 6).

Doreen Lawrence, on the other hand, said this about her family's experience:

> Well, I certainly don't recognise that treatment in what happened to my family at the hands of the police. . . . With us, they spent their time investigating not what had happened, but who we were. They'd never come across a black boy who didn't have a criminal record. They couldn't believe it. And when they finally did, they decided he must have been part of a gang and his death must have been connected to a fight between rival gangs. For two weeks, they concentrated their investigation on us and what we had done wrong.
>
> (1997: 7)

Such is the reality of the public perceptions associated with race. Such are the consequences for Britain's black communities.

CONCLUSIONS

The strengths and weaknesses which exist within the black communities are comparable to those which exist among peoples in the myriad diverse communities which make up society as we know it. The uneven nature of the playing field, however, means that black people's strengths go largely unnoticed, while the weaknesses are magnified ten-fold. The impact this can and does have on the lives of black people can render us invisible, make us ill and lead to a sense of powerlessness and frustration.

Black people are not the only losers in this scenario, however. A society that denies itself in part, weakens the whole. The dilemma in this context is for mainstream society to accept that a re-definition of what is meant by mainstream is fundamental. This should likewise include an acceptance and realisation that the inescapable diversity which exists within it is an opportunity for celebration, rather than a cause for concern.

Chapter 11

The institutional framework

The previous chapter discussed at length the stereotypes assigned to black people. This chapter concentrates on the nature of care and the treatment afforded to black people within the mental health system and on black people's experiences within the criminal justice system. Public policy is discussed in terms of how it operates in shaping services with regard to black people in Britain, that is, within the context of only token acknowledgement of Britain's ethnic diversity and a worldview of Britain's black communities which is framed by an acceptance of stereotypes.

COMMON GROUND?

The fact that black people are largely 'invisible' – to society in general, as well as to psychiatrists trained in primarily Western philosophies and techniques – means that when they present with mental health problems, particularly in the forensic sense, the outsider position assigned to them is reinforced. Sir Roger Ormrod (1990), former Lord Justice of Appeal and former chairman of the Institute of Psychiatry, states that the primary role of forensic psychiatry is 'the advancement of the cause of justice in a court setting ('forum') by making available to the court the skills, knowledge and techniques developed by the discipline' (1990: 1). Consultant forensic psychiatrist Nigel Eastman (1995), speaking at a conference, stated that forensic psychiatry included both 'clinical forensic psychiatry' and 'legal psychiatry' – the latter being the 'application of law to general psychiatry' – but with an additional 'dimension of third party interest in the form of a political dimension'. Robert Blueglass (1990), professor of forensic psychiatry at the University of Birmingham, states: 'In the UK the forensic psychiatrist is primarily a doctor and his or her continued responsibility for the treatment and management of patients is fundamental, but he or she is also a professional expert witness'(1990: 7). He quotes (with apparent approval) a comment by Sir John Wood (1982) in the Maudsley lecture in 1981: 'If the term [forensic psychiatrist] had previously lacked clear definition it might now be said that it should be applied to the psychiatrist with a skill to make complexities and uncertainties of his discipline appear simple and certain to judge' (1982: 552).

The sad reality for black people who are part of the forensic psychiatric system is that the complexities and uncertainties are not simple. The consequent disadvantage which frames black people's experiences within the context of forensic psychiatry occurs for a number of reasons: First, because labels, stereotypes and images associated with black people engender fear, misunderstanding and an accompanying tendency to react repressively; second, because there is frequently little common ground or understanding between, on the one hand, the major players in both the criminal justice system (police officers, magistrates, probation officers) and the mental health system (consultant psychiatrists, social workers, community psychiatric nurses) and, on the other, black people; third, because black people are viewed as having no part in the shaping of the current system of justice in Britain and fourth, because the interface between black communities and the police, governed by suspicion and a lack of knowledge, results in black people being more likely to be 'stopped, searched, arrested, charged, convicted and to receive a custodial sentence than white people' (Edwards, 1992: 249–50). 'The Institute of Race Relations . . . [states that] . . . the suspicion about the West Indian is that he is a criminal, a wild man . . . the suspicion about the Asian is that he has sneaked in under the cover of night' (Edwards, 1992: 259).

Black people experience both law and psychiatry as different and competing methods of controlling (what is seen by society as) antisocial behaviour; both models remove the individual from their social context – the former by playing down the relevance of social problems such as poverty, and the latter by dwelling on a medical 'dysfunctional' model. 'Help' or 'treatment' within the psychiatric system, especially forensic psychiatry, are experienced as punitive, little different to the sanctions imposed by the criminal justice system.

Edwards (1992) discusses two explanatory models of black men's and black women's involvement in crime either as victims or perpetrators. The first concerns a pathological and social predisposition towards crime, or 'the notion that black people are intrinsically the problem . . . [governed by] . . . the belief that the home environment and especially black parenting and black mothering is to blame'. This model utilises what (according to Edwards) is called 'racist logic' devised to 'present black crime as a primary cultural problem, [either] forged in the economic "no man's land" between deprivation and restricted opportunity, or secured in a spurious social biology' (1992: 256–9). The second model focuses on racism in private attitudes and public procedures and illustrates the racism of the criminal justice system by identifying the high proportion of black offending within individual racist attitudes, and the result of the exercise of discretion within institutionalised patterns and processes (1992: 259). It is evident that both models come into play in determinations of forensic psychiatric disposals for black people. For example, 'the response of the government through the Criminal Justice Act 1991 has been to use the family as a means of controlling juvenile crime' (1992: 258). In addition:

> In the courtroom too there is a race blindness which results in racism through racial disadvantage and discriminatory treatment. In the case of *R v. Thomas* (1989) 88 Cr App R 370, Mr. Justice Otton was asked to exercise his power to stand by members of the jury. The application was made as four 'black' youths stood for trial before an all-white jury. Otton's comments are particularly telling: 'At the end I must ask a simple question: is there a real risk that these four youths would not get a fair trial from an all-white jury? The answer is: There is no such risk.
>
> (1992: 259)

However, Deryck Browne (1990) in an exploratory study into the psychiatric remand process as it affects black defendants at magistrates courts concluded that 'coupled with magistrates' lack of experience and unfamiliarity with the provisions of the 1983 Mental Health Act, and the unavoidably subjective nature of decisions they are expected to make . . . decisions are not always made in the best medical interests of mentally disturbed defendants generally, and black defendants in particular' (1990: 28). At the other end of the scale, evidence suggests that black people's access to psychiatric services via their general practitioners is considerably less than that of their counterparts in the larger community (see Wilson, 1993b; Department of Health, 1994a). This may well lead to crisis admission, compulsory treatment and detention in psychiatric hospitals resulting in reinforcing the view of black people as problematic, behaving outside the boundaries of 'normal' behaviour, and 'other'.

Department of Health task force survey

During an eighteen-month period between 1992 and 1994, a task force appointed by the NHS executive consulted with African-Caribbean and Asian communities about their experiences of mental health services under the government's community care policies (Department of Health, 1994a). This survey showed that: (a) African-Caribbeans, including large numbers of women, continue to be over-represented in psychiatric institutions at all levels; (b) psychiatric treatment often does not take account of the impact of race and racism; (c) there is no widespread acceptance of the importance of culturally diverse methods in working with black mental health users and carers; and (d) general practitioners (GPs) fail to respond adequately to black clients' complaints, leading to crisis admissions and compulsory admissions in medium secure units with treatment involving high drug dosages. The result of all this is that: (1) in practice, black people access mental health services at a much later stage than those in the general population, necessitating crisis and therefore, controlling responses; (2) because of the nature of societal attitudes concerning race and crime, there is a high probability that black people will be taken into the criminal justice system; and (3) once they get there, and are deemed to be in mental distress or suffering mental ill health, because of the ways in which their cultures, actions and mores may be interpreted or mis-interpreted, they are more likely to be given more punitive disposals at the severe end of psychiatric treatment.

THE ROLE OF PROFESSIONALS

> For blacks, in general, the criminal-justice system has been a negative experience and this linkage of the mental-health professional to the system has caused many blacks to distrust both the professional and the therapeutic process.
>
> (Owens, 1980a: 1)

Professionals in the mental health field (general psychiatrists, forensic psychiatrists, social workers and others) do not operate within a vacuum when it comes to making pronouncements and judging the mental health of black people with whom they come into contact. They are conditioned – possibly even on a subconscious level – to regard black people as alien, as 'other', inferior, problematic. Thus, when black people who may be suffering mental distress or 'ill-health' present for treatment through a criminal justice system which itself weighs against the rights of black people, they are placed in double jeopardy. The mental health professional's worst fears are realised, and the treatment regime for the black 'forensic patient' is predicated on a basis of fear, apprehension and an inculcated inability or unwillingness (on the part of the professional) to recognise the real nature of the person who is before them.

Black patients, however, are not alone in experiencing the effects of racism. Black people within various professions too face bias against them in employment and promotion within the health service (Fernando, 1988) and discrimination against non-white and female applicants has been clearly shown in the selection of medical students (Commission for Racial Equality, 1988). Yet, both black and white professionals are trained in and operate a system that is inherently racist (Fernando, 1988). Mental health professionals, by virtue of the responsibility placed upon them to contain people with mental health problems, have a stake in maintaining the status quo. In a talk, Aggrey Burke (1995) expresses the concern felt by many black practitioners when faced with a predominantly white mental health system: 'Workers in the psychiatric system, particularly those in secure hospitals, are predominantly white. One wonders if they will be affected by the racial factor as it relates to the victims themselves. One wonders if therapists, and indeed mental health review tribunals, reflect the attitudes and sentiments of judges and jurors in populations where the victim is a white female, as opposed to populations where the victim is a black female instead'.

Fernando (1988) notes the importance of the public face of psychiatry and how an acknowledgement of racism in psychiatry by psychiatric professionals might shake the position of psychiatry and threaten it – a point illustrated by the results of a study which found that psychiatrists perceive a greater risk of violence from a black patient than from a white patient (G. Lewis, *et al.*, 1990) – although surprisingly, the authors of the study concluded that this finding was not indicative of 'racism'. The situation in the UK has parallels with the US experience. One US consultant forensic psychiatrist noted recently that the relationship between stereotypes and care and treatment was evident in that in his experience in the USA 'the presumption is that if a patient is black, 6'2", 230 pounds, he clearly poses a risk for assaultative behaviour; while a frail white woman, who has been responsible for taking out six staff, is free to walk around the hospital' (Phillips, 1997: personal communication).

COMMUNICATION

A study of compulsorily detained patients at the Maudsley Hospital (Moodley and Thornicroft, 1988) showed that all the West Indian patients were detained in a locked ward at the time of admission, compared with half of the white men, and that medication was more likely to be administered immediately to black than to white detained patients. In a study in Nottingham (Chen, *et al.*, 1991) a depot injection was more likely to be given to African-Caribbeans than to other ethnic groups and it was also given earlier in the course of treatment. Seclusion was used more commonly for black patients (compared to whites) at a US university hospital (Soloff and Turner, 1981), explained by the researchers as resulting from 'attribution [to black patients] of violent traits, cultural prejudice, fear and distrust . . . compromising the quality of understanding between patient and staff and contributing ultimately to a system of bias in seclusion practice' (1981: 43).

The widespread failure in communication in general has been outlined by Scott-Moncrieff (1993):

> Psychiatry, in common with other disciplines, has its own jargon and this is extensively used in psychiatric records. The present author has lost count of the number of section papers, psychiatric reports and medical and nursing notes where patients are described as behaving 'violently' or 'being aggressive' or 'being hostile' or 'making threats'. These words and phrases are all terms of interpretation that conceal the words and deeds of the patient.
>
> (1993: 101)

For black patients within the psychiatric system, the potential for being misunderstood and misrepresented because of wrongly attributed racial and cultural characteristics is great. From the moment a black person becomes a patient, he/she enters a milieu which, by its very nature, is designed to exclude, mystify and deny participation on an equal basis.

THE ROLE OF THE MEDIA

The public perception of people with mental health problems in general as violent and dangerous, is ill-founded (see Robertson *et al.*, 1996) and Sayce (1995) cites research evidence which shows 'that a diagnosis of mental illness is not a predictor of violence' (1995: 6). In addition, the vast majority of people with mental health problems are not violent and are very distressed to see constant images of the 'mad axeman' staring back from the pages of newspapers. Nevertheless, notes Sayce, the [public] debate is being shaped by the 'moral panic' that has taken hold of attitudes to mental health – a panic in which highly unusual incidents of homicide have become emblematic of the supposed failure of community care. Saturation reporting of killings – one study found that two thirds of all mental health reporting focused on violence – has heightened public fears about danger, madness and loss of control; and become the rationale for proposals for more repressive mental health law (1995: 6).

Sayce's observations are closely mirrored by the US experience: Steadman and Cocozza (1978) stated at a conference in the 1970s: 'The belief in a strong link between violence and mental illness is firmly rooted in the minds of many US citizens. Television, movies and newspapers regularly foster this view by selective and sensationalized reporting' (1978: 2). And the situation does not appear to have changed, as some years later Monahan and Arnold (1996) wrote:

> One content analysis performed for the [US] National Institute of Mental Health found that 17% of all prime-time American television programs that could charitably be classified as 'dramas' depicted a character as mentally ill. Seventy-three per cent of these characters with mental illness were portrayed as violent, compared with 40% of the 'normal' characters, and 23% of the characters with mental illness were shown to be homicidal, compared with 10% of the 'normal' characters.
>
> (1996: 68)

When the dimension of race is added to the media portrayal of people suffering mental distress, the big, black and dangerous image becomes fused in public perceptions with images of mental illness which are also associated with danger and fear. The result is the mad *and* bad *and* black image: black people as dangerous, hostile, aggressive and inferior, create a climate of fear and mistrust, along with a desire for self-righteous retribution. These distorted views about mental illness and race can and do have disastrous consequences for black people in all walks of society, but particularly when they are suspected perpetrators (of crime), actual victims of crime or thought to be 'mentally ill'.

In the first instance, black people, in particular African-Caribbean men, who may have been patients in the psychiatric system at sometime *and* suspected of having committed a crime (especially a violent crime) are, in effect, tried, convicted and sentenced in the press. The context in which this occurs evokes subtle – and often not so subtle – impressions derived from the times of slavery and the post-slavery period (see Chapter 1). The homily from those times is that black men (whether mad or not) cannot be let loose to ravage white communities, and more particularly, white women. An example of this can be seen in the way the British press dealt with the case of Glen Grant, a convicted rapist who had been discharged in 1996 from a psychiatric unit in south London by hospital managers (a lay panel). Grant's picture was splattered across the pages of several tabloid newspapers using headlines such as 'Scandal of the evil madman let out to rape' (*Sun*, 1996: 2). The *Daily Mail* (1996), under the headline 'How they freed the Beast to rape again' (1996: 17) dubbed him 'the Beast of Belgravia' referring to attacks on middle class women in an upper class district of London: 'When arrested over the 1984 rapes, he said of his two victims: "They had everything and I had nothing. But they're not so good now they have been raped by a black boy"' (1996: 17). Clearly the cruelty and criminal nature of Grant's behaviour were inexcusable (and should not be minimised) but there is little doubt that the tenor of the press reporting about him was influenced by the fact of his blackness counterpoised against the (often implied) whiteness of his middle class victims. Despite his diagnosed 'mental illness', Grant was given a prison sentence.

Another black man with a history of diagnosed 'mental illness' who had much press publicity after criminal activity was Wayne Hutchinson. He was also sent to prison on two convictions for manslaughter, one of attempted murder and three of wounding with intent. The effect of the media emphasising the race of someone who has committed a crime, especially a violent crime, is that repressive measures are taken irrespective of any evidence regarding 'mental illness' because concern (about 'illness') is outweighed by societal pressures for retribution.

The case of Christopher Clunis (discussed in Chapter 12) also reveals the tendency towards alarm and fear (by society) in instances of violent crime when race enters into the picture – although in that instance Clunis was committed to a special hospital and not to prison. In this instance too, a black man (Clunis) was the perpetrator of a crime against a white person.

Although the response to crimes committed by black people is high profile treatment, resulting in punitive approaches towards the criminal, there is discernibly more media ambivalence and often a muted response towards crimes when black people themselves are victims. The contrast – in other words the application of double standards – is shown up by two cases – that of Margaret Bent, a black woman, and that of Perry Southall, a white woman. The former alleged that she was being victimised and stalked by a black man, Dennis Chambers, and gave evidence of incidents of serious harassment by him over a four-year period, including instances of sitting outside her home with a machete, sending threatening letters, and telephoning her ten times a day. Despite the fact that Chambers offered no defence to the charges arising from 'stalking' (which in itself was not an offence at the time), he was cleared of two counts of causing grievous bodily harm and one of affray. Judge Quentin Campbell told Inner London Crown Court that it was 'extremely difficult' to prove intent in cases of 'psychiatric or psychological harm' (*Guardian*, 1996: 1). However, when a black man, Clarence Morris, was charged after stalking a white woman (Perry Southall), he was convicted of causing actual bodily harm 'after a jury decided that the psychological scars suffered by her, Perry Southall, aged twenty, were so severe they were the equivalent of physical injury' (*Guardian*, 1997: 7). And the Judge stated in court that 'if he had his way Morris . . . would be sent indefinitely to Rampton High Security Hospital or jailed for life' (1997: 7). In fact, psychiatric opinion was sought and he was admitted to a medium secure unit and, later, turned down by a special hospital.

THE MENTAL HEALTH ACT

The experiences of black people within forensic psychiatry catalogue a systemic response which is consistently inadequate and inappropriate in meeting the mental health needs of black people who gain mental health treatment through the criminal justice system. The Mental Health Act (Her Majesty's Stationery Office (HMSO), 1983) and the Code of Practice (Department of Health and Welsh Office, 1993) are the tools which govern what happens to people with mental health problems – generally and in a forensic sense. In theory they contain safeguards to protect the rights of individuals. In practice, and in relation to black people's experiences, these safeguards are themselves flawed because of the Act's failure to incorporate a realistic ethos of culture and race.

In its *Fourth Biennial Report*, the Mental Health Act Commission (1991) commented that 'many professionals seem to lack basic knowledge about the different needs of ethnic minority communities and to have little real understanding of institutional racism and the effect of cultural differences in the nature of mental disorder' (1991: 17). A recent review (Cochrane and Sashidharan, 1996) pointed out that 'the powers conferred on psychiatrists (and others) by the 1983 Mental Health Act exceed those available to police officers or virtually anyone else in our society', and went on to state: 'Add the ethnic dimension to this and a very potent brew of racial suspicion and distrust is created' (1996: 107–8).

Provisions

The Mental Health Act (HMSO, 1983) establishes the framework for the compulsory admission of people to psychiatric hospitals and covers a range of provisions in relation to detained patients. Individuals may be admitted under Section 2 of the Act for assessment (twenty-eight days maximum), Section 3 for treatment (six months maximum but renewable), and under Section 4 in situations of urgent necessity (seventy-two hours maximum). The need for detention has to be in the interests of the person's health or safety, or for the protection of other people. The Code of Practice (Department of Health and Welsh Office, 1993) gives guidance on the application of the Act and clarifies the roles of the professionals involved. This Code states that 'people being assessed for possible admission under the Act or to whom the Act applies should receive respect for and consideration of their individual qualities and diverse background – social, cultural, ethnic and religious' (1993: 1). However, apart from calling for the use of 'interpreters' (1993: 14), the Code gives no guidance on the implementation of 'respect' for social, ethnic and religious diversity. What it often means in practice is that black people who are detained under the forensic sections of the Act, are compulsorily committed by practitioners who have only a remote idea in many instances of the diverse cultures represented by the patients with whom they come in contact and more often than not, are not interested (or perhaps do not know how to begin) to incorporate a cultural perspective in interventions which are part of the processes of the Act's requirements. The consequences of this 'head buried in the sand' approach are disastrous for black people who encounter the mental health system. They are detained in secure provision – either in locked wards in psychiatric hospitals, medium secure units or, at the most severe end, special hospitals, but their detention is rarely reviewed by panels which reflect a cultural or ethnic diversity. The bodies that have power to review (for example, mental health review tribunals or hospital managers) are under no obligation to ensure ethnic diversity among their members nor, except rarely, are they trained to assess issues of race and culture. (It is important to point out that there are a few instances of good practice that the author is aware of.)

Some idea of the uphill struggle that black detained patients are faced with can be gained by looking at the problems experienced by detained patients in general. Some detained patients are unaware of their rights under the Mental Health Act 1983, including the right to refuse medication and treatment. A study by City and Hackney MIND on patients at Hackney Hospital, London (Glasman, 1994) found:

> Patients, many of whom were sectioned, were also unaware of their rights. Nineteen had not heard of Mental Health Review Tribunals, while the majority did not know about hospital managers hearings.
>
> (1994: 4)

In the case of people held within the forensic psychiatry system (referred to as 'mentally disordered offenders') many have not been convicted of, or even charged with, an offence (MIND, 1996b). Consequently, they may well harbour a sense of grievance at being detained with people who have been convicted of offences. It is possible that this feeling may be more prevalent among black people than among others, because they are discriminated against in so many other spheres of their lives anyway.

DIVERSION FROM THE CRIMINAL JUSTICE SYSTEM

The process by which people with mental health problems are taken out of the criminal justice system (CJS) – police, courts, prisons – and placed within the psychiatric system is called diversion from custody. MIND's recently published policy on *People With Mental Health Problems and the Criminal Justice System* (MIND, 1996c) notes:

> Since British criminal law does not adequately distinguish between those who should and should not be held responsible, some of the people who are convicted will not have been fully responsible for their crime; others will be. Moreover, the pattern of arrest, conviction and diversion to different types of facility shows clear inequalities on the basis of race and gender. For instance, black men are more likely to be arrested, ordered to hospital by a court and, once in hospital, to be given high doses of medication.
>
> (1996c: 1)

The process

Home Office guidance (Home Office, 1990, 1995) has established a specified structure for managing people who have been earmarked for leaving the criminal justice system in favour of receiving care and treatment within the mental health system. In recent years, the policy of diversion has gained impetus as a way of dealing more effectively with people who do not belong in the CJS. Many practitioners in the criminal justice system, as well as in health and social services, share a consensus that diversion from custody is desirable. The report issued jointly by three organisations (NACRO/Mental Health Foundation/Home Office, 1994) took as its starting-point the view that 'all agencies involved with mentally disturbed offenders should actively adopt the recommendations of the *Home Office Circular 66/90* (Home Office, 1990) to allow for opportunities for diversion from the criminal justice system and discontinuance by the Crown Prosecution Service' (1994: 65). In the consultative document on the diversion of mentally disordered offenders, MIND noted:

> Race and gender form obvious contexts within which to assess the policy of diversion. In particular, we feel it is necessary to question: the basis on which decisions to transfer a mentally disordered offender from the criminal justice system are made; the pathways to secure provision for women and black people and the extent to which an understanding of the relevance of those pathways is understood and incorporated into diagnosis, care and treatment; the extent to which the needs of black people/women labelled as mentally disordered offenders are met by diversion into secure provision; the extent to which they are not; and the extent to which the care of mentally disordered offenders is hindered by diversion policies.
>
> (1996b: 4)

The process of diversion incorporates a variety of legislation (e.g. Mental Health Act 1983; Criminal Procedure (Insanity and Unfitness to Plead) Act 1991; Police and Criminal Evidence Act 1984) and guidance, for example in *Home Office Circular 66/90* (Home Office, 1990) and *Home Office Circular 93/91* (Home Office, 1991) relating to supervision and treatment orders, and 91/92 (Home Office, 1992) relating to pre-sentence and medical reports pertaining to the following stages and considerations (MIND, 1996b).

Legal representation

Legal representatives, e.g. solicitors acting in defence of mentally disordered suspects, have a role to play in helping to ensure that the legal rights, as well as the treatment and care needs of mentally disordered offenders are met. Recent guidance from the Home Office and the Department of Health recommends that all criminal law solicitors, particularly duty solicitors, should find out about local facilities and services for mentally disordered people.

At the police station

The police may be the first contact that mentally disordered people have with the criminal justice system. This may be because intervention is called for under the terms of Sections 135 and 136 of the Mental Health Act 1983 (HMSO, 1983) in the interests of a mentally disordered person who may be thought to be in need of care or control. It may also be because the person is suspected of committing an offence. Evidence suggests a higher incidence of police involvement and assessment at police stations, and a lower involvement of GPs in the initiation of compulsory detention of African-Caribbean people (when compared to whites) (Morley *et al.*, 1991).

The responsibility for the identification of mentally vulnerable suspects lies with the custody officer, where necessary advised by the police surgeon (forensic medical examiner). Options available to the police are arrest for the criminal offence and removal to a place of safety for assessment under Section 136 of the Mental Health Act (Morley *et al.*, 1991) (see Chapter 12).

The aftermath of arrest for a criminal offence may be: (a) no action; (b) a caution; (c) police bail to return to the police station; (d) police bail to attend court (and/or psychiatric referral); or (e) no bail, i.e., custody, appearance in court. The presence of an appropriate adult is required during the questioning of 'mentally disordered' people suspected of committing an offence. The aim of the role of the appropriate adult is to protect the interests and rights of the person. Social workers may act as an appropriate adult for mentally disordered offenders.

In the case of removal to a place of safety for assessment, *Home Office Circular 66/90* calls for agreement to be reached with local hospitals and social services departments so that persons detained under Section 136 are assessed by a psychiatrist and interviewed by an approved social worker (ASW) as soon as possible for the purpose of making necessary arrangements for the person's care or treatment. This can result in formal or informal admission to hospital (with or without further police action). However, here too, evidence points to disproportionate representation of black people. It has been reported that sixteen per cent of requests (under Section 136) for ASWs, involved non-white people (10 per cent related to African-Caribbeans) compared to an estimated 6.4 per cent in the general population in the area studied (MIND, 1996c).

Diversion at the point of arrest

Home Office Circular 66/90 calls, wherever possible, for people who are felt to be mentally disordered offenders to receive care and treatment from the health and social services. A number of schemes are in operation around the country at police stations to accomplish this. If mental disorder is suspected, under the diversion process, an offender should be assessed, ideally, by trained professionals – ASW, psychiatrist or community psychiatric nurse (CPN). Increasingly, many black professionals and others argue that assessment should also take account of race and cultural factors/considerations.

Crown Prosecution Service

If charges are brought, evidence is presented to the Crown Prosecution Service (CPS), which decides whether a prosecution is needed in the public interest. Papers presented to the CPS will include information on a person's mental condition. In serious cases, a prosecution will usually take place unless there are public interest factors against, which outweigh those in favour. The existence of mental disorder is a factor against prosecution, which must be weighed against the seriousness of the offence and the possibility that it might be repeated. The needs of the defendant must be balanced against the needs of society: if the offence is serious, it remains likely that a prosecution will be needed in the public interest. Yet, given what is known about the disproportionate public fears of black men in particular, it is clear that 'it is race which is the underlying issue in crime, danger and mental illness, though the concern is not explicitly stated' (Francis, 1996: 4).

Probation Service

Where prosecution is necessary in the public interest, the probation service should ensure that the CPS and the courts have relevant information to enable the court to decide whether the defendant can be safely bailed or remanded to hospital instead of prison before conviction and sentence, and to decide on the suitability of non-custodial disposals after conviction. Chief probation officers are expected to do the following: (a) review arrangements for cooperation and joint planning of services with local health authorities and social services departments and other agencies, including voluntary agencies, to ensure that: alternatives to prison custody are available so that the court can consider these options before and after conviction, where prosecution is not necessary in the public interest, other effective courses of action are available, and the needs of mentally disordered offenders are considered when partnership plans are drawn up; (b) ensure, where defendants who might benefit from psychiatric assessment are identified, that the court receives appropriate information about the person's condition and the available treatment services; (c) facilitate access to accommodation to help avoid prison custody being used in default of more appropriate accommodation; (d) advise the court on possible options other than imprisonment, both in general and in individual cases in the pre-sentence report.

Magistrates/Crown Court

Magistrates and judges have the following options available to them: (a) court bail; (b) acquittal; (c) absolute or conditional discharge; (d) probation order (with or without out-patient treatment; (e) guardianship order under the Mental Health Act 1983; (f) absolute discharge Criminal Procedure (Insanity and Unfitness to Plead) Act 1991 (CPIA) supervision and treatment order; (g) guardianship order (CPIA). The courts can also: (a) commit for trial and sentence; (b) commit to hospital under Section 37 of the Mental Health Act – with or without conviction; (c) allow court bail (with condition of hospital residence); (d) remand for psychiatric reports under Section 35 of the Mental Health Act; or (e) issue a probation order (with condition of in-patient treatment or as specified). Crown courts can, in addition, issue: (a) an order for remand for treatment; (b) an interim hospital order under Section 38 of the Mental Health Act; (c) a hospital order under Section 37 of the Mental Health Act, with or without restrictions under its Section 41 or CPIA. Under *Home Office Circular 12/95* (Home Office, 1990), which builds on *Home Office Circular 66/90* (Home Office, 1990), magistrates and judges are asked: (a) when making decisions on remands or imprisonment, to bear in mind that custody is inefficient as a means solely to obtain medical reports or to meet treatment needs and (b) that where bail is requested, mentally disordered people have the same right to bail as everyone else.

Court diversion

A number of assessment schemes operate in Magistrates Courts. The aim is to offer psychiatric assessment services based at court to divert people classed as 'mentally disordered offenders' away from prison or remands to prison and to facilitate access to health and care agencies.

Prison

The NHS is responsible for providing treatment for mentally disordered offenders who require treatment in hospital for their mental disorder. The prison service is responsible for the provision of primary health care compatible in range and quality to that provided in the community by general practitioners and out-patient services. Mentally disordered offenders needing psychiatric in-patient treatment should be transferred to hospital for treatment. For prisoners who are regarded as requiring treatment in hospital for mental disorder, arrangements will be made to transfer them to hospital under the provisions of Sections 47 and 48 of the Mental Health Act 1983.

Remand prisoners

Where a remand prisoner is transferred to hospital under Section 48 for treatment, the receiving hospital will wish to consider whether it would be appropriate to recommend to the court detention in hospital after conviction through the making of a hospital order (S37) or the suitability of some other form of treatment-oriented disposal, such as a probation order with a condition of psychiatric treatment or a guardianship order. In the *Home Office Circular 12/95* (Home Office, 1995), prison medical officers are asked to sustain and develop arrangements for identifying and transferring to hospital prisoners needing psychiatric in-patient treatment, with special regard to remand prisoners. Again, the disproportionate representation of black people in relation to their numbers in the population means that they are most likely to enter the psychiatric system through this means.

CONCLUSIONS

The institutions which are brought to bear on the lives of black people – whether mentally disordered or not – are not colour blind, despite the pretence that they are. In any event, a blindness to colour is not what is needed. Instead, an acknowledgement of the existence of and capacity for societal institutions to perpetuate racism within the media, the criminal justice system and the forensic psychiatric system is much more useful. This at least could pave the way for real change in the status quo, and signal to black people that an understanding of their situation within society in general would be part and parcel of creating a fundamental shift in public policy and practice.

Chapter 12

Expectations and experiences

The mechanisms which govern disposals for people with mental health problems who come into contact with the criminal justice system would appear to be straightforward. Injection of the dimension of race, however, creates a more complicated picture.

FORENSIC PATHWAYS INTO THE MENTAL HEALTH SYSTEM

The inadequacies and inequalities which characterise black people's experience of mental health service delivery have been well documented by black mental health professionals and others in recent years (Fernando, 1988, 1991; Sashidharan, 1994a; Wilson, 1993b; MIND, 1993; Mental Health Foundation, 1995; Littlewood and Lipsedge, 1982). Documentation, however, has not led to concerted and consistent attempts to change the status quo to any appreciable extent. Bhui (1997) notes: 'So decades of persuasive research findings, tragedies, working parties, committees, enquiries, "political first aid" and health service restructuring, all designed to deliver effective care to all people, have failed black people. While these facts are well known, the barriers to progress remain diverse, institutionalised and manifest through contradictory ideologies and theoretical frameworks for conceptualising a solution' (1997: 144).

A new training pack (University of Manchester, Department of Health, 1996) intended for use by a wide range of mental health professionals, including psychiatrists, social workers, community psychiatric nurses, etc., identifies the following causes for concern in relation to the care and treatment of black people with mental health problems:

> First, the disproportionate numbers of African-Caribbeans in psychiatric wards, particularly the higher rates for compulsory detention under The Mental Health Act, 1983, for people of African-Caribbean origin, and also for some people of Asian origins;
>
> Second, there have been reports of more compulsory admissions of black patients under the 'forensic' sections of the Mental Health Act, 1983, and more transfers of patients to secure wards for reasons unconnected with violence;
>
> Third, one study found that people from the Caribbean living in stable families were more likely than whites in similar situations to be admitted to hospital by the police, rather than through GPs. The situation has not been helped by the lack of ethnic monitoring of services.
>
> (1996: 102)

A study by Davies *et al.* (1996) concluded that, independent of psychiatric diagnosis and sociodemographic differences, black African and black Caribbean patients (compared to white patients) with a diagnosis of 'psychosis' in south London were more likely to have been detained under the Mental Health Act 1983. At a recent conference, Bartlett (1995) noted, 'the dilemma between custody and treatment stems from the position of the patient, who is subject to a variety of constraints'. These emanate from hospital managers, purchasers of services, the courts, the Home Office and the Department of Health but (according to Bartlett) 'most of the anxieties about control are filtered through the clinical team, which are then brought to bear on the patient'. So clearly, an accurate perspective on black people's experience of the mental health system via the criminal justice system is a perspective that goes beyond the publicly stated policy for practice. In this regard, it is useful to discuss: the use of S136 of the Mental Health Act in relation to African-Caribbean men, risk assessment and legislation and policy changes that result in increasingly punitive and restrictive 'disposals'.

SECTION 136

The legal power authorising the police to detain a 'mentally disordered person' in the community is set out in Section 136 of the Mental Health Act 1983 which states:

> (1) If a constable finds in a place to which the public have access a person who appears to him to be suffering from mental disorder and to be in immediate need of care or control, the constable may, if he thinks it necessary to do so in the interests of that person or for the protection of other persons, remove that person to a place of safety within the meaning of Section 135 above. (2) A person removed to a place of safety under this section may be detained there for a period not exceeding 72 hours for the purpose of enabling him to be examined by a registered medical practitioner and to be interviewed by an Approved Social Worker and of making any necessary arrangements for his treatment or care.
>
> (R. M. Jones, 1996: 354)

Section 136 is the only section in the Mental Health Act which specifically authorises the removal from a public place of a person suspected of being mentally disordered. The police have been given the power to initiate the section because they and not other professionals have traditionally had jurisdiction in public areas (Rogers and Faulkner, 1987). The length of detention allowed under this power 'greatly exceeds the normal maximum period of detention of 24 hours for a criminal suspect' (Roughton, 1994: 2).

Studies in the 1980s found that African-Caribbeans were particularly likely to be detained under S136 and were over-represented under this section compared to their numbers in the general population (Rogers and Faulkner, 1987). A study by the West Midlands police (Roughton, 1994) indicates that this fact still applies: 'According to 1991 census figures, black African/Caribbean groups make up only 3.6 per cent of the overall population of the West Midlands yet accounted for 13.5 per cent of the s.136 sample' (1994: 5). A number of reasons have been advanced (see, for example, Rogers and Faulkner, 1987) for the disproportionate use of S136 in relation to African-Caribbeans. These reasons include the following: (a) black people's behaviour is open to misinterpretation because of ignorance about their culture, language and mores; (b) the view among many black groups and organisations that mental health legislation is primarily used as a means of maintaining law and order, directed in particular towards black people; and (c) black people's routes into mental health service delivery is less often through their GPs and more often at a point of crisis.

A study on race and compulsory detention under the civil

sections of the Mental Health Act (D. Browne, 1997) analysed the records of 224 people in one London borough, who had been compulsorily detained during the twenty-six months from January, 1989 to February 1992. Interviews were conducted with consultants, police divisions and approved social workers, covering three main areas: their responsibilities and the procedures they followed; how they made decisions; and specific race issues. Browne found that, since neither the Code of Practice (see Chapter 11) nor specific guidelines drawn up between health authorities, the local authority and the police, made any reference to race, ethnicity or culture (with reference to an operational policy for S136), the way was left open for professionals to make individual interpretation about behaviour etc. of people who might be 'mentally ill'. This led to the misreading of behaviour of black people and allowed stereotypical assumptions and perceptions to influence decisions. The study quoted the following statement by a policeman as an example of what happens in practice:

> If you can't understand them, they probably won't be able to understand you, and the more likely you are to find yourself using some form of restraint. Violence is more of a factor because persuasion can't be used – and particular groups do tend to be more excitable than others. One race that tends to get excited are Nigerians. It's the same with people from Arab countries. I mean, they really know how to demonstrate don't they. Add to this a 136 situation where a person might be excited anyway.
>
> (D. Browne, 1997:10)

In a similar vein, the West Midlands police study noted that 'given the fact that an arrest under S136 relies heavily on the discretion of the arresting officer, police discrimination is a factor which cannot be completely discounted when attempting to explain this apparent disparity' (Roughton, 1994: 5).

Browne (1997) found that approved social workers considered as a group tended to take greater precautions when dealing with black people (compared to white people), and were therefore more likely to call on the police for help. Interestingly, they felt that the police tended to 'overreact' when they heard that the person who might need sectioning was black. One social worker described an occasion when six police officers arrived in a transit van, instead of the one officer she had asked for, to accompany someone from a largely black housing estate (1997: 10). One black social worker recalled that, as a trainee, she had seen a white social worker signing detention papers for a black client without an interview (ibid.: 11). Most of the fourteen approved social workers interviewed considered there to be a connection between 'race' and mental pathology, the following comment being typical:

> There is a false pathology seen in some cultures by the professionals involved . . . yes, the police are guilty, but so are many GPs, psychiatrists, and social workers. This is bound to affect the way they carry out assessments.
>
> (ibid.: 10)

It is clear from the evidence that professionals' subjective interpretations, based on widely held perceptions about black people, can and do lead to the application of the more controlling and compulsory sections of the Mental Health Act. So the problem for black people is that widely perceived stereotypes hinder their care and treatment. When 'help' is promulgated in mental health, as elsewhere, it is likely to fall wide of the mark because of the motivation and motives of professionals who provide it, and in the outcomes and consequences for black people who receive it. Yvonne Christie (1995), a community worker with a great deal of experience states black people are:

> seemingly the easiest community to understand, and the group that is visually the most assimilated to Western Society and lifestyles. Alas, they are also the most researched and most overrepresented proportionally and the most abused in the field of psychiatry, medium secure units, court diversion schemes and prisons. This statement, although fully evidenced, also tends to be the most dismissed and ignored in service planning and delivery. Why else would this type of response continue?
>
> (1995: 5)

RISK ASSESSMENT

Owen (1992) argues that 'the spectre of dangerousness both defines the function of psychiatry and legitimates its operation' (1992: 239). In any discussion of risk assessment, invocation of the 'spectre of dangerousness' is never far behind. This has particular significance for African-Caribbean men, who are often regarded as dangerous, and therefore, as presenting a high risk for committing violence (see, for example, Francis, 1996). Equally, however, any discussion of risk assessment often begs the question as to whose criteria (for such assessment) are being used. In other words, risk is not an objective exercise, and the committal of people (and in particular black people) to psychiatric institutions on the basis of their perceived risk, must be open to question as to the criteria in operation (as discussed in Chapter 4). In a talk at a national conference on forensic psychiatry, criminologist Herschel Prins (1995) suggested that risk assessment must be discussed in terms of: (a) context, (b) communication, (c) vulnerability, and (d) making assumptions from an adequate baseline. His discussion is relevant to an examination of how risk assessment is used in relation to black people.

Context

Prins (1995) argues that the context in which risk assessment takes place currently represents 'a penology motivated by issues relating to public protection, resulting in an uneasy compromise between penologists and clinicians'. Government legislation on supervised discharge (HMSO, 1995) and *Guidance on the Discharge from Hospital of Mentally Disordered Offenders* (Department of Health, 1994b) emphasise on the need to manage potentially dangerous or difficult people in the criminal justice and health care systems. Prins notes that the dangers of too much prescriptive legislation and guidance can 'cloud the issue and prevent more positive action being taken'. For example, once a patient is placed on a supervision register, it may be considered easier to leave them there and take no further action.

Communication

In assessing risk, there is a need for adequate communication between professionals. including communication between the client/patient/worker. It also includes workers' acknowledging and examining what Prins terms 'their own prejudices and blindspots as regards race/ethnicity; gender; and behaviour that induces fear in us'.

Vulnerability

Risk assessment is concerned with the prevention of vulnerability. The degree to which that vulnerability can be prevented does not just depend on the clinician's skills, but on available resources. In terms of black people and risk assessment, it can also be argued that the notion of vulnerability must also encompass the vulnerability of those being assessed.

Operating from an informed baseline

Prins notes that within the criminal justice system an informed baseline 'means having full details and reports of index offences for prognostic purposes', but emphasises the 'need to carefully analyse data and carry out screening'. When assessing the baseline from which consideration of assessing the risk of black people begins, the inescapable argument is that it is frequently inadequate. MIND (1996c) states in its recent consultation document on mentally disordered offenders that:

> The assessment of risk has been equated with 'flying without instruments'. The public perception is that violence and mental health problems are firmly linked. Media terms such as 'psycho', 'schizo' etc. fuel such perceptions. The public wants certainty and absolute security, yet for professionals charged with making assessments of people classed as mentally disordered offenders, the one real certainty is that there are few predicators as to the risk that people may pose.
>
> (1996c: 22)

People with mental health problems who come into contact with the criminal justice system ('mentally disordered offenders') are regarded by many people – general public and professionals alike – as blameworthy, and generally 'not very nice'. There is an increasing tendency, because of this and because of the high profile given to acts of homicide and other occurrences committed by people with mental health problems, to err on the side of caution when assessing the risk they may pose to themselves or others. Gwen Adshead (1996), forensic consultant at Broadmoor Hospital, states: 'I have no doubt from my own knowledge that patients' discharges are being hampered by concerns about risk, and releases are being delayed because psychiatrists are being asked to put public safety first (1996: 14). Research suggests that as many as two out of three people who are detained in hospital on the grounds that they pose a risk are perfectly safe (MIND, 1996c).

The tendency to lock up mentally disordered offenders who are considered a risk to the public has special significance with regard to race. This is because assessment which is prone to uncertainty and ambiguity leaves too much room for error in relation to black people, who may be assessed on the basis of faulty information, and also because the narrow margins within which such assessment procedures operate – i.e. from the starting-point of the Eurocentric perspective as normality – disadvantage and disregard the realities of black people's lives.

INQUIRY REPORTS

Over the past few years, several inquiries have been launched into untoward incidents involving people who had at some time been diagnosed as suffering from a 'mental disorder'. Many of these have involved black people – as people inquired into (rather than those carrying out the inquiry). Francis (1996) notes:

> Almost every major and heavily reported case involving lapses in community care has involved young black men. They are the most feared sector of our population and their predicament commands a disproportionate amount of attention by the media. Yet legitimate concerns such as unemployment, education, housing, family life are barely mentioned. Readers and television viewers are left with subconscious associations between the spectre of unprovoked, inexplicable murder in the street and black psychiatric patients, a potentially explosive combination.
>
> (1996: 4)

Bennett (1996) argues:

> In the last five years what impresses one is not the stigma of mental illness, but the increased willingness, particularly by the press . . . to scapegoat the mentally ill. There has been *no increase* in the number of homicides admitted to special hospitals when care and treatment in mental hospitals has been transferred to the community. The value of repeated inquiries is also considered, for they do little to lessen scapegoating.
>
> (1996: 300)

Many reports have been followed by some action, usually of a repressive nature and nearly always not involving added expenditure. Here again, perceptions and misconceptions result in public policies which fail to meet black people's needs, and even when black people who are obviously in need present themselves for help, inherent failures in the system mean that their needs are not met. The inquiry into the case of Christopher Clunis (Northeast Thames and Southeast Thames Regional Health Authorities, 1994) provides invaluable insight into this regard.

Christopher Clunis

Christopher Clunis, a young, African-Caribbean man, had a history of psychiatric illness, dating from his early twenties. In December 1992 he attacked and stabbed to death a stranger, Jonathan Zito, at a London tube station.

Christopher Clunis was well known to a range of health, housing and social services agencies because of his history of psychiatric illness, yet despite his repeated incidents of violence and threats of violence, failure to attend appointments and unwillingness to engage with the agencies involved, inadequate action was taken to safeguard both his own interests and those of the public. The inadequacy of the care and treatment provided to Christopher Clunis was in part to do with poor communication and interaction and lack of consistency between health and welfare agencies; in part to do with a system forced to operate at the cutting edge with understaffing and poor resources; and in part, to do with his blackness. The result was that he was allowed to fall victim to the anomalies which can arise both in terms of the misguided, but inconsistent and incoherent attempts not to stigmatise him; and at the same time because of the failure of a majority of those acting on his behalf, to recognise the person who presented to them. Both courses occurred as a result of blinkered views.

The inquiry found failures in the following areas :

> communicating and passing on information and liaison between all those who were or should have been concerned with Christopher Clunis' care; to contact and involve the patient's family and general practitioner in the provision of care; to obtain an accurate history; to consider or assess Christopher Clunis' past history of violence and to assess his propensity for violence

> in the future; to plan, provide or monitor S117 Mental Health Act 1983 aftercare; to provide assertive care when the patient is living in the community and to note and act upon warning signs and symptoms to prevent a relapse; to identify the particular needs of homeless itinerant mentally ill patients on discharge from hospital, to keep track of such persons and to provide for their care even when they cross geographical boundaries; to provide qualified social workers, including sufficient numbers of approved social workers, to assess all new referrals and to provide supervision and leadership; of the police adequately to recognise and deal appropriately with mentally ill people; to conduct an internal inquiry that was fair, objective and independent.
>
> (adapted from pages 105–6 of Northeast Thames and Southeast Thames Regional Health Authorities, 1994)

A signal feature of Clunis' case was that, early on, he was alienated from the system that was meant to help him (Dick, 1994: 6–7).

The inquiry report itself, while acknowledging the extent to which there were 'missed opportunities' on the part of agencies which were meant to help him, notes in its discussion on the assessment of dangerousness, that 'an accurate and verified history of a patient is vital in making such an assessment' (Northeast Thames and Southeast Thames Regional Health Authorities, 1994: 118). It continued: 'the assessment of the risk of violence should never be a hasty guess following a simple examination of the patient's current mental state at interview' (ibid.: 119). The report added: 'We are sure that Christopher Clunis was entitled to better care than he received and that the risk of his danger to the public was not properly assessed' (ibid.: 74). In calling for better training for psychiatrists and mental health workers and other professionals to equip them with the skills necessary to make appropriate assessments, the report stated: 'At the very least, they should be given sufficient training to recognise the limits of their personal knowledge and to understand the role of forensic services' (ibid.: 119). Yet, it is clear that Christopher Clunis slipped through the net and failed to get the care that he needed because he was black. Perhaps the most telling aspect of the report is found in the following passage:

> Accounts of Christopher Clunis frequently refer to his considerable height and powerful build. Yet he was very often referred to

> as a friendly giant, rather than a threat. The fact that he is articulate and well spoken has perhaps meant that he was *not subject to racial stereotyping and pre-conception.* On the other hand it was clear from all we have seen and heard that he was determined to pursue his own goals, and he often actively resisted help. It is a feature of the case that we can find not one occasion when Christopher Clunis attended an out-patient appointment. We recognise that it would be difficult for doctors and social workers to counter such a combination of physical presence, verbal strength and fierce determination on the part of any patient. *The added factor of his blackness may have contributed to the diffident manner in which some professionals treated him, and it may have caused them to defer, against his best interests, to his own expressed wishes.*
>
> (emphasis added, 1994: 8)

The case of Christopher Clunis illustrates the danger of reliance on stereotypical assumptions and perceptions at one extreme. Though Christopher Clunis was clearly a person in need of help, he did not receive it because of contradictory and inadequate assessments, responses and views made and held by health and social services agencies. Although Christopher Clunis was perceived as big and black, mental health and social services did not consider him to be a risk to others, in part because he was – against type – articulate! Also, assessments about what he needed and should have received in terms of care and treatment were hampered because mental health professionals may have been intimidated by both his size and his blackness. The mental health assessment team which attempted to assess Christopher Clunis in November 1992, for example, had no idea of what he looked like, except that he was black (ibid.: 85).

The point to be made here is that the majority of interventions made on behalf of Christopher Clunis, which included assessment and the responses (or lack of responses) which occurred as a result, were inherently flawed because of the propensity to regard Clunis, first and foremost as black, with all the implications and misinformation associated with it. This meant that the fact that he was/is a person with glaring needs, who required sustained and consistent care and attention, was obscured. An obvious need was for housing, yet Christopher Clunis was never found appropriate housing.

Following the death of Jonathan Zito, and after his committal to

Rampton Hospital, Clunis was interviewed by the inquiry team: 'His subsequent memory of admissions to hospitals or hostels and of the care he received, is of needing help, but not knowing how to ask for it; of lack of explanation as to what he was suffering from; of frustration that he was not being involved in the decisions that were being made for him; and an absence of planned help towards settling down in a home of his own' (ibid.: 103).

It must be noted that although the system's failure of Clunis was governed by an apparent consensus *not* to label him, it was nevertheless undertaken within a context which could not regard him as a man in need of help. He was instead regarded as a *black* man who went against type. He should have been regarded as a person with a mental health problem that needed appropriate attention. Because he was not, the opportunity to help him was lost.

The inquiry into the case of Christopher Clunis illustrates an important point that needs underscoring regarding inquiries in general – that is, they take place with the benefit of hindsight. Rather than leading to more effective preventive measures, however (inquiry after inquiry has consistently called for greater communication, more multidisciplinary, multi-agency working practices, etc.), they instead result in harsher and more punitive responses in relation to people who are mentally ill. Because of the realities of who goes into the psychiatric system through the forensic sections of the Mental Health Act 1983, it is clear that it is black men, in particular, African-Caribbean men, who bear the brunt of these policies.

Nevertheless, it cannot fail to be lost on even the casual observer that much of the prescriptive legislation and guidance now on the statute books occurred in the wake of Christopher Clunis' actions.

Orville Blackwood

The case of Orville Blackwood is illustrative of the opposite end of the spectrum in relation to how black men, in particular African-Caribbean men, are dealt with by the forensic mental health system, which regards them as 'big, black and dangerous' – the subtitle of the inquiry report (Special Hospitals Service Authority, 1993). It also indicates the extent to which perceptions based on stereotypical images again hinder black people getting the appropriate help they need. The inquiry team noted: 'The term "big, black and dangerous" seems to be frequently used to describe ethnic minority offender patients, particularly African-Caribbean offender patients.

We think it encapsulates some of the misconceptions which may influence the handling of such patients' (1993: 4).

Orville Blackwood was one of three African-Caribbean men who died between 1984 and 1991 at Broadmoor Hospital, after being placed in the seclusion wing. In July 1984 Michael Martin died on Cromer Ward; in August 1988 Joseph Watts died on Folkestone Ward and in August 1991 Orville Blackwood died in a special care unit. Each death was followed by an inquiry. The first two resulted in recommendations aimed at preventing future deaths. But Orville Blackwood still died.

According to the inquiry report, Orville Blackwood had a history of 'being strong-willed and unwilling to accept advice from his own family'. He had a long criminal history, 'first coming to police attention at the age of ten when he was cautioned for trespass' (1993: 5). Orville Blackwood's crimes included theft, deception, assaulting police, and taking without consent, robbery and burglary. He received cautions, spells in detention centres, prison sentences (e.g. six months in 1985 for actual bodily harm and criminal damage). From 1982 when he received his first admission to Tooting Bec Hospital, initially as an informal patient, and subsequently detained under the Mental Health Act 1959, to his death in 1991, he was in and out of prisons and psychiatric hospitals on a "revolving door" basis.

Although the inquiry into Orville Blackwood's death acknowledged his illness, importantly, the inquiry team also undertook to assess the underlying motives governing how he was dealt with by mental health services.

Insight and IQ

The inquiry noted the conflicting assessments made by black and white psychiatrists on Orville Blackwood. The director of medical services at Broadmoor Hospital said that Orville Blackwood, 'suffered from delusions and had no insight into his illness most of the time'. Dr Aggrey Burke, a black consultant psychiatrist who saw Orville Blackwood, concluded that he was *not* without insight, rather, he had *profound* insight:

> This view was not shared on the ward. The nurses we spoke to often referred to Orville Blackwood's lack of insight, and this incapacity seemed to have applied to other areas of his illness. For example in discussing patients such as Orville Blackwood

> who believed they were only detained in Broadmoor Hospital because they were 'big, black men' we were told that all the patients were there simply because they were mentally ill but they often blamed their detention on other things because of *their lack of insight*. We were told that this was a common theme in all patients, not just African-Caribbean patients.
>
> (1993:17)

The inquiry took evidence from Orville Blackwood's family, which supported Dr Burke's diagnosis: 'His sister said he would compare himself to other people in the hospital and ask himself why he was there' (ibid.:17). 'So Orville Blackwood decided to play along and said he accepted he was mentally ill. But his sister informed us that his doctor told the family that this proved he must be mentally ill' (ibid.:17).

Diagnosis

The inquiry noted differences of opinion regarding Orville Blackwood's precise diagnosis, between the director of medical services at Broadmoor and Dr Burke, although there was agreement that he was suffering from a psychotic illness. Interestingly, however, Broadmoor's medical director diagnosed 'chronic schizophrenic condition', while Dr Burke termed the illness 'stress-related acute psychotic disorder'. While noting diagnosis did not play a significant part in the events leading up to Orville Blackwood's death, the report stated: 'diagnosis did . . . play a very significant role in his admission to secure psychiatric facilities and eventually to Broadmoor' (ibid.: 18).

Violence and dangerousness

The report noted that:

> Orville Blackwood did not believe he should ever have been sent to Broadmoor Hospital. He did not believe that he should have been treated in the special care unit. He did not believe he should have been detained for as long as he had been, given the nature of his index offence. He felt that he had been harshly and unfairly dealt with, and his anger and frustration at this unfairness sometimes manifested themselves through aggression and violence.
>
> (ibid. : 22)

The report concluded that anger and frustration at being detained in Broadmoor had played 'a very significant part in the circumstances leading to his death' and went on to note:

> Special hospitals exist to care for patients who require treatment under conditions of maximum security because of their 'dangerous, violent or criminal propensities'. In order to be deemed suitable for admission to special hospital a patient should 'present a grave and immediate danger to the public' and not be able to be managed under condition of lesser security. The question we have asked ourselves is *whether Orville Blackwood presented such a grave and immediate danger while he was in the community. In other words, was Orville Blackwood inherently dangerous; or did he become frustrated, angry and aggressive because of his incarceration?*
>
> (emphasis added, ibid.: 22)

Dr Burke had concluded that there was no good evidence that Orville Blackwood was a danger to the public when he was in the community; and that furthermore in the two and half years he had known him 'he had never been convinced that he had been properly placed in secure facilities or that if he had he should have remained there'. This was a view reinforced by other psychiatrists who also saw Orville Blackwood.

Racism

An important component of the inquiry report into the death of Orville Blackwood was its noteworthy refusal to shy away from the part played by racism both in attitudes concerning and treatment given to Orville Blackwood. It noted:

> It is important the hospital recognises that racism is not something that happens only 'out there'; in many ways the problem is imported with the admission of patients who feel they have been victimised by the system. Nor is it sufficient to treat all patients the same, as one senior manager told us was the Broadmoor Hospital practice. This implies that all patients are treated as white European men.
>
> (ibid.: 51)

There is no doubt that Orville Blackwood did suffer from mental distress; but mental health professionals chose, in the main, to approach any 'illness' they diagnosed from a perspective which took little account of who Orville Blackwood was – in terms of stresses and conditioning exacerbated by an indifferent society. The labels applied to Orville Blackwood, labels which created a host of expectations and pre-conceptions on the part of those charged with delivering care and treatment to him, set in motion the series of events which led to his eventual death. That labelling process involves racism. The inquiry noted:

> Patients are aware that racism exists, but because the staff and management at the hospital do not recognise the subtle way in which racism can operate they do not see it as a problem and there is a dissonance of viewpoint. Broadmoor Hospital is a white, middle-class institution in rural Berkshire. African-Caribbean patients from poor inner city areas therefore find themselves in an alien environment. The closed, in-bred community of nurses some from a military-type background, has little understanding of the needs and cultural differences of ethnic minority patients. It is not good enough to maintain that all patients are treated the same, regardless of colour or ethnic background. Management and staff alike need to recognise that there are differences, and these differences need to be catered for.
>
> (ibid.: 55)

Stephen Laudat

Stephen Laudat, who fatally injured Bryan Bennett in a social services day centre in the London Borough of Newham in July 1994, pleaded guilty to manslaughter on the grounds of diminished responsibility and was committed by the Central Criminal Court to an indefinite period of treatment in Rampton Hospital in December 1994. An independent review into the health and social care of Stephen Laudat, was commissioned jointly by East London and the City Health Authority and Newham Council (1995).
The press release by Newham Council (1995) noted:

> The report is critical of the psychiatric treatment and care which Stephen Laudat received over a number of years and in particular in the months immediately prior to the fatal accident. . . . There is particular criticism of the lack of communication between the health and social services professionals caring for Stephen following his discharge from hospital. Among the main

> recommendations, the report calls for improved joint working and highlights the need for services which are ethnically sensitive to the needs of the clients they serve.
>
> (1995: 1)

Stephen Laudat had a long history of mental illness from his early twenties. He and his family were well known to health and social services agencies from his birth. The inquiry states: 'In attempting to secure independent accommodation for himself [following a serious assault upon his mother] he committed criminal offences in 1991, for which he was remanded in prison' (East London and the City Health Authority and Newham Council, 1995: 1). However, the inquiry panel considered that he 'should have been transferred to hospital for a psychiatric assessment and court report, and should have been made the subject of a hospital order under the Mental Health Act rather than receive a prison sentence' (1995: 1–2).

In March 1992, Stephen Laudat was transferred from prison under provisions of Section 47/49 of the Mental Health Act 1983 – first to an interim secure unit at Hackney Hospital for assessment, and then to a privately run secure unit at Kneesworth House Hospital for longer term treatment. The inquiry panel considered that the care and treatment of Stephen Laudat at Kneesworth House to have been 'barely adequate', with the exception of specific incidences of work carried out by a probation officer and senior social worker who worked with Stephen Laudat during his stays at Kneesworth House (1995: 36, 39, 43). Although during the eighteen-month period that Stephen Laudat spent at Kneesworth House he was 'usually engageable and cooperative . . . little explorative and therapeutic intervention was attempted. This is despite recognition of a range of social and emotional derivation factors that S.L. had confirmed as significant to him' (1995: 43). The inquiry panel concluded:

> Most of the care provided at Kneesworth House appeared to be solely custodial and lacking a robust focus on preparing patients for discharge back into the inner city. This situation was not helped by a relative lack of sensitivity to his ethnicity.
>
> (1995: 43–4)

And the panel noted that:

> During our scrutiny of the psychiatric services that S.L. had

> used, especially those at Kneesworth House Hospital and those provided by. . . . Newham, the Review Panel became increasingly concerned by their failure to recognise and respond to the cultural dynamics of this case. These failures cluster around two key themes – limiting access to mental health care by restricted opportunities, and limiting access to mental health care by the provision of inappropriate services.
>
> (1995: 133)

Christopher Clunis was not considered a risk (except in hindsight) because he did not fit the stereotype; Orville Blackwood was considered a risk, because he did. Christopher Clunis killed; and Orville Blackwood is dead. Both men became victims, as did Stephen Laudat, to a system which failed to see them and, not only that, failed to recognise and acknowledge its own shortcomings. Public pronouncements which followed in the wake of the Clunis case suggested that a history of being ignored by different local authority and health departments was ironically interpreted to mean that this 'violent man' should have been contained earlier, somewhere in the system (Aveleon Associates, 1994: 2). What this also ignores, or tries to obscure, however, is that, had something been done earlier to meet Christopher Clunis' most basic needs of housing and employment, the entire situation could have been prevented (ibid.). It is important to ensure that assessment is directly linked to care or treatment options and that care packages are designed with the client's health at the top of the agenda, not simply what is most convenient, cheapest or least threatening to the care professionals (ibid.: 4).

Stephen Laudat needed ongoing care and attention which was culturally appropriate and sensitive to his needs. What he got was isolated pockets of good care when a few health professionals took the time and the opportunity to engage with him as a person with severe mental health problems who was in need of help. The path which brought Stephen Laudat to the day centre in Newham, however, and which resulted in his killing of Bryan Bennett, was more often characterised by inadequate and inappropriate care and treatment, and scant attention given to his needs by the service as a whole.

When black people, in particular African-Caribbean men, interface with the forensic psychiatric system, it is crucial for practitioners to have some sense of the realities behind the stereotypes, the images and preconceptions that they hold. This avoids a blinkered approach, which arbitrarily assigns characteristics to black people based on erroneous and superficial information. Such an approach is likely to result in care and treatment which bears some resemblance to the needs of the person who is presenting, rather than lead to greater ill health and more punitive solutions.

Inquiries: what do we learn?

It has been noted that more recent 'inquiries reflect a shift in public feeling and concern that the psychiatric over-control of patients demonstrated in the earlier inquiries [i.e. between 1969 and 1994, most of which considered the ill treatment or neglect of patients, the occurrence of an unusual number of suicides or severe administrative difficulties] has shifted to the under-control suggested in the more recent reports' (Bennett, 1996: 299).

It could be argued that the perceptions of dangerousness associated with black men, combined with the reality of the relatively small number of homicides committed by this group, has formed the basis for a number of recent inquiries which have given impetus to this shift. Yet, an examination of the findings of inquiries points to the inescapable fact that it is more often than not black people who are the victims of the failures of the system, not the cause. They are victimised through lack of communication (both between agencies and with black clients themselves), as a result of the lack of information about, and access to, appropriate services, and by an unwillingness to engage with black people on a basis other than a stereotypical one. These issues are seldom considered when attempts are made to shape public policy through the use of inquiries.

RECENT LEGISLATION AND POLICY

The fallout from the Clunis, Blackwood and Laudat inquiries has led, as noted earlier, to an increasingly restrictive ideological bent in government legislation, with a view to 'fixing' what is wrong with the mental health system via a more punitive and controlling criminal justice system, in order to protect the public. The Mental Health (Patients in the Community) Act (HMSO, 1995), for example, introduced supervised discharge (after-care under supervision), including the power to 'take and convey' people to their residence, place of treatment, work or training (MIND, 1996g). The

Woodley Team Report (East London and the City Health Authority and Newham Council, 1995) noted in its discussion of the legislation before it became law that: 'The Bill is based on the assumption from a few, but serious incidents, that there is a homogeneous group of patients who pose a risk to others, who are non-compliant and need to be coerced. We have found no hard evidence to support these assumptions (1995: 141). In commenting upon assumptions that appear to underlie legislation, the report states:

> The terms 'non-compliance', 'uncooperative', and 'a management problem' are used, predominantly by some health professionals to describe the behaviour of some patients with severe mental health needs and these are recorded in clinical notes. These terms are value laden. They sometimes suggest that non-compliance with treatment is a symptom of mental illness, rather than a rational reaction to the unpleasant and sometimes dangerous effects of these treatments.
>
> (1995: 142)

Supervision registers introduced in spite of objections from the Royal College of Psychiatrists (Isherwood, 1996) represent another strand in the remit to reduce risk to the public from patients discharged into the community. They were implemented under Health Service Guidelines HSG(94)5, issued by the NHS Management Executive in 1994 (see MIND 1996d). In its response, opposing the setting up of supervision registers, MIND (1994b) noted that 'supervision registers will operate in a discriminatory way because women and black people are over-represented among those diagnosed "mentally ill"' (1994b: 3). Within this remit, there is a clear onus upon mental health professionals to assess risk and, in so doing, attach primary importance to the role of public protector. At a recent conference, consultant forensic psychiatrist, Nigel Eastman (1995), argued that 'mental health care is driven by different methods and motives, not least of which, in relation to forensic psychiatry, is the criminal justice system. . . .' This means that 'the judge holds the trump card, and clinicians must bow to the criminal justice view'.

Hybrid orders

The introduction of the hybrid order (HO) was one of a series of significant, recent government initiatives, which are designed to protect the public and entrench the criminal justice view in relation to 'mentally disordered offenders'. The *Report of the Department of Health and Home Office Working Group on Psychopathic Disorder* (1994b) prepared under the chairmanship of Dr John Reed (1994b) cautiously recommended the introduction of a new sentencing instrument, the 'Hybrid Hospital Order', specifically and exclusively in relation to defendants suffering from 'psychopathic disorder' (Eastman, 1996). But the government White Paper – *Protecting the Public: The Government's Strategy on Crime in England and Wales* (Home Office, 1996b) proposed changes in the remand, sentencing and subsequent management of all 'mentally disordered offenders', including those suffering from mental illness and mental impairment (see MIND, 1996c; Eastman, 1996). The HO would enable the courts to pass a prison sentence on an offender and at the same time order his immediate admission to hospital for medical treatment. Under the order, an offender would remain in hospital for as long as his mental condition required, but if he recovered or was found to be untreatable during the fixed period set by the court, he would be readmitted to prison (MIND, 1996c: 11). The order would be made 'where the court is satisfied that there is a need by the defendant to receive treatment in hospital for the time being', but it is not certain that such treatment will sufficiently address the risk to the public posed by the defendant and a punitive element in the disposal is required in order to reflect the offender's whole or partial responsibility (Eastman, 1996: 483).

Eastman (1996) argues that the government proposal for HOs 'proposes *legal culpability* (coincidental with mental disorder) and *public safety* as the essential criteria for the making of HOs' and that the disadvantages of a generally available HO would include 'problems relating to the need to determine degrees of criminal responsibility; inherent problems arising from the nature of mental illness (i.e. its chronic or relapsing nature) and a potential "avalanche effect" on forensic and general and psychiatric services' (ibid.: 487). In other words, psychiatrists would be charged with advising to what extent a person's illness is related to the crime. MIND (1996c), in opposing the introduction of the HO, argues that 'the fundamental issues of criminal responsibility and the justification for detaining people on the basis of future risk should be separated and addressed' (1996c: 2).

For black offenders, who are deemed 'mentally disordered', and who, as has been shown, are over-represented in both criminal justice and psychiatric institutions (see Preface), and whose public *persona* is regarded as being one of hostility and aggression, the consequences are obvious – longer periods of incarceration in prison and the likelihood of longer periods of committal to psychiatric hospitals because of the perceived risk from black aggression. This could effectively spell preventive detention for black people, in particular African-Caribbean men. The tendency to get the criminal, dangerous black male off the streets and out of the public consciousness thus becomes the overriding precept.

Crime (Sentences) Bill

The Crime (Sentences) Bill recently passed by the British House of Commons, is another example of the restrictive intentions with regard to containing mentally disordered offenders and protecting the public. The Bill mandates life sentences on those convicted of second specified sexual or violent offences (so-called 'three strikes and out'), at least seven years for those with two or more convictions for certain drug trafficking offences, and at least three years for second convictions for burglary (Rutherford, 1997). The Bill also provides for a new sentencing instrument for 'mentally disordered offenders': a 'hospital direction' which will be applicable whether or not the defendant is liable for the new mandatory life sentence (Eastman, 1996). The Crime (Sentences) Bill borrows from US criminal policy: a policy encouraged by a 'small group of US conservative political scientists' (Rutherford, 1997) who regard welfare dependency and the under-class (read black Americans) as at the root of much of what has gone wrong in the USA, and to be the main purveyors of crime in the USA. Vivien Stern, former director of the National Association for the Care and Rehabilitation of Offenders (NACRO) and current secretary-general of Penal Reform International, recently outlined the US approach and its consequences, particularly for black people. Describing the impetus to privatise prisons in the USA, he notes:

> The striking feature of these advertisements is the ethos they convey. The prison world is a battleground. The prisoners are the enemy and they will try anything to outwit their jailers. The job of the system is to thwart every attempt of this cunning enemy to fight back against its surroundings. A whole industry is now devoted to stopping this. This is not a society incarcerating some

> of its dangerous citizens and trying to keep them secure while working with them to sort out their problems and eventually return them to society. This is a war, and the prisoners are prisoners of war – people of another country or another ethnic group, nothing to do with us.
>
> (Stern, 1997: 11)

The consequences for black people, whether designated as 'mentally disordered' or not, are inescapable.

CONCLUSIONS

The underlying ethos of public policy in relation to mentally disordered offenders is to go for the quick fix. 'Dangerous' black men can/must be incarcerated in prison or psychiatric institutions. If they are let out into the community, they become subject to compulsory treatment within the community (e.g. supervision registers and supervised discharge). The reality, however, is more complicated. How black people are dealt with in the forensic psychiatric system or in the criminal justice system or in psychiatric institutions in general, cannot legitimately be separated from how they are dealt with in terms of their place in society generally. The inherent fallacy in the system is the refusal to acknowledge this fact in an integral way and to re-configure systems, concepts and practices in order to reflect this fundamental reality.

Chapter 13

Public attitudes, private responses

CARE IN THE COMMUNITY

Care in the community is a vital plank of public policy (Ahmad and Atkin, 1996). It has re-emerged as a prominent feature of public policy in the mid-1980s; and has come to be an accepted part of the hegemony which governs how people with mental illness – whether black or white – are cared for outside of large-scale, segregated long-stay institutions. The main components of community care and attitudes associated with it are summarised and discussed below.

Legislation and guidance in the community

The National Health Service and Community Care Act (1990) has as its ethos the need to make services more relevant, accessible and locally accountable to communities through consultations on care planning between health services and local authority social services departments. Implicit within the Act was an understanding of the importance of proactively involving black communities: .

> The introduction of the current community care reforms cannot be divorced from the existing disadvantages facing minority ethnic communities, especially since empirical evidence suggests that community care services do not adequately recognize and respond to the needs of people from ethnic minorities. . . . Problems of access to, and appropriateness of, community health and social services have been well documented. Three themes emerge . . . first, community service provision often ignores the needs of black and minority ethnic groups; second, community care services often misrepresent the needs of ethnic minorities

> because of a preoccupation with cultural differences; third, racist attitudes on the part of service providers have been reported in a number of studies in health and social services.
>
> (Ahmad and Atkin, 1996: 3–4)

Mention of community care in relation to people with mental illness can unleash a plethora of perceptions, feelings and views about the appropriateness of re-locating people with mental health problems into the community. Newspaper reports of campaigns designed to keep people out of a local community (e.g. NIMBY – Not in My Backyard) and against siting facilities in the community, have become a feature of the discussion surrounding community care.

A Mental Health Task Force report (Department of Health, 1994a), which assessed how well the community care legislation was working in meeting mental health needs, found gaps in service provision and, more worryingly, noted that many black people felt that they were not listened to even when services appropriate for their communities were being planned. The task force concluded that, there was a need 'to make services more responsive to the needs of people from different ethnic and cultural backgrounds' (NHS Executive, 1996: 2).

In April 1991 the Care Programme Approach (CPA) was introduced as the cornerstone of mental health policy (NHS Executive, 1996). It requires health authorities to ensure that everyone in touch with specialist mental health services (including forensic psychiatric services) has their needs assessed, a care plan devised and regular review and monitoring of their progress. For people who are potentially a risk to themselves or others, the introduction of Supervision Registers established in 1994, was made an integral part of the CPA.

Health of the Nation (Department of Health, 1992a) guidelines were another strand to government initiatives which broadly affected community care. This set targets for improvements in health, including mental health, and specifically identified the needs of black and minority ethnic communities as an important component (Balarajan and Raleigh, 1993).

The Mental Health (Patients in the Community) Act (HMSO, 1995), provides for statutory supervision in the community of certain psychiatric patients. It is part of the response to public concern about the potential risks of caring for people with severe psychiatric disorders in the community. The Act specified four types of risk as grounds for an application for supervision: 'harm to the health of the patient; harm to the safety of the patient; harm to the safety of other persons; harm arising from the patient being seriously exploited' (University of Manchester, Department of Health 1996: 66).

A notable component of the Act is the power it gives to mental health professionals to 'take and convey' people who are discharged from hospital. In practice, it means that a person may be required 'to live in a certain place, attend specified places at specified times for medical treatment and for work, education and/or training' (MIND, 1995b: 1). It introduced new statutory powers to establish 'supervised discharge' arrangements for people discharged back into the community following a period of detention for compulsory care under the Mental Health Act (ibid.).

While much of the community care legislation has been welcomed as a positive step, albeit an under-resourced one, there is disquiet about some of the more restrictive aspects of treatment in the community. The tendency towards enforced treatment in the community for people who are considered non-compliant or problematic or 'dangerous' may represent an assault on individual rights and may result in coercive and compulsory treatment in the community (MIND, 1995b: 2). Given the (unwarranted) suspicion with which black people are regarded and the impact this has on the care and treatment they receive, it is clear that these measures may disproportionately affect those communities. Of supervised discharge MIND notes:

> MIND is worried that in the current climate of service provision, the power of aftercare under supervision might result in over-reliance on drugs as the primary tool for the aftercare of patients discharged from hospital. Evidence suggests that all too often patients are offered little other than medication. This is of particular concern in relation to black and other ethnic minorities who, the research shows, are more likely to be subject to coercive powers under the Mental Health Act and are less likely to find services offering health and social support that are appropriate to them in the community.
>
> (1996a: 1)

Earlier, MIND opposed supervision registers on the basis that: 'it will not achieve better community care services;' and in particular in relation to black people, because of fears that supervision registers 'will operate in a discriminatory way because women and black people are over-represented among those diagnosed "mentally ill"' (MIND, 1994b: 2–3).

Does the community care?

Community care does not take place within a vacuum. It is shaped by the attitudes and perceptions which operate within the wider parameters of an interdependent society, whether we like it or not. Matt Muijen (1997) director of the Sainsbury Centre for Mental Health, has noted:

> Nowhere else in the Western world is mental healthcare viewed with such suspicion as it is at the moment in the UK, despite the occurrence of community care throughout the West. . . . Community care was introduced in the UK in the 1950s, when the cult of the individual was at its lowest. The 1980s, when implementation of the policy began to accelerate, was a time of Thatcherite values: individualism and low social responsibility. Elections were won by low taxes, not by promises of state-funded child care. In addition, increased unemployment, perceptions of reduced personal safety and fracturing family ties meant that the time was hardly ideal for 'community care' practice, let alone its ideological underpinnings.
>
> (1997: 19)

The degree of commitment and stakeholding on the part of members of the public, which is necessary for the successful reintegration of people with mental health problems, is a crucial component of community care. The co-existence of the general public and people with mental illness who are discharged into the community is characterised by and large, by a sense of disquiet and dis-ease. Images of 'mad axemen', 'psycho-killers' and, the tag given to Glen Grant, 'Beast of Belgravia' – are indicative of the attitudes held by many people concerned with mental health problems (see Chapter 11). These attitudes are largely fostered by media treatment of people with mental health problems.

Though there are notable successes – for example, in some MIND local associations, where efforts have been made to help counter community objections to having people with mental health problems in their midst with programmes of local education and interaction – the primary attitude regarding people with mental health problems, and especially those who are perceived as violent and dangerous, is that they do not belong in a community of 'normal' and vulnerable people. This attitude, of course, refuses to acknowledge the vulnerability that many people with mental health problems themselves feel; and the fact that they are likely to be more at risk of harm *from* others, than to be a risk *to* others.

Yet, the public perception that mental illness is strongly linked to violence persists, and is the most damaging stereotype faced by the mental health community:

> Public perceptions that mental illness is strongly linked to violent behaviour are important for two reasons. The first is that such beliefs drive the formal laws and policies by which society attempts to control the behaviour of people with mental illness and to regulate the provision of mental health care. . . . The second and perhaps even more important reason why beliefs in the violent potential of people with mental illness are important is that they not only drive formal law and policy toward people with mental illness as a class, but they determine our informal responses and modes of interacting with individuals who are perceived to have a mental illness.
>
> (Monahan and Arnold, 1996: 68)

BLACK COMMUNITY ATTITUDES

Black communities/people are not immune to the viewpoints which characterise the majority reaction to people suffering mental distress. In two companion studies on community knowledge of, and attitudes to, mental illness (Wolff, et al., 1996) one of the striking findings was that of the influence of ethnic origin: Asians, Caribbeans and Africans (compared to other groups) showed greater propensity to favour social control – 'social control' being represented by answers to items such as, 'as soon as a person shows signs of mental disturbance, he should be hospitalised' (1996: 190). The researchers concluded: 'Any intervention aimed at changing attitudes to mentally ill people in the community should be targeted at people with children and non-Caucasians, as these groups are more likely to object' (1996: 183). However, just as black people must struggle against the internalisation of the racist stereotypes which are applied to them, so they must (and, it must be argued, do) work against attitudes in relation to mental illness. In fact, much of the innovation and impetus for creating better mental health services for black people has come from black professionals, users and carers.

Negative attitudes and pre- and misconceptions about people with mental health problems, whether held by black or white communities, have much to do with a lack of information and insight into the nature of mental illness (Wolff, *et al.*, 1996: 191). These negative attitudes and the public pressure generated by them, in turn, account for much of the political trend towards punitive and controlling responses which are currently at the fore in relation to the forensic psychiatric patient. For example, a key recommendation of the *Report of the Inquiry into the Care and Treatment of Christopher Clunis* (Northeast Thames and Southeast Thames Regional Health Authorities, 1994) was to make patients subject to supervised discharge orders. And the inquiry was also a precursor to the Mental Health (Patients in the Community) Act in that it identified a category of patients who needed special supervision: 'The patients we are trying to identify are those who are difficult to care for, and need to be followed up intensively, with assertive and close supervision' (1994: 116).

The tendency to go for the 'quick fix' in the face of considerable public and media pressure is, in all likelihood, the politically expedient public response. The jury is still out, however, as to whether the development of public policy 'on the hoof' is the best way to ensure that vulnerable people get appropriate care in the community. A better option, it can be argued, would be to work within what many view as the already adequate legislation and guidance.

Re-shaping policy, creating change

The above notwithstanding, increasingly it is within black communities that there is a discernible impetus for change in the care and treatment of its members who may have mental health problems, both in the general, as well as forensic sense. The author can recall vividly the passion evident in a gathering of a small, black people's church in Brixton, south London, whose members had applied for and received funds to stage a 1996 world mental health day event. Many of the members of the church had themselves been compulsorily detained in the local mental health hospital. At the event, members used the time-honoured mode of expressing themselves in the black church – testifying. One young black woman described how she had been detained under the Mental Health Act because she had momentarily been floored by the collapse of a relationship. She had tried to explain to the mental health professionals that she just needed a bit of time and someone to talk to. What she got was detention in hospital and treatment with psychotropic (psychiatric) drugs. She was detained initially for six months on Section 3 of the Mental Health Act. This was later extended to twelve months because she was perceived as uncooperative.

The pastor explained that it was experiences such as this which had given his congregation its *raison d'être*. Members of the church made regular visits to the wards of the psychiatric hospital – listening, talking, bringing appropriate toiletries, providing a vital link and a grounding that would be otherwise missing in the lives of a large number of the black patients. In this, the Brixton church was continuing a long tradition of support for black communities provided by black churches in the US context (Anderson, *et al.*, 1990) and equally applicable in the UK:

> The church serves in the maintenance of family solidarity as a conserver of moral values having to do with right or wrong behavior. It confers status to those who very often derive little respect or recognition from the dominant culture. . . . The black church is a source for leadership development and historically has been the center for black protest. In addition, it allows for the release of tension through spiritual expressiveness, and it is a source for social interactions and entertainment.
>
> (1990: 265)

Reclaiming the psyche

> There is a universal psyche and then [there is] hundreds of years worth of damage on top of that.
>
> (Stephen, 1995: 43)

Increasingly, many black mental health professionals and others have come to recognise that solutions to the predicament of black people – whether in forensic psychiatry, the criminal justice system or within society as a whole – will not necessarily be found within the mainstream. This is a fact which black people (both in the UK and in the USA), after long years of attempts at assimilation, integration and of negating aspects of self are beginning to embrace and explore to their advantage. The implications for the mental health of black people are exciting, not least because the impetus for change, growth and development is occurring within a positive ethos which has as its starting-point, the health and healing of black people.

Jahoda (1958) (in Franklin and Jackson, 1990) identified six major dimensions that contribute to defining positive mental health. These included:

1 Attitudes of the individual towards himself/herself.
2 The degree to which a person realises his or her potentialities through action.
3 Unification of function in the individual's personality.
4 The individual's degree of independence of social influences.
5 How the individual sees the world around him/her.
6 The ability to take life as it comes and master it.

Franklin and Jackson (1990: 296–9) argue that these can be translated into the following categories: self-concept and self-esteem; autonomy and control; environmental mastery; perceptions of reality; growth, development and self-actualization.

Self-concept and self-esteem

Though there are mixed views about the extent to which social pathology and mental illness affect self-esteem, Franklin and Jackson (1990) note that the value of a positive self-concept repeatedly surfaces as important in the development of a positive self-esteem for black people. Dr Na'im Akbar, a clinical psychologist at Florida State University, is a pioneer in the development of African-centred approaches to psychology. Akbar spoke at the Million Man March held in the USA in Washington, DC in 1996. He describes the significance of the march for black people in the following terms:

> one of the things that the Million Man March really showed those of us that have been trying hard to argue that we are distinct . . . [is that] we are not deviant Europeans. We have a very distinct identity, we have a very distinct expression as human beings.
>
> (Akbar, 1996: 43)

The Nation of Islam in the USA has played a crucial part in

re-establishing a sense of self-identity and self-worth among black men. Whatever one may think of the politics of the organisation, it is clear that the work of the black Muslims in the USA has led to the generation of feelings of self-worth, black pride and a sense of responsibility, particularly among black prisoners in US jails (Owens, 1980b: 33). The process that many [prison] inmates go through to become Muslim is captured in this extract of a letter from an inmate:

> Within the walls of the prison the Muslims are very powerful in their attracting force. Their principles, conduct and their beliefs made an entirely different society in the walls, from the confined inmates and free officials. . . . In this environment I began to slowly develop a sense of self-concepts which I found to be positive and productive to this day . . . without becoming subject to the debilitating influence that exists there.
>
> (Owens, 1980b: 35)

Owens notes of the Nation of Islam that 'by helping black offenders to develop their racial component, they helped turn blacks who come to prison into self-respecting, responsible, proud individuals',

> Very simply, they gave blacks the opportunity to develop positive racial coping skills in American society. With this resolved, black offenders were ready to move toward positive mental health. What the Muslims did for blacks can be implemented by other mental health professionals. In fact, many of the more directive therapies, such as reality therapy, transactional analysis, and gestalt therapy, tend to use the same type of format. The basic difference is that Muslims realized the importance of one's racial feeling and racial position in the lives of black offenders and consequently their mental health.
>
> (ibid., 1980b: 39)

Autonomy and control

> We must own our own madness and we must own the services/mechanisms for developing mental health care to deal with it.
>
> (Conference participant, 1995: 6)

Black mental health professionals are increasingly seeking to redefine the parameters through which they and others provide care and treatment to black communities. That re-definition includes as an integral component, the reflection of a positive ethos of race and culture. The Ipamo Project is an example of the kind of service delivery which is being created through this approach in south London .

The mental health service to be delivered by Ipamo is one which is grounded in an alternative purpose and emphasises the need for 'understanding the meaning and context of distress, rather than just providing symptom control' (Phillips, 1997: personal communication). It will provide an assessment service; a crisis service with ten acute beds; an eight-bed family respite service; twenty-four-hour advice and advocacy; counselling and outreach and community education. Malcolm Phillips, director of Ipamo, describes the ethos of its service: 'We must develop models of psychotherapy that allow black people to express issues of race without pathologising it. Therefore we must develop a model that is in keeping with the needs, beliefs and values of the people who use it' (King's Fund, 1995: 5). Many of the clients which Ipamo reaches will have experienced the forensic psychiatric system in its more punitive forms – including locked wards, medium and high security hospitals – and will have been given high doses of psychotropic drugs. It is a measure of the caring which exists within the black community – i.e., in this case, black professionals – that Ipamo is being specifically set up to help meet the neglected needs of this patient grouping.

Environmental mastery

Arguing the merits of community based alternatives to institutional psychiatry, Sashidharan notes that mental health workers, service providers and users must examine the possibility of alternatives to institutional psychiatry, 'if we are serious about developing anti-oppressive models and practices' (Sashidharan, 1994b: 4). With his team in Birmingham he has pioneered a 'home treatment model' of care by shifting the focus of acute care into the community by providing all aspects of such care at people's homes. Home treatment was introduced in Ladywood, a deprived inner city area in Birmingham in 1991, psychiatric care in the area having previously been provided at a conventional in-patient facility. The most significant change since its inauguration 'was the setting up of a 24-hour, seven days a week service in the community to provide acute care away from the institutional setting' (1994b). The result was that:

> Over a two-year period, 216 episodes of acute care were completed through home treatment. Over 60 per cent of referrals consisted of individuals who were experiencing acute symptoms of severe mental disorder, achieving a diagnosis of psychosis, mostly schizophrenia. Through home treatment, over 80 per cent of these episodes were successfully treated at the patients' normal place of residence, without recourse to hospital admission.
>
> (1994b: 4)

Sashidharan notes that, 'the intervention model that we have developed emphasises the social context within which much of madness is created and sustained, and the life situation – both contemporary and historical – of those who 'break down'. Consequently, the medical model that has come to dominate psychiatric care in this country is less relevant in providing an understanding of madness, and the practices that have stemmed from such a model ought to be re-appraised or rejected' (1994b: 4).

PERCEPTIONS OF REALITY

Franklin and Jackson (1990) argue that the perception of reality is a fundamental concept in mental health, in that 'it clearly helps to differentiate those who are seriously mentally disturbed and are out of touch with their environment, regardless of the basis of socially agreed upon standards' (1990: 298). They note behaviour 'is judged by a normative standard established by social consensus. One's behaviour is in part the outcome of how one perceives the world':

> This fact is crucial in understanding how blacks achieve positive mental health. A classical controversy in this regard is the debate over levels of paranoia in blacks. In our opinion any model of positive mental health for blacks must include certain features of paranoia as adaptive, although the individual may be classified as deviant by conventional criteria. Living in a racist society requires blacks to evaluate constantly the existence and nature of prejudice and discrimination they face. It is essential for blacks to have a level of vigilance about racism. . . . Vigilance about racism, or what W. H. Grier and P. M. Cobbs call 'cultural paranoia', normalises the perception of reality for blacks, and permits constructive functioning.
>
> (1990: 298–9)

Franklin and Jackson further argue that 'counteracting . . . the "invisibility syndrome"' for black men requires not only vigilance but also validation of experiences. This last point was echoed in a slightly different context, in the NHS Executive Mental Health Task Force report (Department of Health, 1994a), which found that a key desire of black groups and organisations who work with black people in mental distress is that the culturally relevant perspectives they bring should be recognised or validated and incorporated within mainstream service provision.

Growth, development and self-actualization

An essential manifestation of positive mental health is whether life goals are achieved and individuals are satisfied with these accomplishments (Franklin and Jackson, 1990). For black people who are denied entry into the realm of acceptable opportunities in large numbers, because their talents are not recognised or acknowledged, the attainment of positive mental health which is attributable to accomplishment may be difficult.

A growing body of opinion among black mental health professionals has begun to argue that black people must re-define or (perhaps more appropriately) re-claim the basis by which validation, recognition and self-actualisation is sought. Stephen (1996) argues that 'for black people the road to self-actualisation and spiritual development are one' (1996: 31). This school of thought argues that it is only through regaining culture and the strengths generated through it, that the disconnectedness which black communities experience can begin to be re-grounded in terms of relationships with each other, with nature and with the universe. It is what Stephen calls 'a development process that moves one towards the true self, so that one can fulfil our potential as human beings' (1996: 30).

The dilemma lies, notes Stephen, in the fact that 'subjective experiences are not valued by this [wider] community and are considered primitive, in its most negative form' (1996: 30). Because primitive is associated with being 'uncivilised, uneducated, wild and animal or primate', black people in the 1950s and 1960s took the decision either consciously or unconsciously to forgo the aspects of culture which would place them within this construct. Many in the black community would argue that the price that has been paid for that collective denial of black culture has been a loss of connectedness and sense of self-worth, to the detriment of many black people's mental health.

Culture, the new ethnicity and control

Application of the Jahoda/Franklin/Jackson construct to the UK and USA experiences reveals a perceptible shift in the attitudes and, as a consequence, the work of black professionals in their work with black people in mental distress. A crucial component of the alternative models now being formulated is an acceptance of concepts of culture and identity (beneficial to both patient and practitioner alike) to allow for the development of more adaptive and responsive approaches.

Watters (1996) argues that 'identity is not a "fixed core" but shifts in a context in which cultural identities are simultaneously cultures in process' (1996: 121). This ability to adapt, to re-mould the essence of culture and identity, has been the mainstay of black people's survival historically. In part, however, it is also responsible for much of the disconnectedness which many black people experience. Many within black communities are coming to the realisation that it is crucially important to maintain a balance between what is necessary to negotiate a course within wider society, while at the same time continuing to hold true to what is also necessary to maintain a true sense of self and identity. The reclaiming of culture and thus the re-connection of black people's psyches through a process of re-identification is the driving force behind much of the work of black mental health professionals today.

Non-Western approaches

Transcultural psychiatry, transcultural nursing, intercultural therapy (as advanced by Nafsiyat Intercultural Therapy Centre) and Afrocentric counselling are all manifestations of attempts by black professionals to shift the ground to enable the care and treatment of black people suffering mental distress to be undertaken within a positive and healthy environment:

These modern-day solutions have their basis in traditional, ancestral African and Asian healing and philosophical techniques, e.g. Ayurveda in Asia and the 'unity of the spiritual and material worlds' (Fernando, 1991: 162) found in African traditional medicine. The determined consciousness with which a growing school of black professionals has embraced this work underscores the importance of combining the spiritual, emotional and physical.

> Traditional [i.e. Western] models of therapy remove the individual's experiences from the social and political context in which they develop and treat them in isolation. Transcultural therapy transcends this. In this form of therapy, the individual's problems are recognised as being inextricably linked with the wider social context.
>
> (Webb-Johnson, 1991: 54)

CONCLUSIONS

The mainstay of black people and black communities throughout a history of oppression and racism has been the ability to re-group to sustain culture, maintain (a sometimes precarious sense of) wellbeing and stay alive. Despite the vagaries of the systemic responses – e.g. the patchwork effectiveness of community care; the hostility evidenced in the media; the unresponsiveness of the system generally – black people are not bankrupt. The care and attention given to the mental wellbeing of black people who are treated in general and forensic psychiatry is categorically inadequate in a myriad of circumstances. Fortunately for the interests of those black patients who are caught up in the system, however, there are black professionals who are at the cutting edge of service delivery and practice, who are insistent that the way forward is to re-frame the status quo in order to reflect the crucial component of culture.

Part IV

Future prospects

Suman Fernando, David Ndegwa,
Melba Wilson

Chapter 14

The challenge

Today in the UK – and, very likely, in most European countries – forensic psychiatry (or its equivalent) and the forensic thrust within general psychiatry confuse questions of crime and illness and, even more importantly, allow racism to become intimately involved in this amalgam. A vicious circle is created whereby seemingly 'medical' solutions are offered for social ills and social issues get medicalised even more. Forensic psychiatry is developing as a political power in the way psychiatry itself once developed. It has already established a mystique of its own, a part of which is about its ability to diagnose dangerousness. In going about its business, forensic psychiatry naturally uses the tools that are closest to hand, namely, the traditional psychiatric diagnostic system, especially the diagnosis of schizophrenia – modern schizophrenia no doubt, but still a schizophrenia that carries the aura of inherited madness, degeneration and racial imagery (mainly of black people) that derive from its origins in nineteenth-century Europe. As racist stereotypes and myths about black people are incorporated into it and as the powers that control society locate in black people all that is seen as alien and disturbing, forensic psychiatry in conjunction with the criminal justice system functions as a means of control using medical language and pseudo-scientific arguments about illness, especially schizophrenia.

The practice of forensic psychiatry is closely connected with the operation of the criminal justice system. Indeed, the two systems often function as one – at least as far as the people caught up with them as 'mentally disordered offenders' are concerned. Yet, these very people often prefer one or the other (if given the choice) – and it is not always the (medical) psychiatric system that is preferred by black people, one major reason being their perception of the forensic psychiatry system as racist. As the twenty-first century approaches, issues of cultural difference and ethnic identity are of increasing importance. In such a context, racism in psychiatry is likely to be felt even more forcefully through the forensic system unless Western society can bring itself to re-consider not just the place of psychiatry in social control of black people, but wider questions of justice and equity in relation to race and culture. The questions for the final part of this book centre on strategies for achieving changes in psychiatry, especially forensic psychiatry, in order to help in this endeavour

The fact that psychiatry as a discipline needs a fundamental re-appraisal is a major theme of this book. Unfortunately, the Royal College of Psychiatrists, the main organisation that leads the psychiatric profession (through controlling training, influencing research and advising the Department of Health in the organisation of services), has failed so far to provide leadership in reforming the areas of psychiatric practice that relate to issues of race and culture. Since the exercise of power within the forensic field is centred on psychiatrists, the chances of a way forward 'from the inside' alone are remote. Therefore, external pressures (on forensic psychiatry) by other professional organisations, managers of hospital trusts and purchasers of forensic services, together with guidance from the Department of Health and lobbying by voluntary bodies, especially black and ethnic minority organisations, are all essential. Recently, the Mental Health Foundation (a body that dispenses grants for research and service development) took the lead in bringing together national organisations, such as the Transcultural Psychiatry Society, MIND and the National Schizophrenia Foundation (NSF), in order to agree a statement outlining the need for change in the psychiatric services to meet the needs of black and ethnic minorities in the UK (Mental Health Foundation, 1997). The low key and cautious nature of this statement says a great deal about the political state of play in this field. Clearly, direction and pressure from the government is needed and the advent of a new government in the UK which claims to raise the profile of human rights, gives grounds for hope in this direction.

PSYCHIATRIC SYSTEM

Physicians and other practitioners within the health service work in a stable and largely conservative environment. Judgements on reasonableness and good practice are based on the prevailing majority professional opinion and practice. The current ethos within professional circles (in forensic psychiatry) is that opinions voiced by people seen as leaders in the profession are given precedence over all others; theories are only considered credible or worthy of debate if they are generated by these leaders and the opinion of others is discounted. The result is that views which dissent from those of established people are construed as subversive or 'political' and thus marginalised. Also, there is a tendency to regard psychiatry as a science which has advanced to the stage where qualitative research methodologies asking the question 'why' are irrelevant and so research continues to focus on quantitative methodologies which are then applied uncritically to all sections of the population. All this has to change if the psychiatric system is to meet the demands of a multi-ethnic society.

The history of psychiatry, especially forensic psychiatry, shows clearly the political nature of psychiatry from its beginning (see Chapter 2). Even recently, major developments have come about as a result of political action. For example, the institution of 'community care' as the main setting for the practice of psychiatry has led to the care programme approach (Kingdon, 1994) being used by psychiatrists. Administrative changes, such as the introduction of supervision registers (Tyrer and Kennedy, 1995) has led to clinical systems of risk assessment.

Many interventions used as 'treatment' in forensic psychiatry, such as heavy tranquillisation, seclusion, control and restraint, are practised in other settings (than the medical psychiatric one) by people involved in controlling human or animal populations – for example, in prisons, veterinary medicine and farming. These interventions (when used in non-medical settings) are regularly criticised by the public on humanitarian, ethical or (broadly speaking) political grounds. The same critical approach is required in relation to 'treatment' in forensic psychiatry. As bell hooks states:

> conventional mental health care professionals who attend to the needs of black folks often reject any analysis that takes into account a political understanding of our personal pain. This may be true of black mental health care workers as well as everyone else. While there is a growing body of self-help literature that is addressed specifically to black folks, it does not connect political injustice with psychological pain.
>
> (1995: 142)

This statement pinpoints an important issue for professionals in the mental health field, especially those working in a multi-ethnic setting. When practitioners emphasise the non-political nature of their thinking and activity, they emphasise their commitment, and in some cases their sacrifice. While these motivations are laudable and indeed the humanitarian traditions of medicine (to which psychiatrists often try to adhere) must be recognised, the fact is that, as a way of working and a discipline that provides a service, psychiatry, most especially forensic psychiatry, is more political than medical. Therefore, it would seem appropriate – desirable – that political analysis should be brought into quality assessment of service provision and the auditing of clinical practice. In the case of forensic psychiatry, such auditing should be the most important dimensions along which the clinical practice of psychiatrists is measured.

Psychiatrists and others working in forensic services are often subject to enormous pressures from society at large, which to a large extent sees their main duty as that of protecting society from violent and dangerous 'mad' people. However, they are also subject to pressures from the culture in which they practice – the expectations of their fellow professionals that are transmitted overtly and covertly. Unfortunately, societal pressures have influenced the attitudes of professionals within forensic psychiatry to such an extent that many settings are now characterised by a sort of 'macho' culture. An image that some forensic psychiatrists aim to develop for themselves (and admire in others) is one of being 'hard' and 'tough' with a readiness to take firm action usually in the form of high dose medication. It is not unusual to hear some psychiatrists describing as 'soft', colleagues who veer towards using relatively low doses of medication or look to counselling or even just talking to patients considered to be 'dangerous'. Another feature of the current forensic psychiatry scene (and one that affects general psychiatry too) is the blindness among some psychiatrists to the influence upon the decisions they take of their own prejudices and weaknesses. In fact, a tendency to examine one's motivations and feelings about others, especially people labelled as patients – and, most especially, black people with this label – is sometimes seen as a sign of weakness, inconsistent with the 'macho' image that is considered desirable.

Thus, if there is any prospect of change in the way forensic psychiatry is practised, issues at both 'macro' and 'micro' levels must be addressed. Changes are also needed in the political framework of forensic psychiatry, in the culture of the discipline, in attitudes of practitioners that are generated by this culture and in the methods of clinical assessment. Clearly, such a general overhaul of forensic psychiatry is not feasible – at least in one clear swoop. But changes targeted at specific areas are feasible. In other words, opportunities for change that are practical and politically possible are not too difficult to find – some of which will be discussed in the next chapter.

Chapter 15

Opportunities for change

The simple answer to the challenge presented by the issues in forensic psychiatry covered in this book is that fundamental changes are required in the thinking around mental health and mental health problems, together with a remodelling of the criminal justice system *vis-à-vis* mental health: changes designed to counteract racism and ensure that the systems concerned take account of cultural difference. This task is not something that this chapter can even begin to attempt, but some avenues along which progress may be achieved are worth considering. However, any changes, to be effective, must be backed by those in authority through clear policies and their effectiveness being continuously monitored until the changes themselves become institutionalised. The bare bones of a policy to promote 'racial equality' is given in Box 15.1. The rest of this chapter will consider specific areas in which changes can be made – assessing dangerousness, psychiatric assessment and diagnosis, black staff and 'white institutions', black identity and separate services, resistance strategies and mental health, service structure, training, research, combating racism, political/legal changes, forensic psychotherapy, and medication.

ASSESSING DANGEROUSNESS

An earlier book about issues of race and culture in (general) psychiatry (Fernando, 1988) proposed the following strategy for assessing dangerousness:

> Dangerousness to be assessed on the basis of a body of information (about the person being assessed) in which a general psychiatric view is only one part; this information to include

> episodes of observed violence, rather than assumptions about behaviour, and a full knowledge of the person's life circumstances (particularly those at the time when violence occurs) and culture, evaluated against a background of social conditions including racism. Questions of 'mental disorder' to be considered as a separate issue from dangerousness. Specialists to be appointed to advise courts on questions of dangerousness, while multidisciplinary research on the topic is fostered as a matter of urgency.
>
> (1988: 180)

A way forward for forensic psychiatry would be to highlight the limitations in making judgements about (individual) dangerousness and to develop lists of contextual variables that affect such judgements in the clinical field. The items listed in Box 15.2 can be a start. The term 'clinical' must reach out to cover areas much wider than the narrow medical approach may imply – at least into 'wider environmental and close, familial factors that may contribute to further harmful actions by offender-patients' (Prins, 1990: 18). What is described as 'violence' or 'aggression' must always be seen in the context of interpersonal and personal issues, as well as in the context in which people live. Generally, seeing 'aggressiveness'

Box 15.1 Promotion of racial equality

1 Race equality *policy*
   Combating racism
   Promoting equal opportunities

2 *Monitoring* systems
   Employment practices
   Service provision
   Training

3 *Action* at various levels
   Disciplinary procedures
   User involvement

4 Forward *planning*
   Feed in 1, 2 and 3

Box 15.2: Genesis of aggression

Inequalities

Racism

Oppression

Homelessness

Unemployment

INTERPERSONAL

Conflict

Provocation

Hostility

Stereotypes

Power

Prejudice

Misunderstandings

PERSONAL

Frustration

Anger

Retaliation

Psychological problems

Family problems

Imagined fears

Real fears

merely as a reflection of 'illness' or as arising out of the blue, is both unrealistic and misleading.

It is important to bring into any scheme for risk assessment (of dangerousness) a way of allowing for cultural difference and racist stereotyping, while moving away from narrow symptom based or illness based assessments. In analysing episodes of violence, forensic psychiatry must find ways of addressing basic factors around the genesis of aggression. Risk assessment must move away from 'illness analysis' towards real life analysis. In the genesis of aggression, conflict, anger, frustration, provocation, prejudice, stereotypes, etc. are all involved in one way or another, in addition to personal or family problems, imagined or real fears, etc. At a wide contextual level, inequalities, racism, oppression, poverty, unemployment, homelessness all play their parts. In short, risk assessment is about evaluating risks of aggression and, except very occasionally, these are the same for people deemed 'mentally ill' as for others. It is not simply a matter of enumerating episodes of violence or ticking off items about personality, symptoms or whatever the checklist says. Observations have to be sensitive to race, gender and other issues. And finally, an assessment cannot be static: continuous re-examination in the light of changes in the personal psychology of the individual concerned or of his/her circumstances should be mandatory.

The role of psychiatrists in the decision-making processes, which involves assessments of dangerousness leading to the deprivation of a person's liberty or rights or privileges, should be challenged by the profession, and the limitations of psychiatrists/psychologists in this field should be made explicit to the public and operatives of the criminal justice system. Actuaries, psychologists, anthropologists and other professionals with interest in prediction, cultural studies and racism should play a part in risk assessment. The legal profession should have a more critical approach to psychiatrists or psychologists who provide information as 'experts', especially when this is done on the basis of 'clinical judgement' alone. In challenging the opinions of psychiatrists, their professional ideology should be examined openly.

PSYCHIATRIC ASSESSMENT AND DIAGNOSIS

The general public is now largely sceptical about the usefulness of psychiatry and often (at least in the UK) see psychiatrists as people who diagnose and medicate and little else. In this context, forensic psychiatry is seen as practising psychiatry with dangerous people but seldom (if ever) trying to understand their apparent propensity to be – or appear to be – 'dangerous'. To a large extent, psychiatry has brought this upon itself by having allowed itself to become an adjunct of state (social) control systems without complaining very much. Psychiatry needs to become humane, to focus on therapy rather than control, to look for meanings rather than symptoms, to be on the side of people in need (with mental health problems), to oppose racism and all injustice, cleaning up its own house first. A start can be made by examining the use of schizophrenia as a diagnosis.

This book highlights the diagnosis of schizophrenia as playing a central role in the use of psychiatry – especially forensic psychiatry. In the main, the objections to the continuing use of schizophrenia as a diagnosis, in the face of its lack of validity as 'illness' and its excessive use with black people, relate to: (a) the negative effects of 'labelling' (Scheff, 1975) resulting from the diagnosis of a person as 'schizophrenic' – particularly that the door is thereby closed to a consideration of the person as a human being with 'ordinary' problems; (b) the way in which forensic psychiatry colludes with images of dangerousness and fear associated with black people that schizophrenia raises in Western society; and (c) the apparent use of schizophrenia diagnosis as a means of enforcing social control. In short, the diagnosis of schizophrenia is experienced by most black people as a tool for their oppression and control rather than for the alleviation of their suffering and the promotion of their wellbeing.

This criticism of schizophrenia as a diagnosis is not meant to imply that psychiatrists misdiagnose in order to avoid examining problems in depth, to reinforce the image of danger from black people, or to exercise control over other people. The argument presented here is that the availability of schizophrenia as an option in diagnosis with all its historical baggage, including its implications of genetic inferiority (not to speak of racial degeneration), enables *the system* (of psychiatry) to slip into all these behaviours. It may not be feasible for individual psychiatrists to work differently so long as the system promotes such a situation, but they, like all others involved in the field of forensic psychiatry, have a responsibility to strive to change the status quo. The authors, therefore, plead for deconstruction of the schizophrenia diagnosis and taking it out of the classification system as a start towards freeing up psychiatry allowing it to move forward by dealing with its ethnocentricity and racist practices. There is no simple way of achieving this deconstruction, but several approaches already present within the Western systems of thought are worth pursuing. In the application of cognitive therapy (Drury *et al.*, 1966) individual symptoms are considered as 'problems' although the current approach is to continue seeing them as part of an 'illness'. The 'hearing voices' movement (Romme and Escher, 1993) promotes the view that 'the real problem is not so much the hearing of these voices, but rather the inability to cope with them' (1993: 7). What both these approaches have in common is their tendency to try and 'understand' rather than control: to look for meanings rather than 'symptoms'.

Once the over-arching, over-inclusive concept schizophrenia is abandoned, models of health and therapy from Asian and African cultures (see Fernando, 1991) can then be examined and blended into an understanding of mental health that is derived multiculturally. A possible model for re-thinking psychiatry proposed in an earlier book (Fernando, 1995b) uses a basic distress coping model as a central theme which is 'related to a family systems analysis and, more widely, to political and social systems such as education, welfare, policing and psychiatry – the particular emphases depending on the sociopolitical-cultural context of the individual case' (1995b: 201). In the meantime, a change that can be implemented immediately is a shift from the diagnosis based approach in current practice to a needs based approach in psychiatric assessments, winding down (as it were) the predominance of diagnosis and emphasising the perceptions of people who need help. What is being advocated here is not an 'anti-psychiatry' (i.e. a hostility to psychiatry) but a psychiatry that connects with people. In the case of black and minority ethnic communities, this means a psychiatry that is firmly grounded in their experiences (including the experience of racism) and the many cultural strands that make up multi-ethnic societies in Europe and North America.

BLACK STAFF AND 'WHITE INSTITUTIONS'

It may seem that if more practitioners in the psychiatric services were from ethnic minorities this might lead to improvement of services for those minorities who are over-represented in forensic psychiatry services. Although this may well happen in some instances, current experience does not suggest that increasing the numbers of black staff within forensic psychiatry would make much difference overall under present circumstances. First, individual practitioners, however well intentioned, are unlikely to be able to change the way services are delivered because they work within strict constraints. Moreover, black staff working in institutions where the ethos is predominantly 'white' often face considerable problems in having their views heard, quite apart from being acted upon (see Fernando, 1996). Second, the training of psychiatrists fails to address issues of race and culture and most psychiatrists generally do not go much further than following (what is regarded as) 'normal' practice – i.e. ways of working that are institutionalised in training programmes. Indeed, they may well be taken to task if they do not follow such 'normal' practice. In other words, swimming against the tide is difficult for the average person (and most psychiatrists are average people), and reversing the tide is not something an individual can really accomplish, especially if she/he is trained to swim with it. In fact, it is not unusual in psychiatry (as in politics) for people previously identified as radicals to become conservative on entry into higher positions within bodies they were trying to reform. This is particularly evident in the forensic field because of the power structures inherent within it.

In developing services for a vulnerable or disadvantaged group of people, there is a need for those in authority over them to adhere to an ideology that involves respect for human and civil rights – and for this, a deep understanding of the ways in which power can be abused through racist and sexist practices in professional systems is essential (MIND, 1996f). Clearly, personal experience, concern about issues affecting minorities, sensitivity to cultural diversity and identification with people for whom services are provided are all important but they need to operate within a facilitative climate. When the institution of change involves challenging powerful conservative forces within a system such as forensic psychiatry, the chances of success are extremely problematic.

The elitism of psychiatrists is a major factor in shaping the relationship between black people and the psychiatric system – especially so within the field of forensic psychiatry where people who are 'patients' are seriously disempowered. It may appear to the general public that psychiatrists are united in their wish to continue the trend of diagnosing schizophrenia in large numbers among black people (referred to many times in this book). This is not really the case but it is the case that psychiatrists (and perhaps other professionals within the forensic services) calling for a radical re-think within the psychiatric system, or even merely querying the current psychiatric pre-occupation with diagnosing schizophrenia in the way it does, are usually sidelined. Anyone who ventures to deviate from the professional 'norm' is likely to find that she/he will be left in the lurch, unsupported by professional colleagues, if some untoward incident occurs as a result. Although virtually all psychiatrists are caught up in a power situation that perpetuates injustice, the resulting problems at a personal level impact mainly on black professional staff.

BLACK IDENTITY AND SEPARATE SERVICES

The sufferings of black people in the psychiatric system, whether through omission or commission, may draw concern from the dominant white society but the 'victim-role' may not enable lasting change to take place. bell hooks (1995) argues that white society today is comfortable with a victim-focused black identity which places white society in a superior caring (and controlling) position. By accepting and sometimes seeking a victim identity black folk collude in perpetuating white supremacy. She refers to the US scene, but her conclusions on this matter are applicable to the UK too. Although many British white people, especially those in authority, recognise the reality of racism that causes serious disadvantage, they are content to abrogate personal responsibility. bell hooks says, 'many white people are comfortable with a rhetoric of race that suggests racism cannot be changed, that all white people are "inherently racist" simply because they are born and raised in this society' (1995: 270). In calling for a shift 'from a framework of victimization to one of accountability', she accepts that this may involve some degree of 'separation' but believes that it 'need not be rooted in a separatist movement' (1995: 59–61). While arguing that black people need 'to construct places of political sanctuary where we can escape, if only for a time, white domination' (1995: 155), bell hooks advocates a search for a black self-determination that addresses the realities of modern ethnicities:

> There is no monolithic black identity. Many black families have expanded to include members who are multiracial and multi-ethnic. This concrete reality is one of the primary reasons nationalistic models seem retrograde and outmoded. While black self-determination is a political process that first seeks to engage the minds and hearts of black folks, it embraces coalition building across race as it is rooted in a sophisticated understanding of the way in which neo-colonial white supremacy

works and what must be done to effectively challenge and change it. It also recognizes the importance of black people learning from the wisdom of non-black people, especially other people of color.

(1995: 261)

Developing separate systems of mental health care, at least in the short-term, is one way forward for black people. Indeed, several ethnospecific counselling services have already been established in various parts of the UK; some have been listed by the organisation Good Practices in Mental Health (Harding, 1995). A new diploma in black therapy, taught by the Black Therapy Centre, includes in its programme of studies:

> The development from Cross-cultural to Transcultural therapies: A critical Black analysis of the dominant Western modes of Psychotherapy and Counselling: The development of Traditionalist, Reformist and Radical schools of Black Psychology in the USA: Explore and rediscover the traditional talk therapies of Africa, Caribbean, Indian Subcontinent and Central/South America.
>
> (Advertisement 1995: 52)

The authors are aware of other initiatives by black mental health professionals which aim to provide alternatives to ordinary psychiatric hospitals and these may eventually serve people who may otherwise become patients of forensic psychiatry. Some of these services are developing models of mental health that draw from non-Western cultural traditions. The main problem is that they are invariably under-resourced, since the bulk of resources are tied up in statutory services within the British National Health Service.

RESISTANCE STRATEGIES AND MENTAL HEALTH

Although there are many black organisations in the UK and many voluntary groups providing mental health services for minority communities, there is not, as yet, an effective 'common voice' – either over general issues or those concerned with mental health. One reason for this situation may be the lack of coherently articulated ways of opposing the injustices in psychiatry including forensic psychiatry. As bell hooks (1995) says about the USA: 'Until progressive black critical thinkers, especially those who specialize in mental health care, distinguish between habits of survival used to withstand racist assault that are no longer useful and those that were and remain constructive, there can be no collective development of resistance strategies that outline concrete ways to create healthy minds' (1995: 143).

Amos Wilson (1991), writing about the USA, advocates an array of community based strategies for crime prevention that are equally valid as strategies for mental health. He advocates 'Afrikan-centered educational rehabilitation' for African-Americans by which he means a combination of basic education, family support and job training together with psychotherapeutic programmes focusing on what he calls the 'nexus of alienation'. Such therapy addresses not only alienation itself but also includes 'the lack of knowledge of the criminogenic nature and operation of American racism and Euro-American economic imperialism; the sense of powerlessness; inadequate responses to stereotypical projections; unrealistic and self-destructive desires; internalization of racist attitudes; frustration; displacement; imitation of the aggressor; faulty self-concept; dysfunctional self-esteem; hostility; intellectual, social and personal incompetence; . . . other stress-producing and misdirective factors' (1991: 57). Such essentially self-help strategies are important for counteracting elements of self-hatred and internalised racism and for enabling black people to find ways of breaking out of the psychological and social stranglehold of white supremacy, but the wider political setting should not be ignored. Work at a national level to change general systems of society, including those of forensic psychiatry and criminal justice, is crucially important and for this purpose, alliances may need to be worked out with some white people and 'white institutions' – especially in the European (including British) setting.

Independent black religion

There is evidence, as noted earlier, in both UK and US contexts, that black communities are producing solutions and developing strategies to meet current problems related to mental health. There are networks and avenues which black people are using to try and counter-balance the inequities and inadequacies of the forensic system. However, the lack of organised black resistance to the damaging effects of forensic psychiatry is evident and the weakness of the black person's voice within forensic psychiatry, and indeed within mental health services as a whole, is obvious. For example, it has long been recognised (if not acknowledged) that black people are poorly represented in patients' councils in special hospitals – developed specifically with the aim of involving (and possibly empowering) people who are 'patients'. Although this may well be a result of black people experiencing such bodies as racist, it is likely also that the structures themselves do not suit black people.

In such a context, a discussion of the black church/religion is relevant. In the USA and, to some extent in the UK, the black church and other religious bodies have played and continue to play a crucial and integral role in helping to develop and enhance the mental and spiritual wellbeing of its constituency – black communities. Anderson *et al.* (1990) argue that this occurs in the USA despite the existence of other support mechanisms:

> It is understandable that, as other avenues have opened up for black people in terms of social, political and carer opportunities, the all-inclusive function of the church might become somewhat less significant. However, as needs of the community have changed, so has the role of the church. A very recent example of this is the action that black churches have taken in responding to the need for child care by establishing in-house day-care centres.
>
> (1990: 266)

In Britain, the black church has played a similar role, for example, in education. Saturday schools in black British churches have long been a mainstay of support and guidance for black children who are failed, and regarded as failures, by mainstream British schools. In this connection, it should be noted that the spiritual traditions lost to the 'sciences' of Western psychology and psychiatry are still available in the psychologies of Asia and Africa (see Chapter 2); and black people who derive their cultural background from these traditions, however 'Westernised' they may be, still continue to value spirituality. In the authors' view, the leap from day-care and Saturday schools to mental health care is not as wide as might be imagined; the application of ecclesiastical mechanisms with a spiritual dimension can be brought to bear on what goes on within forensic psychiatric services. However, it must be added that support of this kind in practice must be organised in a context that is independent of statutory services. Religion in the hands of the state can indeed be abused and enlisted as an 'opium of the masses'. So, any model for bringing in 'religion' as a means of influencing the forensic system must be administered and controlled by those with the greatest stake in achieving an equitably beneficial outcome, namely black people themselves.

The suggestion here is that religion in its widest all-encompassing sense, can be an influence in bringing about changes in the forensic psychiatry system and/or counteracting some of the damaging effects (on black people) of this system. Therefore, the authors propose that black churches, Muslim, Buddhist and Hindu religious groups, and other religious organisations can and should be allowed to foster links with predominantly 'white' forensic psychiatry institutions as a means of bringing about change. Second, it is suggested that these religious organisations can offer a lifeline to black detained patients in all mental health settings. It must be underlined, however, that such action must be independent of statutory services and both accepted by, and acceptable to, black religious (and other) organisations in the community. The point is that there are networks within black communities that can and do work for black people, and these must be brought into working for black people trapped within the forensic services. However, while suggesting the advantages of religious organisations being involved in the forensic psychiatry scene, it is important that the political setting in which forensic psychiatry functions is not forgotten or played down. Work at a national level to change systems of society, including those of forensic psychiatry and criminal justice, is crucially important.

SERVICE STRUCTURE IN ENGLAND AND WALES

Radical changes in clinical practice within forensic psychiatry are unlikely to come from within the (medical) psychiatric profession – at least without pressure on it to change. Therefore, other ways for initiating change need to be considered. First, it is possible that a privately run service that responds to 'markets' may be more responsive to needs of black people (than the currently complacent state system) if consumers are seen as the public rather than state authorities. Unfortunately, black people are not likely to have the economic means to access such a service and this may not be a viable proposition anyway. Second, litigation by patients, their relatives or advocates, might set legal precedents leading to the setting of 'minimum standards' (that take race and culture on board) for assessment, diagnosis and treatment. Also, the institution of obligatory clinical practice guidelines devised on the basis of evidence from both professionals and service users might initiate change and, incidentally, open up psychiatric practice to public scrutiny. Third, since a recent increase in the sophistication of lawyers in Mental Health Review Tribunals and Managers' Hearings (of appeals against detention) has led to some improvements in ensuring that detention in hospital conforms properly to the Mental Health Act, further legal involvement in the arrangements within forensic psychiatry may help to improve matters. Perhaps the legal profession should take an interest in the legality of compulsory entry into the system by (for example) challenging professionals involved in signing detention forms and close questioning of psychiatrists giving oral evidence where restriction orders under Section 41 of the Mental Health Act are contemplated.

Diversion

Diversion from the criminal justice system (CJS) to forensic psychiatric services (or even the general psychiatric services) of people deemed 'mentally ill' is a policy that is being pursued at present (see Chapter 11). As such diversions gather momentum, there are calls for modification to the Mental Health Act to enable potentially 'dangerous' people to be managed within psychiatric services or by means of surveillance in the community. This is a serious cause for concern as such calls are most vehemently articulated with respect to inner city areas with quite large black populations. As far as black people are concerned, the choice offered between the CJS and forensic psychiatry has been one of the frying pan and the fire. Surveillance in the community is unlikely to be an improvement on compulsory detention in hospital because such surveillance will almost certainly involve heavy tranquillisation.

Supervised discharge

Among the provisions for 'supervised discharge' in the Patients in the Community Act (HMSO, 1995) is the power to impose requirements (on people in the community) 'to attend for medical treatment, occupation, education or training' (1995: 7). Disquiet has been voiced by service users and others about these requirements (see MIND, 1996g), especially if (as seems likely) it is not made clear to people affected that there is no legal compulsion actually to accept the treatment. Moreover, supervised discharge in the community with the spectre of enforced and compulsory treatment in the community, may well focus on black people. In its response to the introduction of supervision registers (which predated supervised discharge) and supervised discharge orders, the Black Mental Health Professionals Network noted (Aveleon Associates and the Black Mental Health Professionals Network, 1994):

> We are categorically opposed to the introduction of the Department of Health policy regarding Supervised Discharge Orders and Supervision Registers on the grounds that this is a repressive and punitive response to the actual care needs of people who may be severely mentally ill. While the policy is intended to ensure that adequate care is provided for those in the community, supervision itself fails to tackle the outstanding need for more appropriate care responses – not only at this sharper end of mental health services, but variously throughout the system.
>
> (1994: 1)

Clearly, the danger is that over-representation of black people in psychiatric institutions will be complemented in the community by disproportionate over-representation of black people among those who are required to 'attend for treatment' under the powers inherent in the Patients in the Community Act. It is imperative that there should be ethnic monitoring of the use of the powers in this Act and that every effort is made to ensure that the Act itself is repealed as soon as possible.

Special hospitals

There is considerable confusion at the time of writing on the future of special hospitals. If the guiding principles in the Reed report (Department of Health and Home Office, 1992a) are followed, professional and geographical isolation of these institutions would be reduced, leading to only rare cases of placement of patients at inappropriate levels of security and patients being managed close to their homes whatever the level of security involved.

At present, the effect of media publicity appears to determine responses that politicians and managers of these institutions make in response to any suggestions for change or (for example) criticism about particular issues such as the granting of leave to patients. In this respect, managements seems to be their own worst enemies particularly when low risk patients with escorted leave in the community fail to return from their leave. The management response in such instances has sometimes been unfair to the patients concerned and demoralising to staff involved. There has been frequent criticism of one of the trade unions that many of the nursing staff belong to: this union appears to venture into national policy-forming on its own. It may be the case that the management style of special hospitals generates trade union activity that takes a narrow view of how best to meet the needs of their members. Therefore, reform may be required right at the very top to change the culture of management. And even before that, it may be necessary to obtain clear and explicit agreement/disagreement on policy between the main policy makers in both the Department of Health and the Home Office. Clearly, issues of cost come into the picture: a narrow view may well suggest that special hospitals are cost effective since they maximise economies of scale and decentralisation and that their replacement with relatively small units closer to where patients come from would be a relatively expensive option. But, a wider view, which takes into consideration the length of stay of patients, therapeutic effectiveness of care and common humanity (all interrelated matters), may well reveal that special hospitals are a relatively expensive option in comparison to small, local units. In any case, people who have the task of determining policy should consider where their priorities lie – cost effectiveness is not the only issue at stake. And the views of the main stake-holders, namely the people who become patients of these hospitals and their relatives, should be consulted in the first place.

Restriction orders (Section 41 of Mental Health Act)

Restriction orders are the gift of the judge in court. They are given when it 'appears to the court having regard to the nature of the offence, the antecedents of the offender and the risk of his or her committing further offences if set at large, that it is necessary for the protection of the public from serious harm so to do' (Jones, 1996: 180). Before a judge imposes such an order he or she is required to hear oral evidence from one of the medical practitioners providing reports for the purposes of the hospital orders, although the judge need not follow the course of action recommended by the medical practitioners. Guidance on the application of restriction orders states that they are not a means of punishment and they are not a mark of the gravity of an offence. It is also made clear that the harm being referred to is serious harm in the future rather than in the past. Patients who are affected by these orders tend to perceive them as the equivalent of a life sentence and resent the fact that they give the Home Office, rather than medical personnel, a final say in matters of such crucial nature as 'parole' (leave to visit the community) and discharge.

It is increasingly common for forensic psychiatrists to make explicit (in their reports to courts) their assessments – inevitably largely subjective in nature – of the seriousness of an offence and then to recommend restriction orders before the court itself has considered the matter; such assessments tend to be taken as 'clinical' judgements, thereby compromising the role of a medical practitioner in court. In other words, this practice muddles a clinician's medical function *vis-à-vis* the patient with a 'policing' function – and black patients are at particular risk of suffering from such a muddle because of the popular stereotypes of dangerousness associated with race. An authoritative legal opinion clarifying the role of doctors in the process that leads to imposition of restriction orders needs to be established, given that a judgement on the seriousness of an offence is *not* a 'clinical' matter at all.

TRAINING

The role of forensic psychiatry as social control means that judgements about people become personalised – a judgement about the person rather than his/her behaviour. Judging the person inevitably involves making (judgmental) decisions about attitudes, beliefs and ways of thinking – in other words about their cultures. In a multi-ethnic society, this is not a simple matter of applying established norms but allowing for differences and, more importantly, ensuring that racist perceptions do not influence the judgements made. Such safeguards do not usually exist within the framework of psychiatric practice and indeed it is difficult to see how they could exist unless there are major changes in the fundamentals of both psychiatry and psychology. However, anti-racist training of staff working in forensic psychiatry together with strongly enforced anti-racist policies (see later) may go some way towards redressing some of the injustices that prevail in the operation of forensic psychiatry.

The training of staff who work in British forensic psychiatry seldom adequately addresses issues of race and cultural difference, quite apart from addressing a political dimension. Changing this situation is of primary importance, not just in the interests of users of psychiatric services, especially those from black and other minority ethnic groups, but in the interest of psychiatry as a discipline. Any major re-structuring of training for professional staff (including psychiatrists) is a large subject that cannot be covered in this book. However, immediate changes could be instituted (if the political will is evoked to do so) with specific training to address issues of racism and cultural difference. An outline of a scheme for this purpose is given in Box 15.3.

Box 15.3: Cultural difference and racism: aims of training

Understanding and identifying racism

e.g.

Related to cultural difference

Related to psychiatric practice, theory and research

Learning to counteract the effects of racism

e.g.

Examining assumptions

Looking at cultures and at cultural differences

e.g.

Ways of seeing illness and health

Effects of stereotypes on evaluations and therapy

Putting the training into practice

e.g.

Social and political pressures

Personal pressures to conform to traditional practice (political correctness)

RESEARCH

Much of the research appertaining to forensic psychiatry published in psychiatric and psychological journals generally reflects two fundamental problems: first, research is often disconnected from real needs of the communities and the people that are being researched (and who are supposed to benefit from the results of the research). On the one hand, many research centres and/or researchers are geared towards ensuring publication in settings where 'peer review' means the satisfaction of so-called scientific criteria (that take measures of 'good' research in the physical sciences as its standard); on the other hand, needs of people and communities reflect real problems of living – very often (in the case of black people) pressurised by stresses of racism. Also, there are generally no structures in place to enable communities to feed in their views and demands to researchers and research centres in any meaningful and effective way – and it often appears to be the case that research centres do not want such structures anyway. Second, research – especially clinical research – uses methodologies based on models of 'illness' and 'health' that do not address cultural differences and racist perceptions. The result is that diagnoses are assumed to be objective facts, rather than concepts that are ethnocentric, and 'findings' are interpreted in terms of biological variations or pathology. In other words, the fact that diagnoses such as schizophrenia have never been cross-culturally validated is ignored and biased stereotypes of black people are allowed free access into research methodology. Consequently, 'findings' of many clinical research studies in the field of race and culture carry no guarantee of freedom from racism – in fact, sometimes, conclusions actually reflect racism (Fernando, 1988).

The situation at present in the UK reflects a considerable gulf between the two 'sides' – researchers and black communities – resulting in distrust and anger (by black people) towards all psychiatric research. However, research cannot be ignored and the main issue about research is the consequence of publication in reputable journals: psychiatric and psychological papers published in well established learned journals have a strong influence on the culture of psychiatry and hence on psychiatric practice. In the case of mental health, so-called conclusions published in 'scientific' journals, quoting 'scientific' research, wield social and political power which effect the lives of people intimately, mainly because something so published is regarded as 'fact'. These 'facts' get translated into action through the systems controlled by psychiatry. In the course of correspondence in the *Psychiatric Bulletin* following the publication of a paper reporting research into schizophrenia among black people (Harrison *et al.*, 1988), a letter urged the adoption by the *British Journal of Psychiatry* of the following criteria for the assessment of scientific worth and usefulness of research (Fernando, 1989):

(a) Research into black people must address the realities of life for *them* in this country and not make assumptions based on the experiences of white people only.
(b) Research that uses white Eurocentric concepts, such as our present concept of schizophrenia, must allow for the fact that their validity as useful cross-cultural concepts is usually unproven – as is the case with schizophrenia.
(c) The presentation of research must be sensitive to the consequences of racism in society, such as inequalities in (psychiatric) service provision and the relatively excessive numbers of black people being detained, and must deal with the likelihood of research findings being used for reinforcing them.
(d) The involvement of psychiatry in social control systems . . . must be addressed, both in research methodology and in the presentation of findings, as an important factor that affects psychiatry's perceptions of black people and *vice versa*.

(1989: 574)

Several years later (1994), another attempt was made to highlight the issues about research into schizophrenia, but letters to the editor were not published (and hence cannot be referenced). The resistance of the psychiatric establishment to consider criticism of its procedures around research requires outside intervention – and this is particularly urgent in the field of forensic psychiatry. Since most of the funds for research are derived from public money, directly or indirectly, this is an area in which government action is justified. The authors propose that a system should be established to regulate psychiatric and psychological research in the mental health field through careful vetting of projects (presented for funding) by committees accountable to the community at large, rather than professional bodies alone. Together with intervention in the procedures for granting research funding, the 'peer review' system for papers submitted for publication requires standardising to incorporate public accountability.

COMBATING RACISM

All attempts to counteract racism must be informed by an understanding of its nature. The recognition of the cultural plurality of society – multiculturalism – is not to be confused with anti-racism. The two are quite different and (as discussed in Chapter 1), multiculturalism itself may be racist. In modern Western societies in both Europe and North America, racism functions today in a context of the recognition of – indeed sometimes the 'celebration of' – 'cultural difference'. Throughout this book, the structural nature of racism – institutional racism – has been emphasised. However, this is not to say that people running the institutions of society (including forensic psychiatry) have no responsibility. It may be true to say that in a European and US setting, everyone is socialised into racism, through education, the media etc. And, as bell hooks (1995) states 'some misguided thinking socializes white people both to remain ignorant of the way in which white supremacist attitudes are learned and to assume a posture of learned helplessness as though they have no agency – no capacity to resist this thinking' (1995: 270). Clearly this is not so and it is not so with regard to racism in forensic psychiatry and psychology. Both black and white people working in the field of forensic psychiatry have a responsibility to counteract white supremacist thinking that informs research, practice and day-to-day dealings with black people. And managers and administrators of the institutions that provide forensic psychiatry too have a definite responsibility to address racism within their domains.

The pervasive nature of institutionalised racism in society means that attempts to combat it in one specific part of the society, such as forensic psychiatry, are necessarily limited and also that any changes resulting from anti-racist measures can well be lost unless they are constantly renewed. Since forensic psychiatry is so closely allied with the criminal justice system, this section will examine briefly issues of combating racism in the latter before dealing with forensic psychiatry itself.

Criminal justice system

The prevalence of racism in the criminal justice system (CJS) is clearly recognised by the (British) Home Office. In the Criminal Justice Act 1991, Section 95 requires the Home Secretary to publish annually information which would help 'persons engaged in the administration of criminal justice' to perform 'their duty to avoid discriminating against any person on the ground of race or sex or any other improper ground'. The Penal Affairs Consortium (1996) lists the following as positive moves made since the implementation of this act:

> In April 1996, ethnic monitoring became mandatory in all police forces for arrests, cautions, stop-and-searches, and homicide.
>
> The CPS has drawn up a sample monitoring scheme for 1996/7.
>
> A pilot project has been initiated to gather information on ethnicity of defendants appearing before courts in order to monitor bail and sentencing.
>
> A national system for ethnic monitoring was introduced in the probation system.
>
> The Prison Service conducts ethnic monitoring within its areas of control.

However, a recent report of the National Association of Probation Officers and Association of Black Probation Officers, *Race Discrimination and the Criminal Justice System* (1996) states:

> There are at present no High Court judges from minority ethnic groups.
>
> In 1995, only 5 of the 514 circuit judges, 2 of the 339 district judges, 13 of the 897 recorders were from minority ethnic groups.
>
> In 1995 there were no black justices' clerks and very few deputy clerks.
>
> In September 1995, 2,223 (1.7%) of the 127,222 police officers were from minority ethnic groups.
>
> In 1995, five (0.49%) of the Prison Service's 1,020 governor grades were from minority ethnic groups.
>
> The representation of ethnic minorities among probation officers (7.6% in 1995) shows a steady rise over the years.

The areas in which action is required are obvious: the question is one of political will and acceptable strategies. Work at ground level (in police and judicial education, monitoring of police and court activity etc.) must be supplemented by attention to issues at the higher echelons of power within the CJS. Ethnic monitoring must continue in order to identify areas that need attention and the effects of any action that is taken.

Forensic psychiatry

It cannot be emphasised too strongly that racism is expressed in diverse ways throughout society, and racism in any one system, be it forensic psychiatry or criminal justice, cannot be seen in isolation from others. Therefore any moves to counteract racism within forensic psychiatry must be taken in the knowledge of all that is going on around it as well as within it. Anti-racist strategies (say) to limit the impact of racism in diagnosis cannot succeed except within an anti-racist approach within the forensic psychiatry system as a whole. The broad basis of an anti-racist approach for an institution (e.g. a Health Service Trust in the case of the UK) is outlined in Box 15.1. Within such a broad general policy, individual strategies need to focus on different parts of the system. For example, in the case of training, a possible outline plan is given in Box 15.3.

This book cannot provide any more than basic guidance/advice for anti-racist work suitable for forensic psychiatry. It is important that an anti-racist approach at any point, policy, training scheme, etc., needs to be fashioned to fit the particular needs, based on, for example, prior assessment of the people involved and the deficiencies of the system. A ready-made, off-the-shelf plan may be worthless or, even more importantly, counter-productive. In the case of professional practice, anti-racist training must be conducted in the context of general training of (medical) psychiatric trainees, nurses and psychologists, although there may be a place in some settings for multidisciplinary training sessions. Further guidance on anti-racist training is contained in the chapter 'Training to promote race equality' (Ferns and Madden, 1995) in the book *Mental Health in a Multi-Ethnic Society: a Multi-Disciplinary Handbook* (Fernando, 1995a), which forms a useful background to any such training.

POLITICAL/LEGAL CHANGES

The fastest route to change forensic services could come from political pressure and/or legal changes. As a result of the demands of service users themselves being heeded by managers of mental health services, user involvement in specification of services and advocacy (on behalf of patients) within general psychiatric services are now well established. Similar developments in the field of forensic psychiatry are now just beginning and may become a significant influence. Although it is unlikely that psychiatrists will welcome any input by black service users (or potential service users) into determining (what they consider) 'clinical' matters, such as methods of establishing diagnosis, the appropriateness of prescribed treatment and decisions about treatment setting, these are areas in which user involvement can be crucial in correcting some of the injustices of the present system – especially those suffered by black people as patients within forensic psychiatry services.

The UK elected a new government (May 1997), which has voiced its intention to advance human rights of British citizens by (for example) incorporating the European Convention on Human Rights into British law. Clearly, any definition of human rights in a society where racism is prevalent (e.g. British society) must address rights of black people to protection from direct and indirect racial discrimination and this in turn should impact on issues in clinical psychiatric practice (including diagnostic bias). If the government decides to revise the Mental Health Act 1983 (HMSO, 1983), it is essential that the areas for change should be clearly set out to start with. The material in this book would argue strongly for the following changes: (a) incorporation into the Mental Health Act of basic human rights based on the European Declaration on Human Rights; (b) re-structuring of the basis for compulsory detention (and appeals against detention) so that biased assessments and a failure to address issues of cultural difference cannot be used to justify compulsory detention. This may be achieved by specific rules about training of professionals involved in detention, obligation to heed the views of families and communities, etc.; (c) incorporation into the Mental Health Act of anti-discriminatory legislation in the provision of services already available in the Race Relations Act (see Home Office and Central Office of Information, 1977) adapted to suit the mental health scene – especially relating to assessments and treatments.

FORENSIC PSYCHOTHERAPY

The idea that psychotherapy for people with a 'forensic' label is qualitatively different from other forms of psychotherapy is highly questionable. In any case, psychotherapy itself falls within the diverse types of help (for people with mental health problems) generally subsumed under the term 'talking therapies' (e.g. MIND, 1995a), which includes both counselling and psychotherapy. Since many of these therapies are derived from Western psychology, their suitability for people whose cultural background is non-Western – or only partially Western – is problematic (Fernando, 1991). Apart from this, however, there are other issues too: it is generally the case that therapists practising counselling/psychotherapy fail to face up to issues of racism and cultural difference except at centres which are explicitly set up for black and other minority ethnic groups. But such centres seldom deal with people actively using the forensic services because they are based in the community (rather than hospital) and, in any case, professionals working in forensic psychiatry seldom refer clients to them. Psychotherapy organised within the forensic psychiatric services themselves, such as the psychotherapy service at Broadmoor Hospital, appears to ignore the fact that many of their potential clients are from black and minority ethnic communities. Anecdotal evidence suggests that few people from these communities are taken on by psychotherapists in the special hospitals.

There are clearly fundamental problems within forensic psychotherapy, relating to issues of racism and cultural difference. It is not possible in this section to do more than attempt to point the way towards some changes that can be made in the foreseeable future.

First, it is essential that the approach in any form of 'talking therapy' should be culturally appropriate and sensitive to racism. So, fundamental changes in the training of therapists are needed in the long run, but in the short and medium term considerable progress can be achieved by (for example) forensic psychiatry services linking up with established counselling services in the community, especially those organised and staffed by black and minority ethnic communities. Such links can be made at various levels. For example, counsellors currently working in black and minority ethnic community projects can be invited (and paid) to work within the psychotherapy departments of (say) the special hospitals. It may be necessary to establish separate subdepartments so that black and minority ethnic therapists can pursue their own ways of working without being dominated by the current 'establishment'. Second, realistic and sensitive counselling should be introduced at a grass-roots level – i.e. at the level of ward management. The present structure is that nurses on the ward are expected to be available for counselling of patients in hospital. In view of the dual nature of their role as both therapists and custodians, it would be appropriate for professionals from outside the hospital to be employed as counsellors for patients. In such a context, patients should be given a choice of where their counsellors come from. In the case of people from black and minority ethnic communities, the counsellors may well come from voluntary organisations dedicated to working with particular communities. No new money needs to be allocated for such a scheme because ward based counselling is already practised (perhaps without much success because it is left to ward based nurses whose role in forensic psychiatry is largely custodial). Third, counselling aimed at preventive work should be pursued actively. Here again black and minority ethnic organisations should be involved and some of the US suggestions by Amos Wilson (referred to earlier) may be pursued through funding derived from forensic psychiatry.

MEDICATION

The most worrying aspect of current psychiatric treatment which affects black people in particular is the disabling effect of medication (usually associated with a diagnosis of schizophrenia) and the coercion involved in ensuring compliance. This is a situation unlike any other in medicine. Psychiatry – in particular forensic psychiatry – is unique in giving users of the services very little say in determining the nature and type of medication they are prescribed and influencing decisions on the type of environment they are treated in. Where patient groups (service users) are well organised – for example in the National Childbirth Trust (NCT) – they can influence the shape of consultation with professionals, the designs of environments in which they are cared for, the treatments on offer and the range of choices in treatment that patients are offered, by campaigning for changes. Unfortunately, psychiatric patients are not well organised and positive action should be taken to remedy this – perhaps by providing government support for the organisations that do exist, such as the Black Users and Carers Network and the recently formed organisation allied to MIND called 'Diverse Minds'.

There is considerable scope for pressure on pharmaceutical companies (for example) to invest in developing drugs that are relatively 'clean' i.e. free of the adverse effects identified as such by patients who are affected. Also it should be mandatory for drug firms to publicise the serious problems that arise from psychotropic medication, especially when used in high dosages. Modern pharmaceutical companies are concerned about the image they project and may well respond to such pressure. Government-sponsored publicity of the disadvantages of medication, perhaps through the Health Education Authority (HEA), both within and outside the mental health field, could change public attitudes and thence psychiatric practice. Further, the threat of litigation for injury caused by treatment may be held as a possible sanction for failure of compliance by hospitals and mental health professionals.

MIND, the National Association for Mental Health, has recently launched a scheme whereby people who have suffered unwanted effects ('side effects') of psychotropic medication may report their experiences using a 'yellow card'. In reporting on information received in the first year of its operation MIND (1996e) states:

> The vast majority of people reporting adverse reactions to MIND believed that they did not receive enough information (87 per cent) and they were not warned of possible adverse effects before taking the drug (86 per cent). While many reported clear and considerable benefits from their drug treatment, less than half (46 per cent) were convinced of the drugs' overall helpfulness, and there were many unequivocal reports that they had caused damage.

An extension of this yellow card scheme with public recognition of the validity of service users' views about the treatment they receive could bring about changes in prescribing habits.

Another approach which could bring about some modification of the over-use of psychotropic medication may be through controls on the activities of pharmaceutical companies, which not only manufacture the drugs that are used by psychiatrists but (understandably) promote their use through advertising aimed at maximising the use of their products. Since these 'products' could be damaging, it would seem appropriate for the activities of these companies to be regulated in the public interest. A government appointed regulator to oversee pharmaceutical companies, similar to regulators that oversee activities of companies providing public utilities, such as water and electricity, could safeguard the interests of the general public if given the necessary legal powers.

CONCLUSIONS

This chapter set out to examine changes that are feasible and practicable *and* likely to alleviate some of the serious injustices inherent in the present system of forensic psychiatry in the UK. However, it should be stated that these are short-term changes; in the long-term, fundamental issues of racism within the psychiatric system need to be challenged and redressed, and psychiatry needs to face up to reforming itself culturally, in order to become appropriate for people of all ethnic groups that form British society.

Bibliography

Adams, W. and Kendell, R. E. (1996) 'Influenza and schizophrenia', *British Journal of Psychiatry*, 169, 252–3.

Adebimpe, V. R. (1981) 'An overview: white norms and psychiatric diagnosis of black patients', *American Journal of Psychiatry*, 138, 279–85.

—— (1984) 'American blacks and psychology', *Transcultural Psychiatric Research Review*, 21, 83–111.

—— (1994) 'Race, racism and epidemiological surveys', *Hospital and Community Psychiatry*, 45, 1, 27–31.

Adebimpe, V. R., Chu, C., Klein, H. E. and Lange, M. H. (1982a) 'Racial and geographic differences in the psychopathology of schizophrenia', *American Journal of Psychiatry*, 139, 888–91.

Adebimpe, V. R., Hedlund, J. L. and Dong, W. C. (1982b) 'Symptomatology of depression in black and white patients', *Journal of National Medical Association*, 74, 185–99.

Adshead, G. (1996), 'Risk and Rights', *Community Care*, 15–21 (February), 14–16.

Advertisement (1995) 'Diploma in Black Therapy' *Journal of Black Therapy*, 1, 1, 52.

Ahmad, W. I. U. and Atkin, K. (1996) '"Race" and community care', Milton Keynes: Open University Press.

Akbar, N. (1984) *Chains and Images of Psychological Slavery*, Jersey City, NJ: New Mind Publications.

—— (1996) 'An interview', *Journal of Black Therapy*, 1, 2, 10.

Albonetti, C. A. (1990) 'Race and the probability of pleading guilty', *Journal of Quantitative Criminology*, 6, 3, 315–34.

Alvarez, A. (1992) 'Trends and patterns of justifiable homicide: a comparative analysis', *Violence and victims*, 7, 4.

Amato, P. R. (1991) 'Parental absence during childhood and depression in later life', *Sociological Quarterly* 32, 4, 543–56.

American Psychiatric Association (1980) *Diagnostic and Statistical Manual of Mental Disorders* (DSM-III), Washington, DC: American Psychiatric Association, 3rd edn.

—— (1987) *Diagnostic and Statistical Manual of Mental Disorders* (DSM-

III-R), Washington, DC: American Psychiatric Association, revised 3rd edn.
—— (1994) *Diagnostic and Statistical Manual of Mental Disorders* (DSM-IV), Washington, DC: American Psychiatric Association, 4th edn.
Amnesty International (1997) *United States of America: Death Penalty Developments in 1996*, London: Amnesty International.
Anderson, L., Eaddy, C. and Williams, E. (1990) 'Psychosocial competence: towards a theory of understanding positive mental health among black Americans', in D. S. Ruiz (ed.) *Handbook of Mental Health and Disorder Among Black Americans*, New York: Greenwood Press, 255–67.
Ardrey, R. (1967) *The Territorial Imperative*, London: Collins.
Arthur, J. A. (1994) 'Correctional ideology of black correctional officers', *Federal Probation*, 58, 57–61.
Aveleon Associates and the Black Mental Health Professionals Network (1994) *Response to Supervision Registers and Supervised Discharge* (September), London: Aveleon Associates.
Babcock, J. W. (1895) 'The colored insane', *Alienist and Neurologist*, 16, 423–7.
Balarajan, R. and Raleigh, V. S. (1993) *Health of the Nation: Ethnicity and Health*, London: Department of Health.
Banton, M. (1987) *Racial Theories* Cambridge: Cambridge University Press.
Banton, M. and Harwood, J. (1975) *The Race Concept*, London: David and Charles.
Bark, N. M. (1985) 'Did Shakespeare know schizophrenia? The case of poor mad Tom in King Lear', *British Journal of Psychiatry*, 146, 436–8.
Barker, M. (1990) 'Biology and the new racism', in D. T. Goldberg (ed.) *Anatomy of Racism*, Minneapolis, MN: University of Minnesota Press, 18–37.
Barnes, D. M. (1987) 'Biological Issues in Schizophrenia', *Science*, 235, 430–3.
Bartlett, A. (1995) 'Comments from Conference at Springfield Hospital', Pathfinder Mental Health Services NHS Trust (26 September).
Battaglia, M. and Torgersen, S. (1996) 'Schizotypal disorder: at the crossroads of genetics and nosology', *Acta Psychiatrica Scandinavica*, 94, 303–10.
Barzun, J. (1965) *Race: a Study of Superstition*, New York: Harper & Row.
Bayer, R. (1981) *Homosexuality and American Psychiatry: the Politics of Diagnosis*, New York: Basic Books.
Bebbington, P. E., Hurry, J. and Tennant, C. (1981) 'Psychiatric disorder in selected immigrant groups in Camberwell', *Social Psychiatry*, 16, 43–51.
Beccaria, C. (1764) *Dei delitti e delle pene* (Crime and Punishment), Livorno; repr. Pick, 1824.
Beck, J. C. (1994) 'Process in the criminal justice system', *Criminal Behaviour and Mental Health*, 4, 84–8.
—— (1996) 'Forensic psychiatry in the USA and UK: a clinician's view', *Criminal Behaviour and Mental Health*, 6, 1, 11–28.
Bell, C. C., Thompson, B., Shorter-Gooder, K., Shakoor, B., Dew, D.,

Hughley, E. and Mays, R. (1985) 'Prevalence of coma in black subjects', *Journal of National Medical Association*, 77, 5, 391–5.

Bennett, D. (1996) 'Homicide inquiries and scapegoating', *Psychiatric Bulletin*, 120, 298–300.

Bentham, J. (1789) *An Introduction to the Principles of Morals and Legislation*, New York: Macmillan, 1982.

Bernal, M. (1987) *Black Athena: the Afroasiatic Roots of Classical Civilisation*, vol. 1, London: Free Association.

Berrios, G. E. and Chen, E. Y. H. (1993) 'Recognising psychiatric symptoms: relevance of diagnostic practice', *British Journal of Psychiatry*, 163, 308–14.

Berry, J. (1969) 'On cross-cultural comparability', *International Journal of Psychology*, 4, 119–28.

Bhabha, H. (1994) *The Location of Culture*, London: Routledge.

Bhugra, D. (1992) 'Psychiatry in ancient Indian texts: a review', *History of Psychiatry*, 3, 167–86.

Bhugra, D., Leff, J., Mallett, R., Der, G., Corridan, B. and Rudge, S. (1997) 'Incidence and outcome of schizophrenia in whites, African-Caribbeans and Asians in London', *Psychological Medicine*, 27, 791–8.

Bhui, K. (1997) 'London's ethnic minorities and the provision of mental health services', in S. Johnson, *et al.* (eds) *London's Mental Health: the Report to the King's Fund London Commission*, London: King's Fund, 143–66.

Birchwood, M., Cochrane, R., MacMillan, F., Copestake, F., Kucharska, J. and Carris, M. (1992) 'The influence of ethnicity and family structure on relapse in first episode schizophrenia', *British Journal of Psychiatry*, 161, 783–90.

Black, M. M. and Ricardo, I. B. (1994) 'Drug use, drug trafficking and weapon carrying among low income African-American early adolescent boys', *Paediatrics*, 93, 6, 1065–73.

Blau, J. and Blau, P. (1982) 'The cost of inequality: metropolitan structure and violent crime', *American Sociological Review* 47, 114–29.

Bleuler, E. (1911) *Dementia Prœcox or the Group of Schizophrenias*, trans. J. Zitkin, New York: International Universities Press; repr. 1950.

Bloombaum, M., Yamamoto, J. and James, Q. C. (1968) 'Cultural stereotyping among psychotherapists', *Journal of Consulting and Clinical Psychology*, 32, 99.

Blueglass, R. (1990) 'The scope of forensic psychiatry', *Journal of Forensic Psychiatry*, 1, 1, 5–9.

Blumenbach, J. F. (1776) *On the Natural Varieties of Mankind*, New York: Bergman Publishers, New York; repr. 1969 and as extracts in Eze, 1997.

Blumstein, A. (1982) 'On the racial disproportionality of the US prison system', *Journal of Criminal Law and Criminology*, 73, 3, 1259–81.

Bolton, P. (1984) 'Management of compulsorily admitted patients in a high security unit', *International Journal of Social Psychiatry*, 30, 77–84.

Bonger, W. A. (1943) *Race and Crime*, trans. from Dutch M. M. Hordyk, New York: Columbia University Press.

Bowden, P. (1985) 'Psychiatry and dangerousness: a counter renaissance?', in L. Gostin (ed.), *Secure Provision*, London: Tavistock, 265–87.

Bowser, B. P. (1995) 'Racism in the modern world community', in B. P. Bowser (ed.), *Racism and Anti-Racism in World Perspective*, London: Sage Publications, 285–309.

Boyle, M. (1990) *Schizophrenia: a Scientific Delusion*, London: Routledge.

Brakel, S. J. and Cavanaugh, J. L. (1996) 'Law and psychiatry in the USA and UK: another perspective', *Criminal Behaviour and Mental Health*, 6, 1, 28–40.

Brand, C. (1996) *The g Factor: General Intelligence and its Implications*, Chichester: John Wiley.

Bright, T. (1586) *A Treatise of Melancholy*, London: Vautrolier.

Brizer, D. A. (1989) 'Overview of current approaches to the prediction of violence', in D. A. Brizer and M. L. Crowner (eds) *Current Approaches to the Prediction of Violence*, Washington, DC: American Psychiatric Press, xi–xxiii.

Brown, D. R., Ahmed, F., Gary, L. E. and Milburn, N.G. (1995) 'Major depression in a community sample of African-Americans', *American Journal of Psychiatry*, 152, 373–78.

Brown, J. S. and Tooke, S. K. (1992) 'On the seclusion of psychiatric patients', *Social Science and Medicine*, 35, 5, 711–21.

Browne, D. (1990) *Black People, Mental Health and the Courts*, London: NACRO.

—— (1997) *Black People and Sectioning. The Black Experience of Detention under the Civil Sections of the Mental Health Act*, London: Little Rock Publishing.

Bryan, B., Dadzie, S. and Scafe, S. (1985) *The Heart of the Race: Black Women's Lives in Britain*, London: Virago.

Burke, A. (1995) 'Talk', *Meeting at St Georges Hospital Medical School* (21 October).

Burton, R. (1621) *The Anatomy of Melancholy*, London: Hodson; 11th edn, 1806.

Bygott, D. W. (1992) *Black and British*, Oxford: Oxford University Press.

Callahan, C. M. and Rivara, F. P. (1992) 'Urban high school youth and handguns: a school based survey', *Journal of the American Medical Association*, 267, 3038–42.

Cannon, M., Cotter, D., Coffey, V. P., Sham, P. C., Takei, N., Larkin, C., Murray, R. M. and O'Callaghan, E. (1996) 'Prenatal exposure to the 1957 influenza epidemic and adult schizophrenia: a follow-up study', *British Journal of Psychiatry*, 168, 368–71.

Carothers, J. C. (1951) 'Frontal lobe function and the African', *Journal of Mental Science*, 97, 12–48.

—— (1953) *The African Mind in Health and Disease: a Study in Ethnopsychiatry,* WHO Monograph Series no. 17, Geneva: World Health Organisation.

Carpenter, M. D., Hannon, V. R., McCleary, G. and Wanderling, J. A. (1988) 'Ethnic differences in seclusion and restraint', *Journal of Nervous and Mental Disease*, 176, 12, 726–31.

Carr, W. (1991) *The History of Germany 1815–1990*, London: Edward Arnold, 4th edn.

Cartwright, S. A. (1851) 'Report on the diseases and physical peculiarities of the negro race', *New Orleans Medical and Surgical Journal* (May), 691–715; repr. in A. C. Caplan, H. T. Engelhardt and J. J. McCartney (eds) *Concepts of Health and Disease*, Reading, MA: Addison-Wesley, 1981.

Castel, R. (1988) *The Regulation of Madness: the Origins of Incarceration in France* (L'Ordre Psychiatrique), trans. W. D. Halls, Berkeley, CA: University of California Press, Berkeley.

Castle, D., Wessely, S., Der, G. and Murray, R. M. (1991) 'The incidence of operationally defined schizophrenia in Camberwell 1956–84', *British Journal of Psychiatry*, 159, 790–94.

Centres for Disease Control (1985) 'Homicide among young black males – US 1970–82: morbidity and mortality', *Weekly Report*, 34, 629–33.

Cernovsky, Z. Z. (1994) 'Rushton's defendants and their hasty rejection of the null hypothesis', *Journal of Black Psychology*, 20, 3, 325–33.

Chen, E. Y. H., Harrison, G. and Standon, P. (1991) 'Management of the first episode of psychotic illness in Afro-Caribbean patients', *British Journal of Psychiatry*, 158, 517–22.

Chidester, T. R. (1986) 'Problems in the study of interracial interaction: pseudo-interracial dyad paradigm', *Journal of Personality and Social Psychology*, 50, 74–9.

Christie, Y. (1995) 'Overview: service delivery to black communities', in C. Harding (ed.) *Not Just Black and White*, London: Good Practices in Mental Health, 4–6.

Cloward, R. and Ohlin, L. (1965) *Delinquency and Opportunity*, New York: The Free Press.

Cobb, W. M. (1942) 'Physical anthropology of the American negro', *American Journal of Physical Anthropology*, 29, 113–223.

Cochrane, R. and Sashidharan, S. (1996) 'Mental health and ethnic minorities: review of literature and implications for services', in Centre for Reviews and Dissemination Report 5, *Ethnicity and Health: Reviews of Literature and Guidance for Purchasers in the Areas of Cardiovascular Disease, Mental Health and Haemoglobinopathies*, NHS Centre for Reviews and Dissemination, York: University of York, 105–26.

Commission for Racial Equality (1988) *Medical School Admission: Report of a Formal Investigation into St George's Hospital Medical School*, London: Commission for Racial Equality.

Conference Participant (1995) 'Comment at conference: alternatives in black mental health – the sanctuary model' (26 October), London: King's Fund, 11.

Conze, E. (1957 *Buddhism: its Essence and Development*, Oxford: Bruno Cassirer, 3rd edn.

Cope, R. (1989) 'The compulsory detention of Afro-Caribbeans under the Mental Health Act', *New Community*, 15, 3, 343–56.

Cope, R. and Ndegwa, D. (1990) 'Ethnic differences in admission to a regional secure unit', *Journal of Forensic Psychiatry* 3, 365–78.

Crow, T. J. and Done, D. J. (1992) 'Prenatal exposure to influenza does not cause schizophrenia', *British Journal of Psychiatry*, 161, 390–93.

D'Andrade, R. G. (1984) 'Cultural meaning systems', in R. A. Schweder and R. A. LeVine (eds) *Cultural Theory: Essays on Mind, Self and Emotion*, Cambridge: Cambridge University Press, 88–119.

Daily Mail (1996) 'How they freed the Beast to rape again' (8. February), 17.

Dalal, F. (1988) 'The racism of Jung', *Race and Class*, 29, 3, 1–22.

Darwin, C. (1859) *On the Origin of the Species by Means of Natural Selection or the Preservation of Favoured Races in the Struggle for Life*, London: John Murray; 1st edn with intro. Ernst Mayr, Cambridge, MA: Harvard University Press, 1964.

—— (1871) *The Descent of Man and Selection in Relation to Sex*, London: John Murray.

Davidson, B. (1984) *Africa in History*, London: Paladin Books; 1st edn, *Africa: History of a Continent*, London: Weidenfeld & Nicholson, 1966.

Davies, S., Thornicroft, G., Leese, M., Higginbotham, A. and Phelan, M. (1996) 'Ethnic differences in risks of compulsory psychiatric admission among representative cases of psychosis in London', *British Medical Journal*, 312, 533–7.

Davis, A. (1971) *If They Come in the Morning*, New York: New American Library.

—— (1982) *Women Race and Class*, London: Women's Press.

Dawkins, R. (1976) *The Selfish Gene*, New York: Oxford University Press.

de Gobineau, J.-A. (1853–5) *Essay on the Inequality of the Human Races* (Essai sur l'inegalité des races humaine), Paris: Gallimard.

Department of Health (1992a) *Health of the Nation: Specification of National Indicators*, London: HMSO.

—— (1992b) *Report of the Committee of Inquiry into Complaints about Ashworth Hospital*, vols 1 and 2, Cm 2028-I and II, London: HMSO (Chairman, Sir Louis Blom-Cooper).

—— (1994a) *Black Mental Health: a Dialogue for Change. NHS Executive Mental Health Task Force*, London: Department of Health.

—— (1994b) *Guidance on the Discharge from Hospital of Mentally Disordered People and Their Continuing Care in the Community*, London: Department of Health.

—— (1994c) *Report of the Working Group on High Security and Related Provision*, London: Department of Health (Chairman, Dr John Reed).

Department of Health and Home Office (1992a) *Review of Health and Social Services for Mentally Disordered Offenders and Others Requiring Similar Services*, Final Summary Report, Cm 2088, London: HMSO (Chairman, Dr John Reed).

—— (1994a) *Review of Health and Social Services for Mentally Disordered Offenders and Others Requiring Similar Services*, vol. 6, *Race, Gender and Equal Opportunities*, London: HMSO (Chairman, Dr John Reed).

—— (1994b) *Report of the Department of Health and Home Office Working Group on Psychopathic Disorder*, London: Department of Health and Home Office (Chairman, Dr John Reed).

Department of Health and Social Security (DHSS) (1974) *Revised Report of the Working Party on Security in the NHS Psychiatric Hospitals*, Glancy Report, London: HMSO.

Department of Health and Welsh Office (1993) *Mental Health Act 1983 Code of Practice*, London: HMSO.

Dick, D. (1994): 'Lessons for us all', *Report on Symposium: Current Issues in Forensic Psychiatry* (5 October), 6–7.

Dolan, B., Polley, K., Allen, R. and Norton, K. (1991) 'Addressing racism in psychiatry: is the therapeutic community model applicable?', *International Journal of Social Psychiatry*, 37, 2, 71–9.

Down, J. L. M. (1866) 'Observations on an ethnic classification of idiots', *Lectures and Reports from the London Hospital for 1866*, in C. Thompson (ed.), *The Origins of Modern Psychiatry*, Chichester: John Wiley, 1987, 15–18.

Drury, V., Birchwood, M., Cochrane, R. and Macmillan, F. (1996) 'Cognitive therapy and recovery from acute psychosis: a controlled trial: I. Impact on Psychotic Symptoms', *British Journal of Psychiatry*, 169, 593–601.

Du Bois, W. E. B. (1904) *The Souls of Black Folk*, New York: Washington Square Press; Chicago: McClurg, 1970.

Dunn, J. and Fahy, T. A. (1990) 'Police admissions to a psychiatric hospital: demographic and clinical differences between ethnic groups', *British Journal of Psychiatry*, 156, 373–8.

Durant, R. H., Cadenhead, C., Pendergrast, R. A., Slavens, G. and Linder, C. (1994) 'Factors associated with the use of violence among urban black adolescents', *American Journal of Public Health,* 84, 612–17.

Eagles, J. M. (1991) 'The relationship between schizophrenia and immigration: are there alternatives to psychosocial hypotheses?', *British Journal of Psychiatry*, 159, 783–9.

East London and the City Health Authority and Newham Council (1995) *Woodley Team Report of the Independent Review Panel to East London and the City Health Authority and Newham Council Following a Homicide in July 1994 by a Person Suffering With a Severe Mental Illness*, London: East London and City Health Authority and Newham Council (Chairman, L. Woodley).

Eastman, N. (1995) 'Comments from Conference at Springfield Hospital', Pathfinder Mental Health Services NHS Trust (26 September).

—— (1996) 'Hybrid orders: an analysis of their likely effects on sentencing practice and on forensic psychiatric practice and services', *Journal of Forensic Psychiatry*, 7, 3, 481–94.

Edwards, S. (1992) 'Perspectives on race and gender' in E. Stockdale and S. Casale (eds) *Criminal Justice Under Stress*, London: Blackstone Press, 246–64.

Ellison, R. (1952) *The Invisible Man*, New York: Random House.

Estroff, S. E. and Zimmer, C. (1994) 'Social networks, social support and violence among persons with severe, persistent mental illness', in J. Monahan and H. J. Steadmen (eds) *Violence and Mental Disorder: Developments on Risk Assessment*, Chicago, IL: University of Chicago Press, 259–95.

Eysenck, H. J. (1971) *Race, Intelligence and Education*, London: Temple Smith.

Eze, E. (1997) (ed.) *Race and the Enlightenment: A Reader*, Cambridge, MA: Basil Blackwell.

Fabrega, H., Mezzich, J. E. and Ulrich, R. (1988) 'Black–white differences in psychopathology in an urban psychiatric population', *Comprehensive Psychiatry*, 29, 285–97.

Fanon, F. (1952) *Peau noire, masques blancs*, Paris: Éditions du Seuil; trans. C. L. Markmann, *Black Skin, White Masks*, New York: Grove Press, 1967, .

Federal Bureau of Investigations (1981) *Uniform Crime Reports*, Washington, DC: FBI.

Fernando S. (1988) *Race and Culture in Psychiatry*, London: Croom Helm; repr. London: Routledge, 1989.

—— (1991) *Mental Health, Race and Culture*, London: Macmillan/MIND.

—— (1995a) 'Social realities and mental health', in S. Fernando (ed.) *Mental Health in a Multi-Ethnic Society: A Multi-Disciplinary Handbook*, London: Routledge, 11–35.

—— (1995b) 'The way forward', in S. Fernando (ed.) *Mental Health in a Multi-Ethnic Society: A Multi-Disciplinary Handbook*, London: Routledge, 193–216.

—— (1996) 'Black people working in white institutions: lessons from personal experience', *Human Systems: Journal of Systemic Consultation and Management*, 7, 143–54.

Ferns, P. and Madden, M. (1995) 'Training to promote race equality', in S. Fernando (ed.) *Mental Health in a Multi-Ethnic Society: A Multi-Disciplinary Handbook*, London: Routledge, 107–19.

Ferrell, J. (1995) 'Racial identity and African peoples' mental health', *Journal of Black Therapy*, 1, 1, 24–30.

Fine, P. R., Roseman, J. M., Constandinou, C. M., Brissie, R. M., Glass, J. M. and Wrigley, J. M. (1994) 'Homicide among black males in Jefferson County Alabama 1978–1989', *Journal of Forensic Sciences*, 39, 3, 674–84.

Fitzpatrick, K. M. and Boldizar, J. P. (1993) 'The prevalence and consequences of exposure to violence among African-American youth', *Journal of American Academy Child and Adolescent Psychiatry*, 32, 2, 424–30.

Fitzpatrick, P. (1990) 'Racism and the innocence of law', in D. T. Goldberg (ed.) *Anatomy of Racism*, Minneapolis, MN: University of Minnesota Press, 247–62.

Flaherty, J. and Meagher, R. (1980) 'Measuring racial bias in in-patient treatment', *American Journal of Psychiatry*, 137, 679–82.

Forshaw, D. and Rollin, H. (1990) 'The history of law and psychiatry in Europe', in R. Bluglass and P. Bowden (eds) *Principles and Practice of Forensic Psychiatry*, London: Churchill Livingstone.

Foucault, M. (1967) *Madness and Civilization: A History of Insanity in the Age of Reason*, London: Tavistock; 1st edn, *Histoire de la Folie*, Paris: Libraire Plon, 1961.

—— (1977) *Discipline and Punish: The Birth of the Prison*, trans. A. Sheridan, London: Allen Lane, The Penguin Press; repr.

Harmondsworth: Penguin, 1991; 1st edn, *Surveiller et punir: naissance de la prison*, Paris: Gallimard, 1975.

—— (1988) *Politics Philosophy Culture: Interviews and Other writings 1977–1984*, L. D. Kritzman (ed.), London: Routledge.

Francis, E. (1996) 'Community care, danger and black people', *OPENMIND*, 80, 4–5.

Franklin, A. J. and Jackson, J. S. (1990) 'Factors contributing to positive mental health among black Americans', in D. S. Ruiz (ed.) *Handbook of Mental Health and Mental Disorder Among Black Americans*, New York: Greenwood Press, 291–305.

Fromm, E., Suzuki, D. T. and de Martino, R. (1960) *Zen Buddhism and Psychoanalysis*, London: Allen & Unwin.

Fryer, P. (1984) *Staying Power: the History of Black People in Britain*, London: Pluto Press.

—— (1988) *Black People in the British Empire: An Introduction*, London: Pluto Press.

Fulford, K. W. M., Smirnov, A. Y. U. and Snow, E. (1993) 'Concepts of Disease and the abuse of psychiatry in the USSR', *British Journal of Psychiatry*, 162, 801–10.

Gelder, M., Gath, D. and Mayou, R. (1989) *Oxford Textbook of Psychiatry*, Oxford: Oxford University Press, 2nd edn.

Gilroy, P. (1987) *There Ain't No Black in the Union Jack: the Cultural Politics of Race and Nation*, London: Hutchinson.

—— (1993) 'One Nation under a groove', in P. Gilroy *Small Acts: Thoughts on the Politics of Black Cultures*, London: Serpent Tail, 19–48.

Glasman, D. (1994) 'Psychiatric patients claim they are unaware of their legal rights', *Health Service Journal*, 4.

Glover, G. and Malcolm, G. (1988) 'The prevalence of neuroleptic treatment among West Indians and Asians in the London Borough of Newham', *Social Psychiatry and Psychiatric Epidemiology*, 23, 281–4.

Goldberg, D., Benjamin, S. and Creed, F. (1994) *Psychiatry in Medical Practice*, London: Routledge, 2nd edn.

Gordon, P. (1991) *Fortress Europe? The meaning of 1992*, London: Runnymede Trust.

Gostin, L. (1986) *Institutions Observed: Towards a New Concept of Secure Provision*, London: King's Fund.

Gottesman, I. I. (1991) *Schizophrenia Genesis: the Origins of Madness*, New York: Freeman.

Gottesman, I. I. and Shields, J. (1972) *Schizophrenia and Genetics: a Twin Study Vantage Point*, London: Academic Press.

—— (1982) *Schizophrenia: the Epigenetic Puzzle*, Cambridge: Cambridge University Press.

Graham, J. and Bowling, B. (1995) *Young People and Crime*, London: Home Office.

Gray, D. B. and Ashmore, R. D. (1976) 'Biasing influence on defendants' characteristics on simulated sentencing', *Psychological Reports*, 38, 727–38.

Gray G. E., Baron D. and Herman J. (1985) 'Importance of medical anthropology in clinical psychiatry', *American Journal of Psychiatry*, 142, 275.

Gray, L. E. and Berry, G. L. (1985) 'Depressive symptomology among black men', *Journal of Multicultural Counselling and Development* (July), 121–9.

Green, E. M. (1914) 'Psychoses among negroes: a comparative study', *Journal of Nervous and Mental Disorder*, 41, 697–708.

Greenberg, M. and Schneider, D. (1994) 'Violence in American cities: young black males is the answer, but what is the question?', *Social Science and Medicine*, 39, 2, 179–87.

Greenland, C. (1985) 'Dangerousness, mental disorder and politics', in C. D. Webster, M. H. Ben-Aron and S. J. Hucker (eds) *Dangerousness, Probability and Prediction, Psychiatry and Public Policy*, Cambridge: Cambridge University Press, 25–40.

Grob, G. N. (1983) *Mental Illness and American Society 1875–1940*, Princeton, NJ: Princeton University Press.

Guardian (1996) 'Law change call after stalking case acquittal' (18 September), 1.

—— (1997) 'Judge says stalker should have got life' (18 February), 7.

Gunn, J. (1996) 'Commentary: comparative forensic psychiatry USA *vs.* UK', *Criminal Behaviour and Mental Health*, 6, 1, 45–9.

Hacker, A. (1995) *Two Nations: Black and White, Separate, Hostile, Unequal*, New York: Ballantine Books.

Hagan, J. and Bumiller, B. (1983) 'Making sense of sentencing: a review and critique of sentencing research', in A. Blumstein, S. E. Martin and M. H. Tonry (eds) *Research on Sentencing: the Search for Reform*, vol. 2, Washington, DC: National Science Foundation, 1–54.

Hall, G. S. (1904) *Adolescence, its Psychology and its Relations to Physiology, Anthropology, Sociology, Sex, Crime, Religion and Education*, vol. 2, New York: D. Appleton.

Hall, S. (1992) 'New ethnicities', chap. 11 in J. Donald and A. Rattansi (eds) *'Race', Culture and Difference*, London: Sage, 252–9.

Hall, S., Critcher, C., Jefferson, T., Clarke, J. and Roberts, B. (1978) *Policing the Crisis: Mugging, the State, and Law and Order*, London: Macmillan.

Hammill, K., McEvoy, J. P., Koral, H. and Schneider, N. (1989) 'Hospitalised schizophrenic patient views about seclusion', *Journal of Clinical Psychiatry*, 50, 5, 174–7.

Harding, C. (1995) *Not Just Black and White*, London: Good Practices in Mental Health.

Harding, T. and Montandon, C. (1982) 'Does dangerousness travel well?', in J. R. Hamilton and H. Freeman (eds) *Dangerousness: Psychiatric Assessment and Management*, London: Gaskell, 46–52.

Hare, E. (1988) 'Schizophrenia as a recent disease', *British Journal of Psychiatry*, 153, 521–31.

Harer, M. D. and Steffensmeir, D. (1992) 'The differing effects of economic inequality on black and white rates of violence', *Social forces*, 70, 4, 1035–54.

Harrison, D. D. (1988) 'An anthropologist's views of the roots of violence in the United States', *Journal of the National Medical Association*, 83, 7, 843–8.

Harrison, G. (1990) 'Searching for the causes of schizophrenia: the role of migrant studies', *Schizophrenia Bulletin*, 16, 663–71.

Harrison, G., Cooper, J. E. and Gancarczk, R. (1991) 'Changes in administrative incidence of schizophrenia', *British Journal of Psychiatry*, 159, 811–17.

Harrison, G., Glazebrook, C., Brewin, J., Cantwell, R., Dalkin, T., Fox, R., Jones, P. and Medley, I. (1997) 'Increased incidence of psychotic disorders in migrants from the Caribbean to the United Kingdom', *Psychological Medicine*, 27, 799–806.

Harrison, G., Holton, A., Neilson, D., Owens, D., Boot, D. and Cooper, J. (1989) 'Severe mental disorder in Afro-Caribbean patients: some social, demographic and service factors', *Psychological Medicine*, 19, 683–96.

Harrison, G., Ineichen, B., Smith, J. and Morgan, H. G. (1984) 'Psychiatry hospital admission in Bristol: II. Social and clinical aspects of compulsory admission', *British Journal of Psychiatry*, 145, 601–5.

Harrison, G., Owens, D., Holton, A., Neilson, D. and Boot, D. (1988) 'A prospective study of severe mental disorder in Afro-Caribbean patients', *Psychological Medicine*, 18, 643–57.

Harvey, I., Williams, M., McGuffin, P. and Toone, B. K. (1990) 'The functional psychoses in Afro-Caribbeans', *British Journal of Psychiatry*, 157, 515–22.

Hawkins, H. and Thomas R. (1991) 'White policing of black populations: a history of race and social control in America', in E. Cashmore and E. McLaughlin (eds) *Out of Order? Policing Black People*, London: Routledge, 65–87.

Helzer, J. D. (1975) 'Bipolar affective disorder in black and white men: a comparison of symptoms and familial illness', *Archives of General Psychiatry*, 32, 1140–3.

Hemsi, L. K. (1967) 'Psychiatric morbidity of West Indian immigrants: a study of first admissions in London', *Social Psychiatry*, 2, 95–100.

Her Majesty's Stationery Office (1959) *Mental Health Act 1959*, London: HMSO.

—— (1983) *Mental Health Act 1983*, London: HMSO.

—— (1995) *Mental Health (Patients in the Community) Act*, London: HMSO.

Hickling, F. W. (1991) 'Psychiatric hospital admission rates in Jamaica 1971 and 1988', *British Journal of Psychiatry*, 159, 817–22.

Hickling, F. W. and Rodgers-Johnson, P. (1995) 'The incidence of first contact schizophrenia in Jamaica', *British Journal of Psychiatry*, 167, 193–6.

Hitch, P. and Clegg, P. (1980) 'Modes of referral of overseas immigrants and native born first admissions to psychiatric hospital', *Social Science and Medicine*, 14, 369–74.

Home Office (1990) *Home Office Circular 66/90*, London: Home Office.

—— (1991) *Home Office Circular 93/91*, London: Home Office.

—— (1992) *Home Office Circular 91/92*, London: Home Office.

—— (1993a) *Youth Lifestyle Survey*, London: Home Office.

—— (1993b) *Criminal Statistics for England and Wales*, London: Home Office.

—— (1994) *British Crime Survey*, London: Home Office.

—— (1995) *Home Office Circular 12/95*, London: Home Office.

—— (1996a) *Race and the Criminal Justice System*, London: Home Office.

—— (1996b) *Protecting the Public: the Government's Strategy on Crime in England and Wales*, White Paper Cm3190, London: Home Office.

—— (1996c) *Ethnic minorities in Great Britain: Ethnic Minority Advisory Committee of the Judicial Studies Board*, London: Home Office.

Home Office and Department of Health and Social Security (1975) *Report of the Committee on Mentally Abnormal Offenders* (The Butler Committee), Cm 6244, London: HMSO.

Home Office and the Central Office of Information (1977) *Racial Discrimination: a Guide to the Race Relations Act 1976* London: HMSO.

Hood, R. (1990) *The Death Penalty: a World Wide Perspective*, Oxford: Clarendon Press.

—— (1992) *Race and Sentencing: a Study in the Crown Court*, Oxford: Clarendon Press.

hooks, bell (1995) *Killing Rage Ending Racism*, Harmondsworth: Penguin.

Hui, C. H. and Triandis, H. C. (1985) 'Quantitative methods in cross-cultural research: multidimensional scaling and their response theory', in R. Diaz (ed.) *Cross-Cultural and National Studies in Social Psychology*, New York: Elsevier, 69–79.

Human Rights Watch (1991) *Prison Conditions in the United States: a Human Rights Watch Report*, New York: Human Rights Watch.

Hunter, R. A. and MacAlpine, I. (1963) *Three Hundred Years of Psychiatry 1535–1860: a History Presented in Selected English Texts*, London: Oxford University Press.

Ickes, W. J., Patterson, M. L., Rakecki, D. W. and Tanford, S. (1982) 'Behavioural and cognitive consequences of reciprocal versus compensatory responses to pre-interaction expectancies', *Social Cognition*, 1, 160–90.

Imlah, N. (1985) 'Silverman inquiry on Handsworth riots', unpublished transcript.

Ineichen, B., Harrison, G. and Morgan, H. G. (1984) 'Psychiatric hospital admissions in Bristol: geographical and ethnic factors', *British Journal of Psychiatry*, 145, 600–4.

Irwin, M., Klein, R. E., Engle, P. L., Yarborough, C. and Nevlove, S. B. (1977) 'The problem of establishing validity in cross-cultural measurements', *Annals of New York Academy of Sciences*, 285, 308–25.

Isherwood, J. (1996) 'Supervision registers and medium secure units', *Psychiatric Bulletin*, 20, 198–200.

Jablensky, A., Sartorius, N., Ernberg, G., Anker, M., Korten, A., Cooper, J. E., Day, R. and Bertelsen, A. (1992) 'Schizophrenia: manifestations, incidence and course in different cultures', *Psychological Medicine*, Monograph Supplement, 20.

Jahoda, M. (1958) *Current Conceptions of Positive Mental Health*, New York: Basic Books.

Jarvis, E. (1852) 'On the supposed increase of insanity', *American Journal of Insanity*, 8, 333–64.

Jenkins-Hall, K. and Sacco W. P. (1991) 'The effect of client race and depression on evaluations by white therapists, *Journal of Social and Clinical Psychology*, 10, 3, 322–33.

Jenner, F. A., Monteiro, A. C. D., Zagalo-Cardoso, J. A. and Cunha-Oliveira, J. A. (1993) *Schizophrenia: A Disease or Some Ways of Being Human?*, Sheffield: Sheffield Academic Press.

Jensen, A. R. (1969) 'How much can we boost IQ and scholastic achievement?', *Harvard Educational Review*, 39, 1–123.

Jeste, D. V., del Carmen, R., Lohr, J. B. and Wyatt, J. (1985) 'Did schizophrenia exist before the eighteenth century?', *Comprehensive Psychiatry*, 26, 493–503.

Jones, A. and Segal, A. (1977) 'Dimensions of the relationship between the black client and the white therapist: A theoretical overview', *American Psychologist*, 32, 850–5.

Jones B. E., Gray, B. A. and Parson, E. B. (1981) 'Manic depressive illness among poor urban blacks', *American Journal of Psychiatry*, 138, 654–7.

—— (1986) 'Problems in diagnosing schizophrenia and affective disorders among blacks', *Hospital and Community Psychiatry*, 37, 61–5.

Jones, J. S. (1981) 'How different are human races?', *Nature*, 293, 188–90.

Jones, R. M. (1996) *Mental Health Act Manual*, London: Sweet & Maxwell, 5th edn.

Jones-Webb, R. J. and Snowden, L. R. (1993) 'Symptoms of depression among blacks and whites', *American Journal of Public Health*, 83, 2, 240–4.

Kallman, F. J. (1938) *The Genetics of Schizophrenia*, New York: Augustin.

Karenga, M. (1986) 'Social ethics and the black family: an alternative analysis', *Black Scholar*, 17, 41–54.

Karpf, A. (1997) 'Fighting talk', *Guardian 2* (27 January), 4–5.

Keisling, R. (1981) 'Under diagnosis of manic depressive illness in a hospital unit', *American Journal of Psychiatry*, 138, 672–3.

Kendell, R. E. (1975) *The Role of Diagnosis in Psychiatry*, Oxford: Basil Blackwell.

—— (1989) 'Clinical validity', *Psychological Medicine*, 19, 45–55.

Kendell, R. E. and Kemp, I. W. (1989) 'Maternal influenza in the aetiology of schizophrenia'. *Archives of General Psychiatry*, 46, 878–82.

Kendell, R. E., Malcolm, D. E. and Adams W. (1993) 'The problem of detecting changes in incidence of schizophrenia', *British Journal of Psychiatry*, 162, 212–18.

Kety, S. S., Rosenthal, D., Wender, P. and Schulsinger, F. (1968) 'The types and prevalence of mental illness in the biological and adoptive families of adopted schizophrenics', in D. Rosenthal and S. S. Kety (eds) *The Transmission of Schizophrenia*, Oxford: Pergamon, 345–62

—— (1976) 'Studies based on a total sample of adopted individuals and their relatives: why they were necessary, what they demonstrated and failed to demonstrate', *Schizophrenia Bulletin*, 2, 413–28.

Kety, S. S., Wender, P. H., Jacobsen, B., Ingraham, L. J., Jansson, L., Faber, B. and Kinney, D. K. (1994) 'Mental illness in the biological and adoptive relatives of schizophrenic adoptees', *Archives of General Psychiatry*, 51, 442–55.

King, D. J. and Cooper, S. J. (1989) 'Viruses, immunity and mental disorder', *British Journal of Psychiatry*, 154, 1–7.

King, M., Coker, E., Leavey, G., Hoar, A. and Johnson-Sabine, E. (1994) 'Incidence of psychotic illness in London: comparison of ethnic groups', *British Medical Journal*, 309, 1115–19.

King's Fund (1995) *Alternatives in Black Mental Health: the Sanctuary Model*, Conference report (26 October), London: King's Fund.

Kingdon, D. (1994) 'Care programme approach: recent government policy and legislation', *Psychiatric Bulletin*, 18, 68–70.

Klaning, U., Mortensen, P. B. and Kyvik, K. O. (1996) 'Increased occurrence of schizophrenia and other psychiatric illnesses among twins', *British Journal of Psychiatry*, 168, 688–92.

Kleck, G. (1981) 'Racial discrimination in criminal sentencing: a critical evaluation of the evidence with additional evidence on the death penalty', *American Sociological Review*, 46, 783–805.

Klein, S., Petersilia, J. and Turner, S. (1990) 'Race and imprisonment decisions in California', *Science*, 247, 812–16.

Kleinman, A. R. (1977) 'Depression, somatization and the "New Cross-Cultural Psychiatry"', *Social Science and Medicine*, 11, 3–10.

—— (1987) 'Anthropology and psychiatry: the role of culture in cross-cultural research on illness', *British Journal of Psychiatry*, 151, 447–54.

—— (1988) *Rethinking Psychiatry: From Cultural Category to Personal Experience*, New York: The Free Press.

Kohn, M. (1995) *The Race Gallery: the Return of Racial Science*, London: Jonathan Cape.

Kraepelin, E. (1896) *Psychiatrie*, Leipzig: Barth, 5th edn.

—— (1904) 'Vergleichende psychiatrie', *Zentralblatt Nervenheilkunde und Psychiatrie*, 27, 433–7; trans. and repr. in H. Marshall, S. R. Hirsch and M. Shepherd (eds) *Themes and Variations in European Psychiatry*, Bristol: Wright, 3–6.

—— (1913) *Manic Depressive Insanity and Paranoia*, translation by R. M. Barclay of *Psychiatrie*, 8th edition, Vols. 3 and 4, Edinburgh: Livingstone.

—— (1921) *Manic Depressive Insanity and Paranoia*, trans. and ed. R. M. Barclay and G. M. Robertson, Edinburgh: Livingstone.

Krebs, R. C. (1971) 'Some effects of a white institution on black psychiatric out-patients', *American Journal of Orthopsychiatry*, 41, 589–96.

Kreiger, N. (1987) 'Shades of difference: theoretical underpinnings of the medical controversy on black/white differences in the United States, 1830–1870', *International Journal of Health Services*, 17, 2, 259–77.

Kringlen, E. (1966) 'Schizophrenia in twins: an epidemiological-clinical study', *Psychiatry*, 29, 173–84.

Langan, P. (1985) 'Racism on trial: new evidence to explain the racial composition of prisons in the US', *Journal of Criminal Law and Criminology*, 76, 666–83.

Lawson W. B., Hepler, N., Holiday, J., *et al.* (1994) 'Race as a factor in in-patient and out-patient admissions and diagnosis', *Hospital Community Psychiatry*, 45, 72–4.

Leff, J (1973) 'Culture and the differentiation of emotional states', *British Journal of Psychiatry*, 123, 299–306.

—— (1981) *Psychiatry Around the Globe: a Transcultural View*, New York: Marcel Dekker.

Leff, J., Sartorius, N., Jablensky, A., Korten, A. and Ernberg, G. (1990) 'The international pilot study of schizophrenia: five-year follow-up findings' (IPSS), in H. Hafner and W. F. Guttaz (eds) *Search of the Causes of Schizophrenia*, vol. 2., Berlin: Springer Verlag.

Leif, H. J., Leif, V. F. and Warren, C. O. (1961) 'Low dropout rate in psychiatric treatment', *Archives of General Psychiatry*, 5, 200–11.

Leighton, A. H. and Hughes, J. M. (1961) 'Culture as causative of mental disorder', *Millbank Memorial Fund Quarterly*, 39, 3, 446–70.

Lewis, A. (1965) 'Chairman's opening remarks', in A.V. S. De Rueck and R. Porter (eds) *Transcultural Psychiatry*, Ciba Foundation symposium, London: Churchill, 1–3.

Lewis, D. O., Pincus, J. H. and Feldman, M. (1986) 'Psychiatric neurological and psychoeducational characteristics of 15 death row inmates in the United States', *American Journal of Psychiatry*, 143, 838–45.

Lewis, G., Croft, C. and Jeffreys, A. D. (1990) 'Are British psychiatrists racist?' (and letters to editor 158, 289–90), *British Journal of Psychiatry*, 157, 410–15.

Lidz, C., Mulvey, E. and Gardner, W. (1993) 'The accuracy of predictions of violence to others', *Journal of the American Medical Association*, 269, 1007–11.

Lieberman, J. A. and Koreen, A. R. (1993) 'Neurochemistry and neuroendocrinology of schizophrenia: a selective review', *Schizophrenia Bulletin*, 19, 371–429.

Lindsey, K. P. and Paul, G. L. (1989) 'Involuntary commitments to public mental institutions: issues involving the overrepresentation of blacks and assessment of relevant function', *Psychological Bulletin*, 106, 171–83.

Link, B. G., Andrews, H., Cullen, F. (1992) 'The violent and illegal behaviour of mental patients reconsidered', *American Sociological Review*, 57, 275–92.

Link, B. G. and Steuve, A. (1995) 'Evidence bearing on mental illness as a possible cause of violent behaviour', *Epidemiological reviews*, 17, 1, 192–82.

Lipsedge, M. (1994) 'Dangerous stereotypes', *Journal of Forensic Psychiatry*, 5, 1, 14–19.

Littlewood, R. and Cross, C. (1980) 'Ethnic minorities and psychiatric services', *Sociology Health Illness*, 2, 194–201.

Littlewood, R. and Lipsedge, M. (1981) 'Acute psychosis reactions in Caribbean born patients', *Psychological Medicine*, 11, 303–18.

—— (1982) *Aliens and Alienists: Ethnic Minorities and Psychiatry*, London: Allen & Unwin.

Lloyd, K. (1992) 'Ethnicity, primary care and non-psychotic disorders', *International Review of Psychiatry*, 4, 257–66.

—— (1993) 'Depression and anxiety among African-Caribbean general practice attendees in Britain', *International Journal of Social Psychiatry*, 39, 1, 1–9.

Lloyd, K. and Moodley, P. (1992) 'Psychotropic medication and ethnicity: an in-patient survey', *Social Psychiatry and Psychiatric Epidemiology*, 27, 95–101.

Lombroso, C. (1871) *L'uomo bianco e l'uomo di colore: Letture sull'origine e varietà delle razze umane* (White Man and the Coloured Man: Observations on the Origin and Variety of the Human Race), Padua.

—— (1911) *Crime: Its Causes and Remedies*, trans. H. P. Horton, London: Heinemann.

Lorde, A. (1984) 'Sexism: an American disease in blackface', *Sister Outsider*, Trumansburg, NY: Crossing Press, 60–5.

Lorence, J. (1996) 'Ida B. Wells denounces southern social control, 1895', *Enduring Voices*, Lexington, MA: D. C. Heath, 16–17.

Loring, M. and Powell, B. (1988) 'Gender, race and DSM III: a study of the objectivity of psychiatric diagnostic behaviour', *Journal of Health and Social Behaviour*, 29, 1–22.

Malik, K. (1996) *The Meaning of Race: Race, History and Culture in Western Society*, Basingstoke: Macmillan.

Marable, M. (1983) *How Capitalism Under-developed Black America*, London: Pluto Press.

Marsella, A. J. and Kameoka, V. A. (1989) 'Ethnocultural issues in the assessment of psychopathology', in S. Wetsler (ed.) *Measuring Mental Illness: Psychometric Assessment for Clinicians*, Washington, DC: American Psychiatric Press, 231–56.

Maudsley, H. (1867) *The Physiology and Pathology of Mind*, New York: D. Appleton.

—— (1874) *Responsibility in Mental Disease*, New York: D. Appleton.

—— (1879) *The Pathology of Mind*, London: Macmillan.

May, R. (1972) *Power or Innocence: a Search for the Sources of Violence*, New York: W. W. Norton.

McGovern, D. and Cope, R. (1987a) 'The compulsory detention of males of different ethnic groups with special reference to offender patients', *British Journal of Psychiatry*, 150, 505–12.

—— (1987b) 'First psychiatric admission rates of first and second generation Afro-Caribbeans', *Social Psychiatry*, 122, 139–49.

—— (1991) 'Second generation Afro-Caribbeans and young whites with a first admission diagnosis of schizophrenia', *Social Psychiatry and Psychiatric Epidemiology*, 26, 95–9.

McGovern, D., Hemmings, P., Cope, R. and Lowerson, A. (1994) 'Long-term follow-up of young Afro-Caribbean Britons and white Britons with a first admission diagnosis of schizophrenia', *Social Psychiatry and Psychiatric Epidemiology*, 29, 8–19.

McKenzie, K., Van Os, J., Fahy, T., Jones, P., Harvey, I., Toone, B. and Murray, R. (1995) 'Psychosis with good prognosis in Afro-Caribbean people now living in the United Kingdom', *British Medical Journal*, 311, 1435–8.

Mednick, S. A., Machon, R. A., Huttanen, M. O. and Bonett, D. (1989) 'Adult schizophrenia following prenatal exposure to an influenza epidemic', *Archives of General Psychiatry*, 45, 189–92.

Mental Health Act Commission (1991) *Fourth Biennial Report 1989–1991*, London: HMSO.

—— (1993) *Fifth Biennial Report 1991–1993*, London: HMSO.

Mental Health Foundation (1995) *Mental Health in Black and Minority Ethnic People: the Fundamental Facts*, London: Mental Health Foundation.

—— (1997) *Race and Mental Health: Joint Policy Statement*, London: Mental Health Foundation.

Miller, D. T. and Turnbull, W. (1986) 'Expectancies and interpersonal processes', *Annual Review of Psychology*, 37, 233–56.

MIND (1993) 'MIND's policy on black and ethnic minority people and mental health', London: MIND.

—— (1994a) 'Dangerousness', MIND information sheet (May), London: MIND.

—— (1994b) 'MIND's response to the Department of Health's guidance on supervision registers and on hospital discharge' (July), London: MIND.

—— (1995a) 'MIND's policy on talking therapies', London: MIND.

—— (1995b) 'Response to the Mental Health (Patients in the Community) Bill' (August), London: MIND.

—— (1996a) '"Supervised discharge": consultation on draft guidance, MIND's Comments' (January), London: MIND.

—— (1996b) '"Race, rights, provision": diversion from custody and secure provision', London: MIND.

—— (1996c) 'MIND's policy on people with mental health problems and the criminal justice system', London: MIND.

—— (1996d) 'Supervision Registers', London: MIND.

—— (1996e) 'MIND's yellow card scheme: reporting the adverse effects of psychiatric drugs. First Report', London: MIND.

—— (1996f) 'Discrimination: mental health and race issues', London: MIND.

—— (1996g) 'Supervised discharge/aftercare under supervision' , London: MIND.

Mohan, D., Murray, K., Taylor, P. and Stead, P. (1997) 'Developments in the use of regional secure unit beds over a 12-year period', *Journal of Forensic Psychiatry*, 8, 2, 321–35.

Molnar, S. (1983) *Human Variation: Races, Types and Ethnic Groups*, Englewood Cliffs, NJ: Prentice-Hall.

Monahan, J. (1981) *The clinical prediction of violent behavior*, Washington, DC: Government Printing Office.

—— (1988) 'Risk assessment of violence among the mentally disordered: generating useful knowledge', *International Journal of Law and Psychiatry*, 11, 249–57.

Monahan, J. and Arnold, J. (1996) 'Violence by people with mental illness:

a consensus statement by advocates and researchers', *Psychiatric Rehabilitation Journal*, 19, 4, 67–70.

Monahan, J. and Steadman, H. J. (1994) 'Towards a rejuvenation of risk assessment research', in J. Monahan and H. J. Steadmen (eds) *Violence and Mental Disorder: Developments on Risk Assessment*, Chicago, IL: University of Chicago Press, 1–17.

Moodley, P. and Thornicroft, G. (1988) 'Ethnic group and compulsory detention', *Medicine, Science and the Law*, 28, 324–8.

Moorhead, J. (1997) 'The other Mrs Lawrence', *Guardian* (20 January), 6–7.

Moorhouse, G. (1983) *India Britannica*, London: Harvill Press.

Morel, B. A. (1852) *Traite des Mentales*, Paris: Masson.

Morley, R., Wykes, T. and MacCarthy, B. (1991) 'Attitudes of relatives of Afro-Caribbean patients: do they affect admission?', *Social Psychiatry and Psychiatric Epidemiology*, 26, 187–93.

Muijen, M. (1997) 'Catching the drift', *Health Service Journal* (16 January), 19.

Mukherjee, S., Shukla, S., Woodle, J., Rosen, A. M. and Olarte, S. (1983) 'Misdiagnosis of schizophrenia in bipolar patients: a multi-ethnic comparison', *American Journal of Psychiatry*, 140, 1571–2.

Mullen, P. E. (1995) 'The specialism of forensic mental health', *Current Opinion in Psychiatry*, 8, 366–70.

Muller-Hill, B. (1988) *Murderous Science: Elimination by Scientific Selection of Jews, Gypsies, and Others in Germany 1933–1945*, trans. G. R. Fraser, Oxford: Oxford University Press.

Mulvey, E. P. (1994) 'Assessing the evidence of a link between mental illness and violence', *Hospital and Community Psychiatry*, 45, 663–8.

Murphy, G. (1938) *An Historical Introduction to Modern Psychology*, London: Routledge & Kegan Paul, 4th edn.

Murray, C. and Hernstein, R. (1994) *The Bell Curve: Intelligence and Class Structure in American Life*, New York: The Free Press.

NACRO/Mental Health Foundation/Home Office (1994) *The NACRO Diversion Initiative for Mentally Disordered Offenders: An Account and an Evaluation*, London: NACRO/MHF/Home Office.

National Association of Probation Officers and Association of Black Probation Officers (1996) *Race, Discrimination and the Criminal Justice System*, London: NAPO/ABPO.

Nelson, J. F. (1994) 'A dollar or a day: sentencing misdemeanants in New York State', *Journal of Research in Crime and Delinquency*, 31, 2, 193–201.

Newham Council (1995) *Newham Council Press Release* (25 September).

NHS Executive (1996) *Mental Health Services in London*, briefing paper no.1 (June).

NHS Management Executive (1993) *Collecting Information about the Ethnic Group of Patients*, letter (October), Leeds: Department of Health.

Nisbett, R. and Ross, L. (1980) *Human Inference Strategies and Shortcomings*, Englewood Cliffs, NJ: Prentice-Hall.

Noble, P. and Roger, S. (1989) 'Violence by psychiatric in-patients: a hospital survey', *British Journal of Psychiatry*, 155, 384–90.

Nobles, W. W. (1986) 'Ancient Egyptian thought and the development of African (black) psychology', in M. Karenga and J. C. Carruthers (eds) *Kemet and the African Worldview: Research Rescue and Restoration*, Los Angeles, CA: University of Sankore Press, 100–18.

Northeast Thames and Southeast Thames Regional Health Authorities (1994) *The Report of the Inquiry into the Care and Treatment of Christopher Clunis*, London: HMSO (Chairman, J. H. Ritchie).

O'Callaghan, E., Sham, P., Takei, N., Glover, G. and Murray, R. M. (1991) 'Schizophrenia after prenatal exposure to 1957 A2 influenza epidemic', *Lancet*, 337, 1248–50.

Office of National Statistics (1996) *Social Focus on Ethnic Minorities*, London: HMSO.

Office of Population Censuses and Surveys (OPCS) (1993) *Health Area Monitor 1991, Census*, Cen 91, Ham 5, London: Government Statistical Service.

OFSTED (1996) *Recent Research on the Achievements of Ethnic Minority Pupils*, London: HMSO.

Oliver, W. (1989) 'Sexual conquest and patterns of black-on-black violence: a structural-cultural perspective', *Violence and Victims*, 4, 4, 257–73.

Onwuachi-Saunders, C. and Hawkins, D. F. (1993) 'Black–white differences in injury: race of social class', *Annals of Epidemiology*, 3, 2, 150–3.

Opler, M. K. (1959) *Culture and Mental Health*, New York: Macmillan.

Ormrod, Sir R. (1990) 'The scope of forensic psychiatry', *Journal of Forensic Psychiatry*, 1, 1, 1–4.

Overall, D. (1969) 'Extrinsic factors influencing responses to psychotherapeutic drugs', *Archives of General Psychiatry*, 32, 643–9.

Owen, D. (1992) 'Foucault, psychiatry and dangerousness,', *Journal of Forensic Psychiatry*, 2, 3, 238–41.

Owens, C. (1980a) 'Victims of justice', in *Mental Health and Black Offenders*, Lexington, MA: Lexington Books, 1–18.

—— (1980b) 'Black offenders: psychopathology and mental health', in *Mental Health and Black Offenders*, Lexington, MA: Lexington Books, 19–41.

Owens, D., Harrison, G. and Boot, D. (1991) 'Ethnic factors in voluntary and compulsory admission', *Psychological Medicine*, 21, 185–96.

Pakenham, T. (1992) *The Scramble for Africa 1876–1912*, London: Abacus.

Panikkar, K. M. (1959) *Asia and Western dominance*, London: Allen & Unwin; repr. New York: Collier, 1969.

Parsons, C. (1996) 'Permanent exclusions from schools in England in the 1990s: trends, causes and responses', *Children and Society*, 10, 3.

Parsons, C., Castle, F., Howlett, K. and Worrall, J., 1996). *Exclusion From School: the Public Cost*, London: Commission for Racial Equality.

Pearsall, J. and Trumble, B. (1995) *The Oxford English Reference Dictionary*, Oxford: Oxford University Press.

Pearson, K. (1901) *National Life from the Standpoint of Science*, London: Adam & Charles Black.

Penal Affairs Consortium (1996) *Race and Criminal Justice*, London: Penal Affairs Consortium.

Perkins, R. and Repper, J. (1996) *Working Alongside People with Long-Term Mental Health Problems*, London: Chapman and Hall.

Petersilia, J. (1983) *Racial Disparities in the Criminal Justice System*, Santa Monica, CA: Rand.

Pfeiffer, J. E. and Ogloff, J. R. (1991) 'Ambiguity and guilt determinations: a modern racism perspective', *Journal of Applied Social Psychology*, 21, 1713–25.

Phillips, D. E. and Rudestan, K. E. (1995) 'Effect of non-violent self-defence training on male psychiatric staff members' aggression and fear', *Psychiatric Services*, 46, 12, 726–31.

Pichot, P. (1984) 'The French approach to classification', *British Journal of Psychiatry*, 144, 113–18.

Pick, D. (1989) *Faces of Degeneration: a European Disorder c.1848–c.1918*, Cambridge: Cambridge University Press.

Pieterse, J. N. (1995) *White on Black: Images of Africa and Blacks in Western Popular Culture*, New Haven, CT: Yale University Press.

Pipe, R., Bhat, A., Matthews, B. and Hampstead, J. (1991) 'Section 136 and African/Afro-Caribbean minorities', *International Journal of Social Psychiatry*, 37, 1, 14–23.

Pollock, N., McBain, I. and Webster, C.D. (1993) 'Clinical decision-making and the assessment of dangerousness in clinical approaches to violence', in K. Howells and C. R. Hollin (eds), Chichester John Wiley, 89–115.

Poortings, J. H. and Van de Vijner, F. J. R. (1987) 'Explaining cross-cultural differences: bias analysis and beyond', *Journal of Cross-Cultural Psychology*, 18, 13, 259–82.

Porter, R. (1987) *A Social History of Madness: Stories of the Insane*, London: Weidefield & Nicholson.

—— (1990) *Mind-Forg'd Manacles: A History of Madness in England from the Restoration to the Regency*, Harmondsworth: Penguin.

Poussaint, A. F. (1972) *Why Blacks Kill Blacks*, New York: Emerson Hall.

Prichard, J. C. (1835) *A Treatise on Insanity and Other Disorders Affecting the Mind*, London: Sherwood, Gilbert and Piper.

Prins, H. (1986) *Dangerous Behaviour: the Law and Mental Disorder*, London: Tavistock.

—— (1990) 'Social factors affecting the assessment of risk; with special reference to offender patients', in D. Carson (ed.) *Risk-Taking in Mental Disorder: Analyses, Policies and Practical Strategies. Proceedings of an Inter-Disciplinary Conference*, University of Southampton (23 March) Chichester; SLE Publications, 18–22.

—— (1995a) *Offenders, Deviants or Patients?*, London: Routledge, 2nd edn.

—— (1995b) 'Comments', National Conference on Forensic Psychiatry (December).

Proctor, R. (1988) *Racial Hygiene: Medicine under the Nazis*, Cambridge, MA: Harvard University Press.

Pryce, K. (1979) *Endless Pressure*, Harmondsworth: Penguin.

Pryor Brown, L. J., Powell, J. and Earls, F. (1989) 'Stressful life events and psychiatric symptoms on black adolescent females', *Journal of Adolescent Research*, 4, 2, 140–51.

Rack, P. (1982) *Race, Culture and Mental Disorder*, London: Tavistock.

Rendon, M. (1984) 'Myths and stereotypes in minority groups', *International Journal of Social Psychiatry*, 30, 297–309.

Ricardo, I. B. (1994) 'Life choices of African-Americans living in public housing: perspectives on drug trafficking', *Paediatrics*, 93, 1055–9.

Richardson, J. and Lambert, J. (1985) *The Sociology of Race*, Lancashire: Causeway Press.

Robertson, G., Pearson, R. and Gibb., R. (1996) 'The entry of mentally disordered people to the criminal justice system', *British Journal of Psychiatry*, 169, 172–80

Robins, L. N. and Regier, D. A. (eds) (1991) *Psychiatric Disorders in America: the Epidemiological Catchment Area Study*, New York: The Free Press.

Rodney, W. (1988) *How Europe Underdeveloped Africa*, revised edn, London: Bogle-L'Ouverture Publications; 1st edn, London: Tanzania Publishing House and Bogle-L'Ouverture Publications, 1972.

Rogers, A. and Faulkner, A. (1987) *A Place of Safety*, London: MIND.

Rogers, J. A. (1942) *Sex and Race: a History of White, Negro, and Indian Miscegenation in the Two Americas*, vol. 2, *The New World*, St Petersburg, FA: Helga Rogers.

Romme, M. and Escher, S. (1993) 'Introduction', in M. Romme and S. Escher (eds) *Accepting Voices*, London: MIND, 7–10.

Rose, S., Lewontin, R. C. and Kamin, L. J. (1984) *Not In Our Genes: Biology, Ideology and Human Nature*, Harmondsworth: Penguin Books.

Rosen, G. (1968) *Madness in Society*, New York: Harper & Row.

Rosenthal, D. and Frank, J. B. (1958) 'The future of psychiatric clinic outpatients assigned to psychotherapy', *Journal of Nervous and Mental Diseases*, 127, 330–43.

Roughton, A. (1994) *An Investigation into the Operation of Section 136 of the Mental Health Act 1983 in the West Midlands*, Birmingham: West Midlands Police Community Services Department,

Rüdin, E. (1916) *Studien über Vererbung und Entstehung geistiger Störungen. 1. Zur Vererbung und Neuentstehung der Dementia præcox* (Studies into the Inheritance and Genesis of Mental Disorders: 1. The Inheritance and Outcome of Dementia Præcox), Berlin: Julius Springer.

Ruiz, D. S. (ed.) (1990) *Handbook of Mental Health and Mental Disorder Among Black Americans*, New York: Greenwood Press.

Rushton, J. P. (1995) 'Race and crime: international data for 1989–1990', *Psychological Reports* , 76, 307–12.

Rutherford, A. (1997) 'Prisons only work for politicians', *Observer* (19 January).

Rwegellera, G. G. C. (1977) 'Psychiatric morbidity among West Africans and West Indians living in London', *Psychological Medicine*, 7, 317–29.

Safaya, R. (1976) 'Indian psychology', *A Critical and Historical Analysis of the Psychological Speculations in Indian Philosophical Literature*, New Delhi: Munshiram Manoharlal Publishers.

Sartorious, N., Jablensky, A., Korten, A., Earnberg, G., Anker, M., Cooper, J. E. and Day, R. (1986) 'Early manifestations and first contact incidence of schizophrenia in different cultures', *Psychological Medicine*, 16, 909–28.

Sashidharan, S.P. (1993) 'AfroCaribbeans and schizophrenia: the ethnic vulnerability hypothesis re-examined', *International Review of Psychiatry*, 5. 129–144.

—— (1994a) 'Public stereotypes of race and madness', MIND Conference (November).

—— (1994b) 'The need for community based alternatives to institutional therapy', *Share Newsletter*, 7 (January), 3–5.

Sashidharan, S. P. and Francis, E. (1991) 'Epidemiology, ethnicity and schizophrenia', chap. 6 in W. I. U. Ahmad (ed.) *'Race' and Health in Contemporary Britain*, Milton Keynes: Open University Press, 96–113.

Sayce, L. (1995) 'An ill wind in a climate of fear', *Guardian* (18 January), 6.

Scheff, T. J. (1975) 'Schizophrenia as ideology', in T. J. Scheff (ed.) *Labelling Madness*, Englewood Cliffs, NJ: Prentice-Hall, 5–12.

Schmied, K. and Ernst, K. (1983) 'Seclusion and emergency sedation: opinions of patients and nursing staff', *Archiv für Psychiatrie und Nervenkrankheiten*, 233, 221–2.

Schneider, K. (1959) *Clinical Psychopathology*, New York: Grune & Stratton.

Schoenfeld, C. G. (1988) 'Blacks and violent crime: a psychoanalytically oriented analysis', *Journal of Psychiatry and Law* (Summer), 269–301.

Scott-Moncrieff, L. (1993) 'Injustice in forensic psychiatry', *British Journal of Forensic Psychiatry*, 4, 1, 97–108.

Scull, A. (1984) *Decarceration, Community Treatment and the Deviant. A Radical View*, Cambridge: Polity Press, 2nd edn; Englewood Cliffs, NJ: Prentice-Hall, 1st edn.

—— (1993) *The Most Solitary of Afflictions: Madness and Society in Britain 1700–1900*, New Haven, CT: Yale University Press.

Selten, J. P. and Sleats, J. P. J. (1994) 'Evidence against maternal influenza as a risk factor for schizophrenia', *British Journal of Psychiatry*, 164, 674–6.

Shakoor, B. H. and Chalmers, D. (1991) 'Co-victimisation of African-American children who witness violence: effects of cognitive emotional and behavioural development', *Journal of National Medical Association*, 83, 3, 233–8.

Sim, J. (1990) *Medical Power in Prisons: the Prison Medical Service in England 1774–1989*, Milton Keynes: Open University Press.

Simon, B. (1978) *Mind and Madness in Ancient Greece: the Classical Roots of Modern Psychiatry*, London: Cornell University Press.

Simon, R. J., Fleiss, J. L., Garland, R. J., Stiller, P. R. and Sharpe, L. (1973) 'Depression and schizophrenia in hospitalised black and white mental patients', *Archives of General Psychiatry*, 28, 509–12.

Skilbeck, W. M., Yamamoto, J., Acosta, F. X. and Evans, L. A. (1994) 'Self-reported psychiatric symptoms among black, Hispanic and white out-patients', *Journal of Clinical Psychology*, 40, 5, 1184–9.

Slater, E. (1953) *Psychotic and Neurotic Illness in Twins*, London; HMSO.

Slater, E. and Roth, M. (1969) *Clinical Psychiatry*, London: Balliere Tindall and Cassell, 3rd edn.

Smith, D. J. (1994) 'Race, crime and criminal justice', in M. Maguire, R.

Morgan and R. Reiner (eds) *The Oxford Handbook of Criminology*, Oxford: Clarendon, 1041–119.

Soliday, S. M. (1985) 'A comparison of patients and staff attitudes towards seclusion', *Journal of Nervous and Mental Disease*, 173, 5, 282–6.

Soloff, P. H. and Turner, S. M. (1981) 'Patterns of seclusion: a prospective study', *Journal of Nervous and Mental Disease*, 169, 1, 37–44.

Special Hospitals Service Authority (SHSA) (1993) *Report of the Committee of Inquiry into the Death in Broadmoor Hospital of Orville Blackwood and a Review of the Deaths of Two Other African-Caribbean Patients: 'Big, Black and Dangerous?'*, London: SHSA (Chairman, Professor H. Prins).

Spohn, C. (1990) 'The sentencing decisions of black and white judges: expected and unexpected similarities', *Law and Society Review*, 24, 5, 1197–216.

Spohn, C., Gruhl, J. and Welch, S. (1981–2) 'The effect of race on sentencing: a re-examination of an unsettled question 16', *Law and Society Review*, 72, 71–88.

Stack, L., Lannon, P. B. and Miley, A. D. (1983) 'Accuracy of clinicians' experiences for psychiatric rehospitalisation', *American Journal of Community Psychology*, 11, 1, 99–113.

Stanton, B. and Galbraith, J. (1994) 'Trafficking among African-American early adolescents: prevalence, consequences and associated behaviours and beliefs', *Paediatrics*, 93, 6, 1039–44.

Stark, E. (1990) 'Rethinking homicide: violence, race and politics of gender', *International Journal of Health Services*, 20, 1, 3–27.

Steadman, H. J. and Cocozza, J. J. (1978) 'Selective reporting and the public's misconceptions of the criminally insane', *Public Opinion Quarterly*, 41, 4, 523–33.

Steadman, H. J., Monahan, J., Appelbaum, P. S., Grisso, T., Mulvey, E. P., Roth, L. H., Robbins, P. C. and Klassen, D. (1994). 'Designing a new generation of risk assessment research', in J. Monahan and H. J. Steadman (eds) *Violence and Mental Disorder: Developments in Risk Assessments*, Chicago, IL and London: University of Chicago Press, 297–318.

Stephen, S. (1995) '"Therapy in black and white", 1991, Jafar Kareem and Sonia Francis with Anthony Clare', *Journal of Black Therapy*, 1, 1, 41–4.

—— (1996) 'The need for the re-education of the Black community', *Journal of Black Therapy*, 1, 2, 29–31.

Stern, V. (1997) 'Crime pays big dividends', *Guardian* (15 January), 11.

Strakowski, S. M., Shelton, R. C. and Kolberner, M. L. (1993) 'The effects of race and co-morbidity on clinical diagnosis in-patients with psychosis', *Journal of Clinical Psychiatry*, 54, 96–102.

Stromgren, E. (1974) 'Psychogenic psychosis', in S. R. Hirsch and M. Shepherd (eds) *Themes and Variations in European Psychiatry*, Bristol: Wright, 97–120.

Subsachs, A. P. W., Huws, R. W., Close, A., Larkin, E. P. and Falvey, J. (1995) 'Male Afro-Caribbean patients admitted to Rampton Hospital between 1977 and 1986: a control study', *Medicine, Science and Law*, 35, 4, 336–46.

Sun (1996) 'Scandal of the evil madman let out to rape' (8 February), 2.

Sunnafrank, M. and Fontes, N. E. (1983) 'General and crime related racial stereotypes and influence on juristic decisions', *Cornell Journal of Social Relations*, 17, 1–15.

Susser, E., Lin, S. P., Brown, A. S., Lumey, L. H. and Erlenmeyer-Kimling, L. (1994) 'No relation between risk of schizophrenia and prenatal exposure to influenza in Holland', *American Journal of Psychiatry*, 151, 922–4.

Sussman, L. K., Robins, L. N. and Earls, F. (1987) 'Treatment seeking for depression by black and white Americans', *Social Science and Medicine*, 24, 187–96.

Swanson, J. W., Holzer, C. E., Ganju, V. K.and Jono, R. T. (1990). 'Violence and psychiatric disorder in the community: evidence from the epidemiological catchment area surveys', *Hospital and Community Psychiatry*, 41, 701–70.

Thomas, A. and Sillen, S. (1972) *Racism and Psychiatry*, New York: Brunner/Mazel.

Thomson, D. (1966) *Europe Since Napoleon*, Harmondsworth: Penguin.

Tienari, P. (1963) 'Psychiatric illness in identical twins', *Acta Psychiatrica Scandinavica Supplement*, 171.

Todorov, T. (1993) *On Human Diversity: Nationalism, Racism and Exoticism in French Thought*, trans. C. Porter, Cambridge, MA; Harvard University Press.

Tomlinson, S. (1981) *Special Education: Policy Practice and Social Issues*, London: Harper & Row.

Tonks, C. M., Paykel, E. S. and Klerman, G. L. (1970) 'Clinical depressions among negroes', *American Journal of Psychiatry*, 1217: 329–35.

Torrey, E. F. (1973) 'Is schizophrenia universal? An open question', *Schizophrenia Bulletin*, 7, 53–7.

—— (1980) *Schizophrenia and Civilization*, New York: Jason Aronson.

—— (1983) *Surviving Schizophrenia: a Family Manual*, New York: Harper & Row.

—— (1994) *Schizophrenia and Manic Depressive Disorder: the Biological Roots of Mental Illness as Revealed by the Landmark Study of Identical Twins*, New York: Basic Books.

Torrey, E. F., Rawlings, R. and Waldman, I. N. (1988) 'Schizophrenic births and viral disease in two states', *Schizophrenia Reseearch*, 1, 73–7.

Tuke, D. H. (1858) 'Does civilization favour the generation of mental disease?', *Journal of Mental Science*, 4, 94–110.

—— (1890) 'French Retrospect', *Journal of Mental Science*, 36, 152, 117–22.

Tyrer, P. and Kennedy, P. (1995) 'Supervision registers: a necessary component of good psychiatric practice', *Psychiatric Bulletin*, 19, 193–4.

Umbenhauer, S. L. and De Witte, L. L. (1978) 'Patient race and social class attitudes and decisions among three groups of mental health professionals', *Comprehensive Psychiatry*, 19, 509–15.

University of Manchester, Department of Health (1996) *Learning*

Materials on Mental Health, An Introduction, Manchester: University of Manchester.

Van Putten, T. (1974) 'Why do schizophrenics refuse to take their drugs?', *Archives of General Psychiatry*, 31, 67–72.

Venkoba Rao, A. (1969) 'History of depression: some aspects', *Indian Journal of History of Medicine*, xiv, 46.

Wadeson, H. and Carpenter, W. T. (1976) 'Impact of the seclusion room experience', *Journal of Nervous and Mental Disease*, 163, 318–28.

Walker, N. and McCabe, S. (1968) *Crime and Insanity in England*, Edinburgh: Edinburgh University Press; vol. 2, *New Solutions and New Problems*, 1973.

Warheit, G. J., Holzer, C. E. and Schwab, J. J. (1973) 'An analysis of social class and racial differences in depressive symptomatology: a community study', *Journal of Health and Social Behaviour*, 14, 291–9.

Watters, C. (1996) 'Representations and realities: black people, community care and mental illness', in W. I. U. Ahmad and K. Atkin (eds) *'Race' and Community Care*, Milton Keynes: Open University Press, 105–23.

Webb-Johnson, A. (1991) *A Cry for Change: an Asian Perspective on Developing Quality Mental Health*, London: Confederation of Indian Organizations.

Weindling, P. (1989) *Health, Race and German Politics Between National Unification and Nazism*, Cambridge: Cambridge University Press.

Weiss, B. L. and Kupfer, D. J. (1974) 'The black patient and research in a community mental health centre; where have all the patients gone?', *American Journal of Psychiatry*, 131: 415–18.

Weitz, S. (1972) 'Attitude, voice and behaviour: a repressed affect model of interracial interaction', *Journal of Personality and Social Psychology*, 24, 14–21.

Wellman, D. (1977) *Portraits of White Racism*, Cambridge: Cambridge University Press.

Wessely, S. (1993) 'Violence and psychosis', in C. Thompson and P. Cowen (eds.), *Violence: Basic Clinical Science*, London: Butterworth Heinemann/Mental Health Foundation, 119–35.

Wessely, S., Castle, D., Der, G. and Murray, R. M. (1991a) 'Schizophrenia and African-Caribbeans: a case-control study', *British Journal of Psychiatry*, 159; 795–801.

Wessely, S. and Taylor, P. (1991b) 'Madness and crime: criminology vs. psychiatry', *Criminal Behaviour and Mental Health*, 1, 193–228.

Whitehead, T. L., Peterson, J. and Kaljee, K. (1994) 'The "hustle": socioeconomic deprivation, urban drug trafficking and low income, African-American male gender identity', *Paediatrics*, 93, 6, 1050–5.

Williams, P. (1991) *The Alchemy of Race and Rights: the Diary of a Law Professor*, Cambridge, MA: Harvard University Press.

Wilson, A. (1990) *Black-on-Black Violence*, New York: Afrikan World Infosystems.

—— (1991) *Understanding Black Adolescent Violence: its Remediation and Prevention*, New York: Afrikan World Infosystems.

Wilson, M. (1993a) *Crossing the Boundary*, London: Virago Press.

—— (1993b) *Mental Health and Britain's Black Communities*, London: King's Fund.

Wilson, M. and Francis, J. (1997) *African-Caribbean and African Users' Views and Experiences*, London: MIND.

Wing, J. K. (1978) *Reasoning about Madness*, Oxford: Oxford University Press.

—— (1996) 'SCAN and the PSE tradition', *Social Psychiatry and Psychiatric Epidemiology*, 31, 50–4.

—— (1989) 'Schizophrenic psychoses: causal factors and risks', in P. Williams, G. Wilkinson and K. Rawnsley (eds) *The Scope of Epidemiological Psychiatry*, London: Routledge, 225–3.

Wing, J. K., Cooper, J. E. and Sartorius, N. (1974) *Measurement and Classification of Psychiatric Symptoms: an Instruction Manual for the PSE and Catego Program*, London: Cambridge University Press.

Wolff, G., Pathare, S., Craig, T., and Leff, J. (1996) 'Community knowledge of mental illness and reaction to mentally ill people', *British Journal of Psychiatry*, 168, 191–8.

Wood, Sir J. (1982) 'The impact of legal modes of thought upon the practice of psychiatry', *British Journal of Psychiatry*, 140, 551–7.

World Health Organisation (1973) *Report of the International Pilot Study of Schizophrenia*, vol. 1, Geneva: WHO.

—— (1992) *The ICD-10 Classification of Mental and Behavioural Disorders*, Geneva: WHO.

Worsley, P. (1972) 'Colonialism and categories', in P. Baxter and B. Sansom (eds) *Race and Social Difference*, Harmondsworth: Penguin, 98–101.

Xiaoming, L. and Feigelman, S. (1994) 'Recent and intended drug trafficking among male and female urban African-American early adolescents', *Paediatrics*, 93, 6, 1044–50.

Yamamoto, J., James, Q. C., Bloombaum, M. and Hattem, J. (1967) 'Racial factors in in-patient selection', *American Journal of Psychiatry*, 124, 630–6.

Zarin, D. A. and Earls, F. (1993) 'Diagnostic decision-making in psychiatry', *American Journal of Psychiatry*, 150, 179–206.

Zatz, M. S. (1987) 'The changing forms of racial/ethnic biases in sentencing', *Journal of Research in Crime and Delinquency*, 24, 69.

Zung, W. W. K., MacDonald, J. and Zung, E. M. (1988) 'Prevalence of clinically significant depressive symptoms in black and white patients in family practice settings: clinical and research reports', *American Journal of Psychiatry*, 145, 7, 882–3.

Index